Reshaping the Psychoanalytic Domain

Also by Judith M. Hughes

To the Maginot Line:
The Politics of French Military Preparation in the 1920's (1971)

Emotion and High Politics:
Personal Relations at the Summit in Late Nineteenth-Century
Britain and Germany (1983)

Reshaping the Psychoanalytic Domain

The Work of Melanie Klein, W. R. D. Fairbairn, and D. W. Winnicott

Judith M. Hughes

UNIVERSITY OF CALIFORNIA PRESS
Berkeley   Los Angeles   London

University of California Press
Berkeley and Los Angeles, California

University of California Press, Ltd.
London, England

Library of Congress Cataloging in Publication Data will be found at the end of this book.

PBC offers cassettes and books. For information and catalog
write to PBC, 230 Livingston Street, Northvale, NJ 07647

In memoriam

W. H. and T. K. L.

Contents

Preface

The protagonists of this study, Melanie Klein, W. Ronald D. Fairbairn, and Donald W. Winnicott, are sometimes referred to as object relations theorists, sometimes as the British or English School. (Fairbairn was born and lived in Scotland, so "English" cannot be correct.) Under one name or another, their work has become familiar to clinicians in the United States and elsewhere. But it has been taken up by them in piecemeal fashion without an adequate appreciation of its internal coherence. It is this coherence that I want to establish, and in so doing, I hope to elucidate the strand of psychoanalytic theory which constitutes at once the soundest and the most thoroughgoing revision of Freud.

Two books, both published after my own was already launched, bear mentioning. The first is Phyllis Grosskurth's *Melanie Klein: Her World and Her Work;* her subtitle conveys her aim.[1] Grosskurth is particularly strong on psychoanalytic politics in London, and my first chapter, which serves as a prolegomenon to my main argument, benefited greatly from her meticulous investigations. The second book close to mine is Jay Greenberg and Stephen Mitchell's *Object Relations in Psychoanalytic Theory.*[2] With object relations as their principal theme, they compare disparate and dissonant traditions in psychoanalysis. To this end, they cross-examined the theorists about matters they, the authors, considered relevant (while failing to pursue "evidence" about what the theorists themselves thought they were doing). Thus Greenberg and Mitchell have produced something of a compendium and, for that very reason, a useful contribution.

Despite unavoidable overlaps—principally in materials exploited, published and unpublished alike—each book has its distinctive agenda. Mine is as follows. Taking Freud's overarching paradigms as the point of departure for both my protagonists and my readers, I have set out to chart the course followed by people struggling with specific intellectual difficulties. In successive chapters I have traced the issues my protagonists grappled with, and the accompanying modification of theory, concepts, and terminology. In short, I have tried to map the steps they actually took.

Along the way I have tried as well to be alert to clinical issues and clinical practice. In chapters 3, 4, and 5 I have interwoven my protagonists' experience in the consulting room and their reshaping of the psychoanalytic domain. With Klein, I have concentrated on her account of her analysis of "Richard," a ten-year-old boy. With Fairbairn, I have exploited Harry Guntrip's unpublished 400-page distillation of his more than 1,000 analytic sessions. With Winnicott, I have used his case history entitled *The Piggle* and the case of a psychotic woman in which he himself was deeply involved but which was handled by his close colleague Marion Milner. The consulting room has, after all, provided the empirical base for the psychoanalytic enterprise, and nowhere has this been more apparent than in Britain.

There is intrinsic interest to the tale, and, as with most historical accounts, a moral also. In line with Santayana's maxim that those who do not remember their past are condemned to repeat it, historical knowledge of psychoanalysis allows one to see the how and why of the growth of the discipline, the reasons for its intellectual shifts, for discarding particular theoretical items and reformulating others. At the same time, tracing out the transformation of Freudian paradigms not only demonstrates that some lines of research have proved fruitful; it may also suggest where further investigations might profitably be pursued. And since no consensus has been reached, the following study inevitably takes its place within the ongoing debate.

Beyond that, I have a more general purpose in mind: to help dispel the air of mystery which surrounds psychoanalysis. Two sources contribute to that mystery: first, the difficulty in sorting out the paradigms that constitute psychoanalytic theory, especially when those paradigms are articulated in arcane terminology; second, the clinical setting itself, which to the outsider remains an enigma. For arcane terminology and the like, the only remedy is lucidity, and I have attempted a presentation clear enough to put the outsider—and the insider also—at ease. As for the consulting room, my inclusion of clinical material should serve to mitigate its awesomeness. In sum, I hope that my study may aid in overcoming the barriers that keep analysts and the interested public from communicating with each another.

One of the pleasantest things about finishing a book is having a chance to acknowledge those who have been helpful along the way. Given the nature of my project, it was appropriate to make contact with analysts in Britain who had worked with my protagonists—and what an exhilarating experience that turned out to be! I would like to thank Paul Roazen, Sydney Smith, and Robert L. Tyson for facilitating those contacts; I would also like to thank Enid Balint, Eric Brenman, William Gillespie, Martin James, M. Masud R. Khan, John Padel, the late Herbert Rosenfeld, Charles Rycroft, Joseph Sandler, Hanna Segal, and the late Clare Winnicott for the intellectual stimulation and encouragement that came with meeting them. To John D. Sutherland I owe an additional debt: he alerted me to unpublished Guntrip manuscripts and urged me to make use of them. And Marion Milner was particularly generous in helping me understand what she had written about "Susan."

In London I worked at the Institute of Psycho-Analysis, and there Jill Duncan, the library's executive officer, gladly put at my disposal the materials growing out of the controversial discussions of 1943–1944. In New York, courtesy of the Archives of Psychiatry, the New York Hospital–Cornell Medical Center, I consulted the Winnicott Papers, and in this connection I would like to thank Eric T. Carlson, director of the archives.

At home I have had the good fortune to participate in the Psychoanalytic Interdisciplinary Seminar sponsored by the Department of Psychiatry at the University of California, San Diego. Over a period of years I have profited from its monthly discussions of clinical and theoretical issues. Among the seminar's members I would like to thank Melford E. Spiro specifically. He read a first version of the first chapter and tactfully conveyed to me his judgment that it would not do. He was right, and the present version bears absolutely no resemblance to the original.

I should note that material from the following chapters has been presented in lecture form: chapter 2, to the Psychoanalytic Interdisciplinary Seminar; chapter 3, to the Southern California Psychoanalytic Society; chapter 4, to the Department of Anthropology, University of California, San Diego; chapter 5, to the Psychoanalytic Interdisciplinary Seminar; chapter 6, to the Seminar on the History of Psychiatry and the Behavioral Sciences, Department of Psychiatry, Cornell University, and to the San Diego Psychoanalytic Society.

How does one thank one's analyst? An unadorned statement may suffice. I simply acknowledge a debt of gratitude to Allan D. Rosenblatt.

Once again, I want to express deep appreciation for the aid and comfort given me by my husband, Stuart. He has listened as I have tried to refine lines of argument and choose among organizational alternatives; he has read successive versions and offered editorial suggestions; most of all he has been patient and kind.

CHAPTER 1

Reshaping the Psychoanalytic Domain

The British Psychoanalytic Community

In the summer of 1912 Ernest Jones consulted Sándor Ferenczi and sounded him out about forming a "small group of trustworthy analysts" around Sigmund Freud. Visions of "Charlemagne and his paladins," of a secret society standing "to Freud . . . in the relation of a bodyguard," danced in his head.[1] Ferenczi liked the idea; so too did Freud, who responded warmly to the "romantic element." Thus the strictly secret "committee," which Freud expected to watch over his "creation" and whose watchfulness would make "living and dying easier" for him, began its decade-long existence.[2]

How did Jones carry out his self-appointed mission? How did he go about ensuring what Freud called the "continuation" of psychoanalysis "along the right lines"?[3] Two items stand out. In 1913 Jones entered upon a "didactic" analysis, and in so doing became the first analyst to be analyzed. What was meant by "didactic," how such an analysis differed from the ordinary therapeutic variety, remained unclear; in fact there is no reason to believe that there was any difference at all. The analyst in this case was not Freud. The "master" was hard at work with Jones's longtime mistress (who in the course of her treatment ceased to be his mistress) and hence was unavailable to his paladin. So Jones journeyed to Budapest, and there Ferenczi analyzed him in two hour-long sessions a day for a period of a few months. The analysis, he wrote to Freud, gave him "more self dependence and freedom by diminishing what was left of my father complex." He felt certain that Freud would welcome such a development: who could doubt that it was better to have a "permanent attitude of respect and admiration than a kind of veneration which brings with it the dangers of ambivalency?"[4] These particular dangers Jones claimed that he managed to avoid from then on.

When he returned to Britain that autumn, he took a second step toward carrying out his mission: he proceeded to establish the London Psycho-Analytical Society. He acted in haste and soon came to regret what he had done. Quantity and quality alike he found disappointing. Of the fifteen original members, five lived outside Britain, and of the remaining ten, only four, including Jones himself, actually practiced psychoanalysis—the rest had merely an academic interest in it. Still more, the smallness of the society proved no bar to dissension. Before long, Jones's second-in-command showed himself disloyal—he began openly to display Jungian sympathies—and he was not alone in straying from the Freudian fold. In short, the society was incapable of guaranteeing the continuation of psychoanalysis "along the right lines," and during the First World War, with most of the members away, meetings were suspended. Jones thus had a chance to start all over again at the war's end.[5]

And it was the right time to begin. "In every country," he wrote, "there seemed to have been a psycho-analytical moment . . . when interest in the newness of psycho-analysis became acute." Britain's "moment" arrived during the five years after the First World War.[6] In February 1919 Jones invited a select group to meet at his rooms. Forthwith they dissolved the London Psycho-Analytical Society and formed in its stead the British Psycho-Analytical Society, to be affiliated with the International Psycho-Analytical Association. Jones was to preside over this new body for the next thirty-five years. In 1920 he shepherded through the press the first issue of the first psychoanalytic review in English, *The International Journal of Psycho-Analysis;* before long Leonard Woolf and the Hogarth Press were publishing psychoanalytic literature as well. In 1924 the Institute of Psycho-Analysis was launched and with it the educational mission of the society. When two years later the London Clinic of Psycho-Analysis opened its doors, the scientific and clinical accoutrements of the British Society were in place.

In founding the British Psycho-Analytical Society, Jones was intent on putting into practice the lessons that earlier failure had taught him: to control carefully the number and character of the new members. The numbers in fact were never large: by the end of 1919 the society had thirty associate and full members on its roster; thereafter it grew in incremental fashion. Potential recruits usually attended as visitors before being formally proposed, nominated, and voted upon. During the first year of their associate membership, the new associates, who were required to face annual reelection, were frequently asked to read a paper, thereby giving Jones ample opportunity to rectify a mistaken judgment. Initially there was considerable turnover on the periphery of the society, but the center was holding firm. By mid-decade Jones had gathered around him James and Edward Glover, Joan Riviere, James and Alix Strachey, Ella Sharpe, Susan Isaacs, John Rickman, and Sylvia Payne—all of whom were to loom large in the history of psychoanalysis in Britain.[7]

Who were the members of the British Psycho-Analytical Society? Where did they come from, that is, intellectually? As for Jones, his self-description as "a medical student handling the human brain" and committed to "evolutionary perspectives" offered a comprehensive, if thumbnail, sketch of his educational equipment and outlook. "As far back" as he "could remember" he had "wanted to be a doctor," and when that goal was within his grasp, he decided to reach further and specialize in neurology. "The brain," he wrote, "in its position of supreme control" obviously occupied a privileged position. So too would the person who had knowledge of that organ. With the assurance of a clear-sighted materialist, he scorned riddles of metaphysics. In similar fashion he dismissed works of sociology and ethics as lacking "the necessary basis in biology."[8] Only after professional misadventures had forced him to renounce his neurological ambitions did Jones move toward psychiatry, psychology, and Sigmund Freud. He did not, however, renounce his attachment to medicine.

Among the early luminaries, the Glovers followed a course most nearly approximating that of Jones. The sons of a Scottish schoolteacher—Jones had come from a modest Welsh background—they had, one after the other, with James taking the lead and setting the pace, pursued medical studies; migrated to London, where they encountered psychoanalysis immediately following the First World War; and then journeyed to Berlin to be analyzed by Karl Abraham.[9] (That experience left its mark, at least on James's technique; when Sylvia Payne started analysis with him in 1919, she sat "in a chair facing him and he wrote down every word" she said. "After he had had training with . . . Abraham . . . the patient lay on the couch, the analyst sitting behind him. Interpretations were given mainly at the end of the session but not exclusively. . . . The analyst was very passive.")[10] Next to Jones, James Glover ranked as Britain's leading analyst in the early 1920s: indeed James Strachey considered him "the only possible conceivable person" to go to for a second round of analysis, his first having been conducted by Freud himself.[11] The second round did not last long; James Glover died prematurely in 1926, and his less talented younger brother, Edward, fell heir to his position as Jones's right-hand man.

There was a marked contrast, intellectual and social, between, on the one hand, Jones and the Glovers and, on the other, Joan Riviere and the Stracheys. The latter three came, as James Strachey put it, "from the same middle-class, professional, cultured, later Victorian box."[12] (He ought to have said upper middle class.) According to Jones, Riviere had a "strong complex about being a well-born lady":[13] she was a member of the Verral family, a family much involved in the Cambridge-based Society for Psychical Research, which James Strachey joined and to which in 1912 Freud contributed a paper.[14] James Strachey was himself a Cambridge graduate and inhabitant of Bloomsbury, whose presiding spirit was his older brother Lytton—scant preparation, in his own opinion, for psychoanalytic candidacy:

A discreditable academic career with the barest of B.A. degrees, no medical qualifications, no knowledge of the physical sciences, no experience of anything except third-rate journalism. The only thing in my favour was that at the age of 30, I wrote a letter out of the blue to Freud, asking him if he would take me on as a student. For some reason he replied, almost by return post, that he would.[15]

When James Strachey wrote to Freud, he was on the verge of marrying Alix Sargent-Florence, a graduate of Newnham College, Cambridge; Bloomsbury resident; and friend of assorted Stracheys, Stephens, and Woolfs, as well as John Maynard Keynes. Together the newlyweds proceeded to Vienna and analysis with Freud—so too did Joan Riviere, after many years with Jones. Alix subsequently went on to Berlin for treatment with Abraham, whom she considered the "sounder person as an actual analyst."[16] These three—the Stracheys and Riviere—possessed the wide culture requisite for translating Freud's work into English, and it was James, ably assisted by Alix, who undertook the monumental task of editing the *Standard Edition*.

Was there, in the British psychoanalytic community of the 1920s, a correlation among class, gender, and medical or nonmedical background; that is, were male analysts likely to be doctors of lower-middle-class origin, whereas female analysts were likely to be nonmedical and upper-middle-class? The women were not all from the same social milieu: Ella Sharpe and Susan Isaacs, the first a former English teacher steeped in English literature, the second a leader in progressive nursery school education, did not come from that same "later Victorian box." Yet John Rickman, a doctor, did. And while the lay analysts were predominantly women, James Strachey and Sylvia Payne (a medical doctor) were both exceptions. (Payne succeeded Jones as president of the society and was in turn succeeded by Rickman.) Taken all in all, however, there was a strong correlation between cultural outreach and lay status.[17] As a result, when the standing of lay analysts came to be hotly debated in the mid-1920s, the British among them found themselves in a relatively strong position.

In the spring of 1926 Theodor Reik, a prominent nonmedical member of the Vienna Psycho-Analytical Society, stood accused of violating an Austrian law against quackery—"a law which made it illegal for a person without a medical degree to treat patients."[18] (His case never came to trial: after a preliminary investigation, the charges were dropped.) The assault on lay analysis, Freud wrote, seemed "to be only an offshoot of the old resistance against analysis in general. . . . I regard the whole movement as an expression of annoyance at the benevolent interest my seventieth birthday aroused . . . , and . . . feel partly responsible for it."[19] So he fired off a pamphlet entitled *The Question of Lay Analysis,* which had immediate repercussions in the psychoanalytic world; it flushed out, as James Strachey put it, "the strong differences of opinion on the permissibility of non-medical psycho-analysis . . . within the psychoanalytic societies themselves" and prompted the publication of a "long series of reasoned statements (28 in all) by analysts from various countries."[20]

    In sounding the clarion, Freud staked out an extreme position, or rather a succession of extreme positions. What linked them was his grandiose claims for psychoanalysis and an equally grand vision of its future. On the most obvious issue, whether psychoanalysis should be considered a specialized branch of medicine, he was adamant: he did not want to see it "swallowed up by medicine"; he did not want it "to find its last resting place in a text-book of psychiatry under the heading 'Methods of Treatment.' " "The possibility of its application to medical purposes," he argued, should not lead one "astray. Electricity and radiology also" had "their medical application, but the science to which they both" belonged was "none the less physics." If psychoanalysis did not belong to medicine, of what was it a part? Psychology was the answer Freud gave, "not . . . the psychology of the morbid processes, but simply . . . psychology." Still more, "as a 'depth-psychology', as a theory of the mental unconscious," it could "become indispensable to all the sciences . . . concerned with the evolution of human civilization and its major institutions such as art, religion and the social order."

In line with his magnificent dreams, Freud played with the fantasy of creating a college of psychoanalysis and outlined a curriculum for that imaginary institution. He obviously did not regard medical education as obligatory for future analysts. Did he consider it at least desirable? He sounded dubious: it offered an analyst much that was "indispensable" to him; but it burdened "him with too much else" of which he could "never make any use," and there was "a danger of its diverting his interest and his whole mode of thought from the understanding of psychical phenomena." What Freud dreamed of instead was a curriculum that included "elements from the mental sciences, from psychology, the history of civilization and sociology, as well as from anatomy, biology and the study of evolution."[21]

Freud occupied one end of the spectrum; his followers in New York occupied the other. In fact nowhere was opposition to his stand as united as in the American metropolis: Berlin and Vienna were divided; New York spoke with one voice. And that voice insisted on limiting "the practice of psycho-analysis for therapeutic purposes . . . to physicians" who were "graduates of recognized medical schools."[22] (In 1926 this regulation became New York state law.) Above all, New Yorkers were moved by practical considerations or by what Freud referred to as "the local conditions in America."[23] In their opinion too many of their countrymen traveled to Europe, received perfunctory training, returned home, and "degenerated into quacks"—or, at best, became "second-raters."[24] Then there were those who had no training at all: the novice who presumed "to call himself an analyst when surfeited with the boredom of social functions, or the scamp" who saw "an opportunity for financial gain" through charlatanry—"such as the correspondence school psychoanalyst."[25] Against types of this sort, so the argument ran, the honest and the reputable needed the protection that medical education—backed up by the law—alone provided.

In this debate the British occupied a middle position, or rather Jones, Edward Glover, and Rickman found a middle position thrust upon them. Their hearts lay with the doctors, and James Strachey, for one, suspected that they were "more or less . . . anxious to exclude non-medical analysts altogether."[26] Jones's dreams, only a shade less grand than Freud's, were of conquering the medical world. "Once psycho-analysis had obtained a secure foothold in the more psychological departments of medicine," he wrote, "the rest would automatically follow: that is to say, the gradual penetration of psycho-analytical doctrine among the ranks of the profession, and the incorporation of truly psychological, i.e., psycho-analytical, points of view into general medical education."[27] Those dreams depended upon recruiting physicians. In point of fact, with more than forty percent of the British Society already lay, Jones predicted that if medical and nonmedical candidates were "admitted equally without reservation," in a few years, the society would be "composed mainly of laity," and divorce from the medical profession would follow willy-nilly.[28] Yet because of the number and prominence of that laity, Jones did not press for exclusion: he settled for prohibiting the lay analyst from working "independently"; that is, the lay practitioner should consult with a physician at the outset and remain in contact with one during the course of treatment. (Even Freud agreed that the responsibility for a diagnosis belonged to a doctor.)[29] Thus Strachey and his like were allowed to remain.

Strachey thought he had Freud to thank; rather, if one person were to be singled out for gratitude, it should have been Melanie Klein, who had arrived in London in 1926 and had immediately begun analyzing Jones's children.[30] Here a further correlation made itself amply apparent: that between nonmedical female analysts and a practice that included children. At the point when James felt most discouraged about the prospects of lay analysts, he advised Alix that treating children "would evidently be the line to take"—if she could overcome her "disinclination to dealing with the little dears."[31] (Evidently she could not.) The argument may have been about lay analysis; the unintended result was that where lay analysis flourished, so too did the analysis of children.

———   ———   ———   ———   ———

The disputants might not agree about the importance of medical preparation for treating patients; they did, however, agree that psychoanalytic preparation ranked as an absolute necessity. As Freud put it, "[N]o one should practise analysis who has not acquired the right to do so by a particular training." And by the mid-1920s, the particularity of that training had been defined. To transmit theory, the Berlin Psychoanalytic Society, followed by the Viennese and the British societies, organized institutes that offered candidates seminars and lectures. As for praxis, the "older and more experienced" analysts supervised the candidates when they made "their first trials" with what one and all hoped would be "comparatively slight cases."[32] To ensure that the complexes of the practitioner would not interfere with those trials, the candidate was now obliged to follow the course Jones had initiated more than a decade earlier: he was obliged to undergo a didactic or training analysis, in actuality, a personal analysis of his own. This last requirement constituted the most distinctive feature of psychoanalytic training.

Did a training analysis inhibit a candidate's intellectual independence? Ella Sharpe, for one, thought it did not—at least not in the 1920s. She attributed some of the "freedom" she "took for granted," however, to the fact that she and her colleagues "were separated" from their analysts "by the English Channel." (She herself had been analyzed by Hanns Sachs in Berlin.) As the British came to train their own, analyst and candidate found themselves cheek by jowl in a small society, with "that small number consisting . . . of mainly analysts and the people" they had analyzed. It was "almost inevitable," she went on, that if students should "continue moving too long in the orbits of their analysts," they would "be unable to make approximately independent judgments for themselves."[33] Susan Isaacs echoed these concerns: the residue of the attachment between analysand and analyst she considered "more intense and troublesome . . . than the influence of relationships such as teacher and pupil among other scientific workers."[34] In the 1940s, when the society was wracked by dissension, Edward Glover remarked bitterly, "No objective observer of discussions at scientific meetings of the Society could fail to note the existence of training allegiances, even of the phenomenon of postponed obedience."[35]

What about "postponed obedience" to Freud himself? No doubt it was fostered by the training in both its theoretical and its practical aspects. In Britain, however, such obedience figured less prominently than on the Continent—perhaps owing, once again, to the protection the English Channel afforded.

Dramatis Personae

The three protagonists of this study stand as prime examples of independence prospering under the protection of the English Channel. Though Melanie Klein received her psychoanalytic training on the Continent, she was not analyzed by Freud, she did not belong to the circle around him, she never practiced in Vienna—and it was in England that she flourished and her theory grew luxuriantly. W. R. D. Fairbairn and D. W. Winnicott, the one a Scot, the other an Englishman, were far removed, geographically and intellectually, from the center of psychoanalytic orthodoxy. Still more, not one of the three came to psychoanalysis with a conventional psychiatric background. In short, they were on the fringe, so to speak, and this fringe location may well have lessened their commitment to Freudian solutions and prompted a readiness to entertain alternatives.

▬▬ ▬▬ ▬▬ ▬▬ ▬▬

Melanie Klein's origins resembled Freud's. She was born Melanie Reizes in Vienna in 1882 at a time when her family's fortunes were at a low ebb. Her father, brought up in a strict Jewish milieu and originally trained to be a student of the Talmud, had broken away from this tradition and had, without much success, pursued a medical career instead; indeed upon moving to Vienna shortly before Melanie's birth, he found himself largely reduced to a dental practice. Because of her husband's precarious financial circumstances, Melanie's mother was obliged to open a shop and, in so doing, to see her dreams of status disappear. Those dreams never came close to being realized; the family never did thrive, though for a few years during Melanie's childhood, it fared better. As a breadwinner, the father provided a poor model; as a man of learning, however, he set his children a high standard—a standard his indomitable wife could not approach.

Melanie was the youngest of four children, and it was through two of her older siblings that her father's intellectual aspirations reached her. Both died young—her sister at the age of eight, when Melanie was only four. The sister, a shadowy figure, apparently had the time and the temperament to teach Melanie the fundamentals of reading and arithmetic, and for that and similar kindnesses, Melanie remained in her debt. Her brother, five years her senior, exerted a more obvious influence. From about the age of nine, she allowed herself to be guided by him. She turned to him as "confidant," "friend," and "teacher"; he responded by expecting great things of her in the abstract, and, concretely, by coaching her in Greek and Latin and thus helping her pass the entrance examinations to the Lyceum.[36] Beyond there she did not go; what she later claimed had been her dream, to enter medical school and to specialize in psychiatry, remained just that—a dream. Such ambitions were not, after all, appropriate for a lower-middle-class Jewish girl. By the time she began to set more realistic goals, her brother had left Vienna and begun a wandering life. He died when Melanie was twenty.

By then she was already engaged. Her father had died shortly after she met her future husband, and the family's uncertain finances no doubt weighed heavily in her decision to marry. In worldly terms, Arthur Klein ranked as the most suitable of Melanie's admirers. An industrial chemist in training, he had prospects, but it was not until 1903 that his training was completed and that the marriage took place. It was not a success. Almost from the very beginning, Melanie's distress and dissatisfaction were evident. She found her surroundings trying: in their first seven years together, Arthur's profession took him and his wife to a series of small towns in Slovakia and Silesia. She found her children—Melitta, born in 1904, and Hans, born in 1907—likewise trying; in those years she regularly took refuge from her family in cures and seaside spots of one sort or another. And in that family her mother loomed increasingly large; Melanie's widowed parent more and more took over the management of her household and the rearing of her children. When in 1910 Arthur got himself transferred to Budapest, he may have hoped that this change would free Melanie from the depression that threatened to paralyze her.

Liberation was slow in coming. The earliest it can be dated is 1914, the year her third and last child, Erich, was born, her mother died, and Arthur went to war. In the course of the conflict, Melanie extricated herself unofficially from the marriage—it did not legally end until the mid-1920s. During the same period, she became an adherent of the psychoanalytic movement—though by what stages remains obscure. When the Fifth International Psycho-Analytic Congress was held in Budapest in late September 1918, she attended and caught her first glimpse of Freud. The following July she read a paper to the Hungarian Psychoanalytic Society and was immediately granted membership. Along the way, she had analysis with Ferenczi.

What went on in that analysis? What went on in her subsequent analysis with Abraham in 1924 and 1925? From Klein's fragmentary comments, the two—and the analysts also—seem to have been quite different. Ferenczi's preference for encouraging and reassuring the patient, coupled with the relaxed atmosphere of the Hungarian Society—Klein's daughter, Melitta, was, at fifteen, allowed to attend meetings—provided her a supportive therapeutic and professional environment. And she appreciated it. Positive feelings for Ferenczi developed, and, as she later remarked, their effect should not be underrated—but positive feelings alone could "never do the job."[37] Abraham, in contrast, appears to have been punctilious about what was becoming standard psychoanalytic protocol. The setting was more formal, and in it, negative as well as positive feelings emerged; both were analyzed. Whether or not Klein owed her technical rigor to

Abraham is unclear, but it was in Berlin that her strict notions of how to treat children took shape.

Klein had begun working with children in Budapest, following Ferenczi's advice. He drew her attention, she wrote, to her "great gift for understanding children" and suggested that she devote herself to analyzing them.[38] He made the same suggestion to other female colleagues; he may have simply assumed that all women had a similar gift. Child patients—or perhaps any patients—were not, however, readily available to Klein; so she turned to her son Erich.[39] The paper she presented to the Hungarian Society derived from work with him—his identity was concealed in later versions under the pseudonym of "Fritz." Could this work be regarded as analysis? After all, for more than a decade Freud had been urging his "pupils and . . . friends to collect observations of the sexual life of children," and, no doubt, many children of first-generation analysts were intently scrutinized.[40] By the time Alix Strachey met Klein in Berlin in 1924—political turmoil had forced her to leave Budapest, and in 1921 she had settled in the German capital—she had become "absolutely firm" on "keeping parental influence . . . apart from analysis" and on reducing it to "its minimum." That minimum was "to keep the child from actually poisoning itself on mushrooms, to keep it reasonably clean, and teach it its lessons."[41]

It was Alix Strachey who brought Klein to the attention of the British Society. When in the fall of 1924 she arrived in Berlin for her analysis with Abraham, Klein already belonged to the Berlin Society—she had become a full member in 1923. But she was not thriving; she later complained that the "only patients sent to her were children and the deeply disturbed relatives . . . of other analysts."[42] Nor did she meet a warm reception when she "propounded her views and experiences" of child analysis. On one such occasion, Alix reported, "the opposition showed its hoary head—and it really was *too* hoary. The *words* used were, of course, psycho-analytical. . . . But the *sense* was purely . . . anti-analysis" (don't "tell children the terrible truth about their repressed tendencies"). At that meeting Abraham came to Klein's rescue, as apparently he did more than once.[43] After his premature death in December 1925, which brought her analysis (and Alix's as well) to an abrupt end, her position in Berlin became quite uncomfortable. If England would have her, she was ready to go.

England had been forewarned: Klein had lectured there in the summer of 1925, thanks to Alix and James Strachey. Alix's account of Klein's talk in Berlin had aroused James's interest. In London, he wrote, "the little ones" were stirring "people's feelings" to such an extent that discussion of them occupied successive meetings. To that discussion James thought an abstract of the talk would make a fine addition. He proved correct: when he read the document Alix provided, Klein received universal acclaim, with Jones turning out to be "an absolutely heart-and-soul whole-hogging pro-Melanie." James then prepared Jones for Klein's proposal, vigorously supported by Alix, of a lecture series. Again he reported positively:

Jones announced at the meeting that he'd had a letter from Frau Klein but that he hadn't answered it, so that he might first discover what the society thought about the matter. He then, very haltingly, read out her letter. When he got through her scenario, or whatever you call it, he muttered to himself 'very interesting programme'. . . . I had the impression, which afterwards turned out to be true, that he himself was very anxious that it should be put through but felt doubtful of what other people would think. Anyhow, after some talk, he said in very dubious terms: 'Well, as to the number that are likely to attend . . . I'm afraid it's much too early yet to ask people now if they'll be prepared to come . . . h'm? . . . well, perhaps I might ask . . . 'm? . . . those who think they will to hold up their hands.' It was a rather unusually small meeting: only 15 or 16 altogether. Without an instant's hesitation every single hand rose in the air. Jones's whole manner instantly changed. He became wreathed in smiles and exclaimed: 'Oh, well! come!' . . .

   There couldn't be any question at all that there was a most unusual amount of interest at the prospect of her visit; quite a stir, in fact. So you can pile it on as thick as you please.[44]

   How did Klein fare in the British Society? Very well indeed. She had been "sniffed at" by people in Berlin;[45] she was fussed over in London—in fact, within a year of her arrival, Ferenczi, after visiting the British capital, wrote to Freud of "the domineering influence . . . Frau Melanie Klein" had "on the whole group."[46] She attended her first meeting in October 1926 and presented her first paper the following month. After she became a member in 1927, she played an equally active role in the administrative and educational life of the society; in 1929 she was named a training analyst, started to work with her first candidate, and was elected a member of the Training Committee—a position she held for many years.[47] With the publication of *The Psycho-Analysis of Children* in 1932, Klein reached her high point of acceptance within the British Society. Even Edward Glover, later a savage antagonist, found her book full of substance and merit—witness the laudatory review he wrote. He had "no hesitation" in stating that it was "of fundamental importance for the future of psycho-analysis," indeed that it constituted "a landmark in analytical literature worthy to rank with some of Freud's own classical contributions."[48]

In the mid-1930s misfortune struck. In April 1934 Klein's older son, Hans, fell to his death in a mountain-climbing accident. Her surviving son maintained that his brother's death "was a source of grief to her for the rest of her life." At the time her depression was amply apparent to those around her; it prompted her to see Sylvia Payne professionally, though only briefly, and it also prompted her to write the two papers that marked her break with Freudian orthodoxy, "A Contribution to the Psychogenesis of Manic-Depressive States" (1935) and "Mourning and Its Relation to Manic-Depressive States" (1940).[49] In the second of these, Klein drew upon her own experience, thinly disguised as that of "Mrs A," "to illustrate . . . a normal mourner's" distress. A few weeks after her son's death,

Mrs A went for a walk with her friend through the familiar streets, in an attempt to re-establish old bonds. She suddenly realized that the number of people in the street seemed overwhelming, the houses strange and the sunshine artificial and unreal. She had to retreat into a quiet restaurant. But there she felt as if the ceiling were coming down, and the people in the place became vague and blurred. Her own house suddenly seemed the only secure place in the world.[50]

And even "her own house" was no longer safe. In the controversy that erupted after Anna Freud's emigration to Britain in 1938—as companion to her dying father, who had only a year and a half to live—Klein's daughter, Melitta, joined the opposition. Melitta and, along with her, her analyst, Edward Glover, went over to Anna's camp. They were not so much pro-Anna as viciously anti-Melanie. And vicious it was. As one German émigré noted, "At the meetings I could only see something quite terrible and very un-English happening, and that was a daughter hitting her mother with words and this mother being very composed, quite quiet, never defending herself." A British member concurred: "It was horrible at times, *really* horrible."[51]

Who measured up to the demands for undivided loyalty that Klein now made? Alix and James Strachey drifted away; neither turned out to be "an absolutely heart-and-soul whole-hogging pro-Melanie." Nor did Jones for that matter: once the Freuds had crossed the English Channel, Klein could no longer reckon Jones her paladin. Of the early members of the British Society, Joan Riviere and Susan Isaacs proved the most faithful and the most prolific. John Rickman, who had begun a seven-year analysis with Klein in 1934, regarded himself, at least during the war years, as a Kleinian; the Kleinians themselves were less sure. Few émigrés joined their camp; Paula Heimann, another analysand and perhaps a surrogate daughter, stood out. Hers was an intimate relationship with Klein, and their parting, just a few years before Klein's death in 1960, was painful on both sides.[52] Among a younger generation of Klein's analysands, Hanna Segal, Herbert Rosenfeld, and, subsequently, Wilfred Bion explored the territory Klein had opened up in her major postwar paper "Notes on Some Schizoid Mechanisms" (1946). In short, it was from the ranks of those she had trained that her chief lieutenants emerged.

Neither W. R. D. Fairbairn nor D. W. Winnicott had such a "training allegiance" to Klein. Still, both were intellectually in her debt. And it was in large measure thanks to the stimulus of her ideas that they managed to escape the "postponed obedience" to Freud which constrained the world of psychoanalysis.

"He spoils" his good work by the claim "that he is knocking Freud over"—such was the pithy judgment Winnicott passed on Fairbairn.[53] How had Fairbairn come to knock Freud over—leaving aside whether that colloquialism does justice to his heterodoxy? Fairbairn himself provided a clue in describing his life during the war years, when he was both most productive and most "cut off . . . from . . . other analysts":

During these years I suffered from all the disadvantages of working in comparative isolation; but perhaps a sojourn in the wilderness is not altogether without its compensations. For, if the isolated worker lacks the stimulus that comes from exchanges of thought with his fellow-workers, at any rate he does not lack the stimulus that comes from the necessity to work out for himself the problems which he encounters. He is also to some extent delivered from the temptation to fall back too readily upon authority for the solution of these problems. He is thus afforded an unusual opportunity to reconsider classic problems from a new approach.[54]

"Comparative isolation" was a marked feature of his entire life. Born in Edinburgh in 1889, William Ronald Dodds Fairbairn, more familiarly called Ronald, was the only child of prosperous middle-class parents. His father was Presbyterian, his mother Anglican; his father was hard-working, if not hard-driving; his mother has been described as "a bit of a martinet" and intensely ambitious for her son, and it was she who was the dominant figure in his life. (Her death in 1946 quite unstrung him.) Apparently she wanted him to enter the clergy of her husband's church and the church of his childhood; in his maturity, however, he embraced Anglicanism.[55] The strictness of a Calvinist upbringing—typified by Sundays with long morning sermons, which Fairbairn claimed not to mind, and with "afternoons when ordinary activities were suspended and there seemed nothing to do," which he very much disliked—no doubt contributed to the loneliness he experienced as his parents' only child.[56]

When he was nine years old, he was sent to Merchiston Castle School in his home city. There he remained until the age of eighteen, following a curriculum of mostly Latin and Greek, and also following a regimen of a cold shower, an hour of class, and chapel before breakfast each day.[57] After leaving school he went to Edinburgh University, where in 1911 he took an M.A. degree with honors in philosophy. He then spent three years of postgraduate study in divinity and in Hellenistic Greek at the universities of Kiel, Strasbourg, and Manchester, in addition to Edinburgh.[58] This focus on Greek, besides its relevance for his intended clerical vocation, may have betokened a search for something more cheerful than dour Presbyterianism.

In the course of the First World War Fairbairn "decided to go in for medicine with a view to specializing in psychotherapy." What prompted this career choice? The war itself removed him from his normal environment: initially, as a territorial in the Royal Garrison Artillery, he was stationed near home "on the Forth defenses; . . . after volunteering for service overseas," he served in Egypt and took part in the Palestinian campaign.[59] At last, he may have felt, he had gotten away, particularly from mother, but he may also have come to appreciate that getting away was a conflict-ridden process. During the Second World War he was to have ample opportunity to study dependent people suddenly deprived of "accustomed props and supports."[60] Perhaps he had been personally prepared for that study by his experience in the first war.

Upon returning home to Edinburgh at the end of 1918, Fairbairn set about implementing his decision. He immediately began a somewhat abbreviated four-year course in medicine which had been specially designed for veterans. In 1923 he took his M.B.Ch.B. (the normal first degree in medicine, sufficient for practice), and in 1927 he obtained the additional qualification of M.D. As for his plan to specialize in psychotherapy, after taking the first degree, he had a year's psychiatric experience in the Royal Edinburgh Hospital. Beyond that, in 1923 he went into analysis with Dr. Ernest Connell, seeing him several times a week for roughly a year.[61] Not much is known about Dr. Connell except that he was a civilized man, with leanings toward Jung, who had set himself up in practice in Edinburgh. By the 1940s Fairbairn's sketchy training, similar to much of what had gone on two decades earlier, was to count against him: within the British Psycho-Analytical Society, "unconsciously people were graded as more or less trained, more or less real analysts, . . . and Fairbairn . . . was regarded as someone who had trained after a fashion, but it wasn't really adequate."[62]

In the late 1920s Fairbairn launched a new family as well as a new profession. In neither venture was he particularly successful. He married for the first time in 1926 and for the second in 1959, seven years after he had become a widower. Three children, born between 1927 and 1933, survived his first marriage. From 1927 to 1935 he served as lecturer in psychology at Edinburgh University, and for most of that period he also acted as psychiatrist to the University Psychological Clinic for Children. With the academic psychologist James Drever the dominating figure in both the department and the clinic, Fairbairn found himself in a hostile environment. Still, according to John D. Sutherland, who was in analysis with Fairbairn in the 1930s, this hostility did not "knock him down."[63] Along with Harry Guntrip, Fairbairn's best-known analysand of the 1950s, Sutherland would do his utmost to introduce his mentor into the wider psychoanalytic world.

Sutherland did not become his analyst's "agent in London" until after the Second World War.[64] In the 1930s Fairbairn had been in touch with both Ernest Jones and Edward Glover, and he presented at least two papers to the British Society, the first in 1931, after which he was elected an associate member; a few years later he was made a full member. It is possible that he would have enjoyed the society in the early part of the decade; it is certain that he would have been horrified by the fight between Melanie Klein and Anna Freud.[65] From that controversy he kept his distance: he made only one contribution to the society's wartime debate, and that was read for him by Glover.[66] The distance was intellectual as well as physical. In his prewar clinical papers, though there were hints of future deviance, Fairbairn fitted his material into the Freudian mold. In a paper delivered in 1946, in which he provided a condensed summary of the major theoretical departures he had published without arousing much attention during the war itself, his deviance became fully apparent. In the meantime he had been grappling with the work of Melanie Klein.

What was the response of the Kleinians? "There's a story about Fairbairn reading a paper to the Society, and Melanie Klein stomping out in indignation, saying 'That isn't what analysis is!' "[67] Regardless of the Kleinians' reputation for rudeness, for being "contemptuous of other people's viewpoints," such an account defies belief. Fairbairn was not treated impolitely or roughly; rather "he was treated coolly."[68] And with what the Kleinians considered good reason. As Susan Isaacs commented, "Dr. Fairbairn . . . overemphasizes and distorts certain parts of Mrs. Klein's theories to the point of caricature." His "position is not to be taken as representing Mrs. Klein's work or conclusions."[69]

Did Fairbairn knock over Klein as well as Freud? Far from it. In his opinion he was simply pushing Klein's views to their logical conclusion, and in so doing undertaking a major revision of Freudian theory.[70] Did such a revision itself constitute "knocking Freud over"? Again the answer should be no. Winnicott's phrase is inappropriate for describing the relation of one investigator to his scientific forebear. To his London audience, however, Fairbairn's dissection of the formulations of those whom he acknowledged as predecessors and his practice of proposing alternatives seemed to smack of hubris. That he was perceived in this light goes a long way to explain the cool reception his work, as well as his person, encountered. In fact he combined almost ruthless intellectual honesty with painful shyness and reserve.

In his final years Fairbairn succumbed to a combination of depression, drink, and Parkinson's disease.[71] He died in 1964.

━━━━ ━━━━ ━━━━ ━━━━ ━━━━

Winnicott's own allegiance to Freud was less than complete. He felt bound, he wrote, to follow the main lines of Freud's developing ideas and to justify variations on them.[72] Yet he was quite cavalier about interpreting those main lines and about vindicating his modifications. As late as 1960 he confessed an inability to cope with these matters:

Whereas I used to be absolutely unable to take part in a metapsychological discussion, I am now just beginning to be able to see a glimmer of light, so that if I live long enough I feel I might be able to join in from time to time. I do feel, however, that I shall always think that it is relatively unimportant the way Freud contradicted himself and gradually stimulated thought by making new suggestions. In a decade or two the people who mind about this will all be dead.[73]

Despite, or perhaps because of, this inability, Winnicott's approach came across as "typically British and totally beyond the comprehension of the Teutonic Hartmann style of theorist."[74]

"Typically British," or rather English, is a phrase frequently applied to him. Donald Woods Winnicott, a third and youngest child, and an only son, was born in Plymouth in 1896 to parents of "simple" (Methodist) faith. (Subsequently, as a medical student, he entered the Anglican fold.)[75] His parents were also prosperous; his father was twice mayor of Plymouth and was eventually knighted. Nonetheless the father had a streak of diffidence: "[H]e was sensitive about his lack of education (he had had learning difficulties) and . . . because of this he had not aspired to Parliament, but had kept to local politics." That diffidence made itself felt within the family as well: in his younger years, Winnicott wrote, his father was "extremely preoccupied" with town and business matters and he left his son "too much to all" his "mothers." Among those mothers Winnicott counted his sisters, five and six years older than he, and a devoted nanny. "Things," he continued, "never quite righted themselves."[76]

The result, by his own admission, was a strong maternal identification—and a lack of emotional investment in the paternal and perhaps even the sexual. At the same time he was quite insistent on distinguishing between the maternal and the female; the expression "female identification" was "not something" he would ever apply to himself. At the very least, he commented, it started "people thinking along the wrong lines":[77]

I think that the study of man's identification with woman has been very much complicated by a persistent attempt on the part of psycho-analysts to call everything that is not male in a man homosexuality, whereas in fact homosexuality is a secondary matter or less fundamental and rather a nuisance when one is trying to get at man's woman identification.[78]

At the age of thirteen Winnicott left his multiple mothers and went off to the Leys School in Cambridge. While there he determined to become a doctor: recuperating from a broken collarbone, he decided that the only way out of dependency on doctors—which he seemed to imagine as a chronic state—was to become one himself. So he went on to Jesus College, Cambridge, and took a degree in biology. By then Britain was at war, and Winnicott became restless remaining on the sidelines as a medical student. He wanted to enter the conflagration that had already claimed the lives of so many of his friends. Coming from Plymouth, he naturally opted for the navy and applied for and was accepted as a surgeon probationer. Once the war was over, he went straight to St. Bartholomew's Hospital in London to continue his study of medicine and stayed on there, after qualification, for a year as casualty officer. During his training he had become deeply interested in working with children, and in 1923 he obtained appointments at two hospitals, one of which, at Paddington Green Children's Hospital, he was to hold for forty years.[79]

By the time Winnicott had taken up his hospital appointments and opened a Harley Street office, he had discovered psychoanalysis. Personal motives impelled him. In recalling his first meeting with Ernest Jones, in 1923—the year in which he married—he described himself as a "rather inhibited young man asking whether anything could be done about it."[80] To do something about it he entered upon analysis with James Strachey. Strachey, in what would subsequently have been regarded as a serious breach of confidentiality, commented to Alix occasionally about his analysands—for a number of years there were only two. When he thought of ditching them in order to join her in Berlin, she cautioned against giving them up "in the middle" and went on to add, "perhaps . . . W[innicott] will die or f-ck his wife all of a sudden," as if either event would have served to bring his analysis to an end.[81] In fact the analysis lasted ten years.

Strachey was not Winnicott's only analyst. In 1940 he began analysis again, this time with Joan Riviere. The second treatment lasted six years, though the war must have imposed frequent interruptions. According to his widow, Winnicott had wanted to have a second analysis with Melanie Klein, but he had already, from 1935 to 1939, analyzed her son Erich. It would have been improper for the son's analyst to go to the mother for treatment; here Klein and Winnicott obeyed proprieties. It would have been equally improper for the mother to supervise the son's analysis; here Winnicott resisted Klein's encroachment. She had supervised a number of his child cases and wanted to do the same with his analysis of Erich—or at least do a bit of supervision.[82] (Winnicott's close associate Marion Milner was less successful in resisting when it came to the case of Klein's grandson, Michael.)[83]

Before the war Winnicott was very close to Klein. On Strachey's advice he had sought her out: his analyst had told him that if he was applying psychoanalytic theory to children, he must meet her. In the 1920s "no other analyst was also a paediatrician," and he considered himself a pioneer. Overnight he "changed from being a pioneer into being a student with a pioneer teacher."[84] And Klein was generous, and, in view of her later reputation, undogmatic. As Winnicott affectionately reminisced:

She was always having ideas, . . . and they were tremendously important to her when she had them. At one time she endeared herself to me by the concept of internal chaos because of the fact that she insisted on pronouncing this CHOUS, rhyming with the word COWS except that the S was short and sharp! . . . I refrained from correcting this one word . . . because it was such fun![85]

In later years Winnicott made it clear that because he "had never had analysis by her, or by any of her analysands," he "did not qualify to be one of the group of chosen Kleinians."[86] And he preferred it that way. Yet even as he kept his distance from Klein, he remained enormously attracted by her. They have been described as performing a *pas de deux* in the late 1940s and 1950s: "Klein was the ballerina to whom Winnicott was constantly offering something, which she rejected with a toss of her head as if to say that she had it already."[87] In those years he implicitly addressed his papers to her. One cannot "truly understand" them, it has been claimed, "unless one is aware that they have [the] . . . secondary aim of getting her to modify something."[88]

In those same years Winnicott was emerging as an outstanding independent within the British Psycho-Analytical Society, independent, that is, from both the Kleinians and the Anna Freudians. In the aftermath of the wartime controversies, a "middle group," including both Fairbairn and Marion Milner and owing allegiance to neither female chieftain, became recognizable, albeit not institutionalized. And though Winnicott's independence did not prevent him from twice serving as president of the society, from 1956 to 1959 and again from 1965 to 1968, it did bar him, for a long time, from instruction. "[N]either Miss Freud nor Mrs. Klein," he wrote, "would use me or allow their [*sic*] students to come to me for regular teaching even in child analysis."[89] Clearly he paid a price for his independence, a price he was quite willing to pay: "[H]e firmly refused either to found a school of his own or to become the leader of a group, for he held that independents should be independent, not reliant on a leader."[90]

Meantime, after long self-questioning, Winnicott and his first wife ended their marriage, which had remained childless. In 1951 he married Clare Britton, a psychiatric social worker who had been his colleague during the war. (In the 1950s Clare went through psychoanalytic training, including an extended period as one of Melanie Klein's last analysands.)[91] This second marriage was also childless. Yet until the end of his life Winnicott worked with children and played with them as well. In a session with a little girl, prompted by the material she offered, he found himself "ready with the idea of linking birth and death." In response to her question about his birthday, he asked, "What about my death day?"[92] That day came in 1971, and, as he had wished, he "was alive" when he "died."[93]

The Controversial Discussions

British independence—and tolerance—were called into question by the arrival of the émigrés from central Europe. The British Society had accorded the newcomers "immediate membership and, where appropriate, training analyst status"; it had also taken steps to assure their financial security by making arrangements for them to establish private practices.[94] By 1938 over one-third of the analysts in the British Society had come from the Continent.[95] (Six years earlier full and associate members had totaled 74.)[96] "A comparison of the 1937 and 1938 membership lists shows the number of new names that were added—Bibring, Eidelberg, Hitschmann, Hoffer, Isakower, Kris, Lantos, Stengel, Schur, Stross, Sachs, Straub—and of course Sigmund and Anna Freud." Though many of these Central Europeans subsequently moved on to the United States, their presence profoundly altered the climate of the British Society. Melanie Klein, for one, lamented that it "would never be the same again." She told Winnicott, "This is a disaster."[97] Her forebodings were amply confirmed.

To persuade the British "to open their doors to the influx of members from Vienna, i.e., to colleagues who held different scientific views from their own and [who] could only be expected to disrupt peace and internal unity," Anna Freud commented, had been no mean achievement on the part of Ernest Jones.[98] What did he do thereafter? What did he do to mitigate the baleful consequences for peace and internal unity? Very little. With the appearance of the Freuds, Jones seemed to retreat into the background, and when the

Second World War broke out, in September 1939, he retired to the country, coming up to town for business meetings of the society. (The move was in part motivated by financial worries. With only five patients left, he was "terribly hit.")[99] The administrative work he largely delegated to Klein's chief adversary, Edward Glover, and as the native-born left the capital, prompted by either military service or German bombs, Glover and the Continental analysts (who, as aliens from an enemy country, were not allowed to travel beyond the London area) found themselves in command. Jones might sympathize with Klein in private—he wrote to her that Anna was "certainly a tough, and perhaps indigestible morsel"—but he did nothing to defend her in public.[100]

When in 1927, only a year after Klein's arrival in Britain, Anna Freud had criticized Jones's protégée in print, his behavior had differed markedly. (What had been at issue then—and will be explored in due course—was the technique of child analysis.)[101] In his eagerness to champion Klein, Jones had taken the offensive. "It is a pain to me," he wrote to Freud, "that I cannot agree with *some* of the tendencies in Anna's book and cannot help thinking that they must be due to some imperfectly analysed resistances; in fact I think it is possible to prove this in detail." Jones had overstepped the bounds: it was, Freud retorted, a "breach of good taste" to suggest that someone "had not been sufficiently analysed"—and he claimed that Anna had been "more deeply and thoroughly analysed" than Jones himself. (Freud had, in fact, been his daughter's analyst.) Yet for his part, Freud felt free to impugn the motivation behind what he regarded as "a veritable campaign against Anna's child analysis." Anna was his daughter, and hence, he asked, was this "hasty, violent and unjust reaction" really aimed at him? He answered his own rhetorical question in the affirmative: "A fine motive amongst analysts who demand from others that they control their primitive urges!"[102]

Anna was indeed her father's daughter. She too responded to intellectual disagreement as if it were a personal attack—an attack on her father. And it was to consecrate his memory that she entered the lists against Klein. Whether or not Strachey was correct in asserting that she considered psychoanalysis a "Game Reserve belonging to the F. family," he was clearly on target in claiming that she saw "Mrs. K's ideas" as "fatally subversive." In her view, according to Sylvia Payne, her own work and that of her collaborators was "Freudian analysis, and . . . Mrs. Klein's work" was "not psycho-analysis but a substitution for it."[103] In equating psychoanalysis with Freud's legacy, she skillfully shaped the agonistic field: the central issue became loyalty to the master's formulations.

Klein found herself on the defensive. Though her adherent Susan Isaacs publicly objected to the implicit injunction "that Freud's work and his conclusions" were "never to be developed any further and that no-one" was "to formulate theories which he himself had not yet framed,"[104] and though Klein firmly believed that she was "entitled to continue" Freud's findings, she did not voice such sentiments very often or very loudly. Rather, she took what seemed the safer course of disputing Anna's claim to represent "her father's views." And with this object in mind, Klein urged her followers, "both for the discussions in the Society and with Anna Freud and for our own sake, to refresh our memory on every word Freud has written. . . . Then we might be able . . . to meet the 'Viennese Freudians' on their own ground."[105]

In July 1942 the British Society decided to devote one scientific meeting a month to an examination of theoretical differences—a series that came to be known as the controversial discussions.[106] The following October, the format of those meetings was determined. Glover insisted—and Klein acquiesced—that it behooved those who advanced "new theories" to "make clear in what respects . . . their views . . . amplified accepted Freudian teaching" or called "for a modification of it." Hence it was up to Klein and her supporters to give the opening papers, and that task devolved on Susan Isaacs and Paula Heimann, as well as Melanie Klein herself.[107] All three took pains, as Joan Riviere subsequently commented, to show "that many of the concepts . . . developed by Melanie Klein were already inherent in the earliest psycho-analytical theory and observations, and that her work" progressed "by natural and logical steps from them." With "each side appearing to claim to be more Freudian than the other," she added, the effect was sometimes "farcical."[108]

The discussions, which were held in 1943 and 1944 and which focused on previously circulated papers, were actually serious and even promising—and, in comparison with the business meetings of the previous year, relatively free from nastiness and acrimony. Sylvia Payne, Ella Sharpe, and Marjorie Brierley stood out for their combination of intellectual sophistication, good sense, and tolerance.[109] If left to their own devices, they and other members of an emerging middle group who refused to align themselves with either Anna Freud or Melanie Klein might have been able to explore further the feasibility of coexistence. But such an enterprise was anathema to Anna Freud.

From the start of the discussions she was emphatic in maintaining that "compatibility" was not the question, that "the two theories could not co-exist."[110] At that time she reminded her listeners of the so-called exchange lectures—a program designed in the mid-1930s for mutual explanation of the differences developing between London and Vienna.[111] And by her intransigence, Anna Freud made certain that, at the very least, this second attempt at conceptual clarification would be equally inconclusive.

To what extent and in what respect do false or defective views about the findings or theories of psycho-analysis imply incompetence to carry out a training analysis, to do control work, to conduct a seminar or to give a course of lectures?

In this fashion Strachey posed the question over which the fiercest battle raged. For his part, he tried valiantly to limit the strife to the field of clinical practice:

I suggest that the essential criterion of whether a person is fit to conduct a training analysis is not whether his views on aetiology or theory are true, but whether his technique is valid. If his technique is valid, then any gaps in his knowledge (and there are sure to be many) and any mistakes in his deductions (and they are not likely to be few) will have only what I may call a *local* effect, they will not lead to any *generalized* distortion of the analytic picture, and it will moreover be possible for the gaps to be filled in and the mistakes corrected.

To justify his choice of terrain, Strachey invoked past experience:

It is, indeed, in some such way as this that we must account for all the successful analyses carried out in the period before Freud made his later discoveries and also for all of our own successful analyses to-day—since I am rash enough to believe that in the course of the next hundred or thousand years some further facts will be discovered about the human mind of which we are ignorant to-day.

By shifting the ground from valid theory to valid technique ("valid" was intentionally left vague), Strachey hoped to avoid what he regarded as the greatest danger: "that those who hold one set of views may feel tempted to declare that those who hold the contrary set of views are on that account incompetent to carry out training activities."[112]

He did not succeed. Anna Freud refused to be drawn from her position. Strachey suggested that analytical training might "be based on an 'open forum' where candidates would be introduced to a variety of psychoanalytical tendencies."[113] Anna Freud countered that "if such a teaching procedure had been adopted from the beginning of psychoanalytic development, psychoanalysis of the present day would include the theoretical and technical teachings of, for instance, Stekel, Adler, Jung, Rank, etc. A psychotherapeutic Institute of this type," she continued, "was actually set up in Berlin in 1934, under pressure and according to the express wish of the Nazi regime."[114] With the specter of Nazi Germany before her, she defended her inheritance. With that specter before her, she nonetheless asserted that "if there are two controversial views . . . it is not possible to compromise. . . . Nowhere in the world do people use only legitimate methods. . . . Someone . . . convinced of his views will use all the methods available."[115] In February 1944, following much discussion and memorandum writing, a majority of the Training Committee—and subsequently of the society as well—came to the conclusion that divergences in technique did exist, but that such differences could be contained within existing psychoanalytic practice.[116] In short Anna Freud and Edward Glover found themselves rather than Melanie Klein in a minority, and they resigned from the Training Committee forthwith.[117] (Glover also resigned from the British Society.)

"Freud's daughter has had to resign," one member declared dramatically.[118] Before long, Sylvia Payne, who shortly thereafter was elected president of the society, approached Anna Freud and elicited from her the conditions under which she and her supporters would take an active part in the training program. During the war that program had already begun to split: it had become customary for the Training Committee to assign a Kleinian analyst to candidates wishing Kleinian training and to assign a Freudian analyst to those preferring Freudian training.[119] Payne now agreed to institutionalize this split. In 1946 the society introduced two parallel courses: Course A, organized as formerly on an eclectic basis, with a strong Kleinian element, and Course B, to be taught by Anna Freud and her adherents. (Both courses would come under one Training Committee, which would also take charge of the selection and qualification of candidates.) For a student's first training case, the supervisor was to be chosen from the student's own group; the second was to be selected from the group of analysts—the middle group—who did not identify themselves as either Kleinian or Anna Freudian. "The society remained one, but divided into three separate groups with two training courses."[120]

What effect did this compromise—or stalemate—have on the job of conceptual clarification which had scarcely begun? At the very least, it meant that there would be no public avowal of theoretical shifts. At the very least, it meant that there would be no explicit agreement on the transformation of Freudian paradigms already underway. And to this day no consensual resolution has been acknowledged.

Freudian Paradigms

An assessment of how Klein, Fairbairn, and Winnicott transformed Freudian paradigms dictates some discussion of Freud's own views as points of comparison.

Two strategies for so doing suggest themselves, and since they are not mutually exclusive, I have adopted both. The first is to refer to Freud piecemeal, that is, to take up his ideas where, and to the extent that, Klein, Fairbairn, and Winnicott grappled with them. Such a plan of action promises to capture how the three protagonists of this study conceived their agreement or disagreement with the founder of psychoanalysis. This strategy has been followed in the individual chapters devoted to them.

The second strategy is one of selective recapitulation—of summarizing those strands within the Freudian corpus which rank as paradigmatic. This strategy has been adopted for the present chapter. An irony lurks here: Freud's first attempt to deal with issues of structure, "The Project for a Scientific Psychology," though ignored by the protagonists of this study, of necessity figures as a benchmark for discussion of subsequent work.

Structural theory has been granted the status of paradigm; so too has developmental theory. The first two sections of this chapter sketch Freud's beginnings in late nineteenth-century neurology and how he defined and carried out the model-building task he assigned himself. The last two sections outline his account of sexuality and along with it a developmental paradigm.

Freud and *Fin de Siècle* Neurosis

What was the state of neurology when Freud entered the field in the mid-1880s? How were so-called nervous disorders conceptualized and explained? The word neurosis itself was introduced by one of Britain's most important eighteenth-century physicians, William Cullen, in an attempt to establish a classification of diseases. According to Ilza Veith, "All diseases," in his view, were

disorders of the nervous system, and since only two deviations of this system could be envisaged—namely, excessive or diminished tonus—the limits for nosological arrangement . . . were extremely narrow. . . . Yet, somehow a category of disorders characterized by spasm or atony was segregated from the rest and included under the term "neurosis." It was for this reason, and not because of its psychic concomitants, that hysteria, obviously a spastic or convulsive disorder, fell under the heading of "neurosis."[1]

Through most of the nineteenth century, as psychiatry moved out of the asylum and into the university, research focused not on the nervous system but on the brain. Scientists within the mainstream sought anatomical explanations for psychiatric disorders. In France, despite an emphasis on heredity and mental degeneration, physicians claimed that an anatomically identifiable brain lesion produced mental diseases. In Germany the slogan "mental diseases are diseases of the brain" epitomized professional wisdom; still more, it was widely believed that even those mental disturbances that appeared to be unaccompanied by anatomical lesions "would, if allowed to progress, eventually display such changes."[2] And in Vienna, Freud's own teacher, Theodor Meynert, continued very much in this tradition: his work on cortical localization seemed full of promise to those intent on anatomical specificity. Meynert himself "saw no limits to the potential for correlating the clinical symptoms of psychiatric disorders with local anatomical lesions."[3]

Meynert's optimism was misplaced; the localized lesions could not be found; the correlations could not be made. This is to suggest not that anatomists chalked up no successes but simply that in entire categories of cases autopsies failed to reveal the expected structural changes in the brain. The failure with regard to the neuroses in general and to hysteria in particular was glaring. At this point Jean-Martin Charcot, who already had a distinguished career of elucidating the anatomical lesions associated with a variety of diseases, led the way in rejecting an anatomical basis for hysteria. In so doing Charcot adopted the view that the pathology of hysteria involved a neurodynamic abnormality, "that is, some purely physiological disturbance of the nervous system."[4] Charcot's physiological emphasis echoed that of Cullen, though, in fact, not until Charcot had the notion of physiological abnormality as opposed to an anatomical lesion did he make much headway on the Continent.

What was the "hysteria" that Charcot was exploring? The essential feature, both then and now, has been the existence of physical symptoms for which no demonstrable organic cause can be found. In Charcot's day the cause had been understood to be anatomical, and indeed the fact that the symptoms of hysteria did not resemble those produced by anatomical lesions weighed heavily in his turning away from anatomy; currently what is not demonstrable extends to "known physiological mechanisms" as well.[5] (The American Psychiatric Association's *Diagnostic and Statistical Manual*, third edition, classifies what was once hysteria under the heading "somatoform disorders"; the term "hysterical" in its colloquial meaning of excessively emotional, as in "hysterical female," has been dissolved into "histrionic personality disorder.") The symptoms themselves were legion, and it was Charcot's intention to arrange them in coherent fashion. According to Freud, reporting on the winter of 1885–1886, which he had spent studying with Charcot in Paris, the French neuropathologist succeeded admirably:

I will venture to sum up in a few words what Charcot has achieved. . . . Up to now, hysteria can scarcely be regarded as a name with any well-defined meaning. . . . During the last few decades a hysterical woman would have been almost as certain to be treated as a malingerer, as in earlier centuries she would have been certain to be judged and condemned as a witch or as possessed of the devil. . . .

In his study of hysteria Charcot started out from the most fully developed cases, which he regarded as the perfect type [i.e., "the consciously and intentionally schematized extreme form"][6] of the disease. In these typical cases he next found a number of somatic signs (such as the character of the attack, anaesthesia, disturbances of vision, . . . etc.), which enabled him to establish the diagnosis of hysteria with certainty on the basis of positive indications. . . . Rapidly increasing experience with the most excellent material soon enabled him to take into account as well the deviations from the typical picture. . . . Thus, by his efforts, hysteria was lifted out of the chaos of the neuroses, was differentiated from other conditions with a similar appearance, and was provided with a symptomology which, though sufficiently multifarious, nevertheless makes it impossible any longer to doubt the rule of law and order.[7]

During the course of the following decade Freud became less confident that "law and order" truly ruled. The neuroses—and the neurotics—he encountered seemed to be mixed cases, and he concluded that "it was not right to stamp a neurosis as a whole as hysterical because a few hysterical signs were prominent in its complex of symptoms." He continued:

Whenever a hysterical sign, such as an anaesthesia or a characteristic attack, was found in a complicated case of psychical degeneracy, the whole condition was described as one of 'hysteria', so that it is not surprising that the worst and the most contradictory things were found under this label.[8]

The work of specifying the various neuroses remained far from complete. But Freud's aim went beyond clarifying the clinical picture; he wanted to elucidate the motive that governed the ailment as well.

At the very outset Freud introduced intention into his work on the neuroses.[9] It was embedded in his central concept: defense—the effort of will or the intention to push away or fend off a painful thought. Why should a thought be painful? Once again Freud couched his explanation in purposive terms by stressing a second crucial concept: incompatible ideas. His neurotic patients, he argued, began their attempts at defense

the moment . . . *an occurrence of incompatibility took place in their ideational life*—that is to say, . . . [when] their ego was faced with an experience, an idea or a feeling which aroused such a distressing affect that the subject decided to forget about it because he had no confidence in his power to resolve the contradiction between that incompatible idea and his ego by means of thought-activity.[10]

With defense playing the crucial role, it was but a short step to group together, and then to contrast, the neuroses that seemed to have this function in common—those which Freud called the neuropsychoses of defense. What was vital to the distinctions Freud made among them was the notion of an idea and the affect it aroused as separable, and hence subject to differing fates. "In hysteria, the incompatible idea is rendered innocuous by its *sum of excitation being transformed into something somatic.*" For this process Freud used the term "conversion." In obsessions and phobias the affect remains in the psychical, rather than the somatic, sphere. It "attaches *itself to other ideas which* are *not in themselves incompatible; and, thanks to this 'false connection', those ideas turn into obsessional ideas.*"[11]

Where Freud stressed defense, Josef Breuer, his senior coauthor in *Studies on Hysteria*, stressed hypnoid states. For Breuer, as for Freud, the central issue was, What kept affect-laden ideas from being deprived of affect by associative contact, that is, by the influences "of thinking, or corrections by reference to other ideas"? The answer, Breuer claimed, was this: the idea remained "exempt from being worn away by thought . . . because it originally emerged and was endowed with affect in states in respect of which there" was "amnesia in waking consciousness— . . . in hypnosis or in states similar to it." "The importance of these states" lay "in their power to bring about the splitting of the mind" which was "of fundamental significance for 'major hysteria'." And so it had been, Breuer suggested, since time immemorial: the split-off mind was none other than the devil who, in superstitious eras, had been thought to possess anyone mentally disturbed. It was true "that a spirit alien to the patient's waking consciousness" had held "sway in him; but the spirit" had not been "an alien one, but a part of his own."[12]

Freud became adamant; he claimed that he had never "met with a genuine hypnoid hysteria":

Any that I took in hand has turned into a defence hysteria. It is not, indeed, that I have never had to do with symptoms which demonstrably arose during dissociated states of consciousness and were obliged for that reason to remain excluded from the ego. This was sometimes so in my cases as well; but I was able to show afterwards that the so-called hypnoid state owed its separation to the fact that in it a psychical group had come into effect which had previously been split off by defence. In short, I am unable to suppress a suspicion that somewhere or other the roots of hypnoid and defence hysteria come together, and that the primary factor is defence.[13]

In insisting on defense, Freud had no intention of severing the psychical and psychological from the physiological. Indeed he was far from certain that the processes he had elucidated were psychical at all; it might be more appropriate, he intimated, to think of them as the "psychical consequences" of physical processes.[14] What were those physical processes? How could psychical consequences be explained in mechanistic terms? Freud made a valiant, albeit abortive, effort to answer these questions.

Mind: Psychological Speculation

That effort, which absorbed Freud in the latter part of 1895, resulted in what is now known as "The Project for a Scientific Psychology" and what Freud originally entitled "Psychology for Neurologists." He had started out with high hopes, confident that he could get his mechanical model of the mind to run of its own accord, and after a period of intense, indeed frantic, intellectual activity, he sent off the manuscript to Wilhelm Fliess. By the end of the year, however, Freud's hopes had vanished: he wrote to his friend that he could "no longer understand the state of mind" he had been in when he had composed the "Project."[15] With the exception of an addendum dated January 1, 1896, Freud simply allowed the work to be buried, and so it remained until it appeared, along with the bulk of his correspondence with Fliess, in a German edition in 1950 and was translated into English four years later. Though Freud judged the "Project" a failure and certainly intended to keep it from view, it haunted "the whole series" of his "theoretical writings to the very end"[16]—indeed this sketch, as he sometimes referred to it, stands as the initial statement of a structural paradigm. Hence any assessment of how subsequent work (even work done in ignorance of the "Project" itself) transformed Freudian paradigms must start with that document.[17]

Freud's mechanistic explanation began with energy. In his "Project," energy, represented by "Q," was material and subject to the "laws of motion." What sort of material Freud thought Q was made of was not altogether clear: James Strachey argued that Freud simply did not know.[18] Karl Pribram and Merton Gill maintained that Freud had something neurochemical in mind, which in 1895 could be described only in terms of its electrical manifestations.[19] (The neurochemical interpretation has the advantage of giving "energy" a meaning that would link it to modern neurophysiology.) As for the "laws of motion," what interested Freud was the principle of inertia, that is, the tendency of the apparatus to divest itself of energy. To assure compliance with this principle, he fastened on the mechanism of discharge (a formulation subsequently undermined by Cannon's classic work on homeostasis). The point that is crucial to an explication of the "Project" is not the current repute of Q but the fact that it appears in two distinguishable forms: flowing and static, or free and bound.

That Q was material stood as Freud's first theorem; neuron theory figured as his second. (Here Freud was building on previous developments in histology; in 1891 Waldeyer had used the term "neuron" to denote the basic unit of the nervous system.) Taken together these two theorems could account for what Freud regarded as the primary and secondary activities of the nervous system: discharge and accumulation. Discharge implied "a *current* passing from the cell's path of conduction or processes [dendrites] to the axis-cylinder." Accumulation assumed resistance to discharge, and resistance itself, Freud argued, was probably "located in the *contacts* [between one neurone and another]," which thus served as *"barriers."*[20]

Freud was correct in considering the hypothesis of contact-barriers as "fruitful in many directions." (Two years later the term "synapse" was introduced by Foster and Sherrington.) It allowed him to differentiate two classes of neurons, those which behaved as if they had no contact-barriers, that is, offered no resistance and were permeable, and those "whose contact-barriers" made "themselves felt," that is, offered a great deal of resistance and were impermeable. Though Freud was ready to admit that "histologically" nothing was "known in support of the distinction" he was making, it nonetheless seemed to fit well with the double task the nervous system had to perform: the handling of both exogenous and endogenous stimuli, the first accomplished by the system of permeable neurons, the second by impermeable neurons.[21] Thus, in rough summary, external stimuli, permeable neurons, losing Q, and discharge formed one cluster; endogenous stimuli, impermeable neurons, retaining (or "cathecting") Q, and accumulation formed another.

Two further complications must be introduced, each an apparently extreme form of one of the two neuronic systems already outlined, and each in consequence a further elaboration of the hypothesis of contact-barriers. The extreme form of the impermeable system Freud called the "ego." Its neurons he depicted as constantly cathected, hence serving as a storehouse of Q.[22] From it Q could be drawn to boost the flow of energy. Less obviously it could also retard the passage of Q. (In fact, in mammals at least, excitatory and inhibitory systems of neurons are now conceived of as separate.)[23] Note that from the beginning Freud assigned a directing or executive role to the ego. (By the same token, he was unable to provide it with a developmental history: the ego had to be more or less there from the beginning.)

The extreme form of the permeable system Freud marked off as a third system of neurons, giving it its own Greek letter, ω. This system was designed to transform "external quantity into quality," and since quantity was, by definition, allowed no place in it, its neurons had to be conceived of as completely permeable. What allowed quantity to be transformed into quality? At this point Freud invoked a temporal characteristic of the flow of Q, periodicity, that could be transmitted without resistance from contact-barriers. What is crucial here is that he ascribed responsibility for consciousness to the ω system through excitation by periodicities. Note the attenuated role of consciousness in his model of the mind.[24]

Where did intention fit into this mechanistic scheme? Along with Q, the motive force in the mechanistic scheme, Freud set up memory, construed in terms of Q, as a motive force in the purposive scheme. To establish the rules of translation so that one could easily switch between the two, Freud again exploited the hypothesis of contact-barriers:

A psychological theory deserving any consideration must furnish an explanation of 'memory'. Now any such explanation comes up against the difficulty that it must assume on the one hand that neurones are permanently different after an excitation from what they were before, while nevertheless it cannot be disputed that, in general, fresh excitations meet with the same conditions of reception as did the earlier ones. It would seem, therefore, that neurones must be both influenced and also unaltered, unprejudiced. We cannot off-hand imagine an apparatus capable of such complicated functioning; the situation is accordingly saved by attributing the characteristic of being permanently influenced by excitation to one class of neurones, and, on the other hand, the unalterability—the characteristic of being fresh for new excitations—to another class.[25]

The former class was the ψ system (impermeable neurons), and it offered a *"possibility of representing memory."* The state of those contact-barriers (and recall that contact-barriers, not neurons themselves, served to distinguish the two systems of neurons) was permanently altered by the passage of an excitation, making them more capable of conduction. This capability Freud described as "their degree of facilitation." Not all contact-barriers, he added, were equally well facilitated, and indeed differentiation was essential. It would therefore be more accurate to say that memory was *represented by the difference in the facilitations between the* ψ *neurones*"—in effect, grooved into the mental apparatus and acting as a normal motive force.[26]

So far nothing has been said about defense. It was, after all, Freud's desire to provide a physical substrate for the neuropsychoses of defense which had propelled him into theory building. More particularly, he had hoped to draw a distinction between normal and pathological defense. Here he was to reach an impasse.

The crucial question for Freud was how to describe a process that most of the time prevented an eruption of extremely large quantities of Q—i.e., of pain—but that on occasion failed to do so. (Recall that he had already made it clear in his clinical writings that he conceived of defense as an ego activity.) His answer, as he himself fully appreciated, was far from satisfactory. Normal defense (or defense proper) he characterized as entailing what he called side-cathexis: the interference with the flow of Q through its being channeled into neurons adjacent to the pathway it would otherwise have followed. (Side-cathexes, in fact, constituted Freud's mechanistic explanation of the ego's inhibitory function, and hence defense and inhibition proved to be one and the same.) As for pathological defense, he did no more than point to the deficiencies of side-cathexes: these proved able to provide a counterweight to the passage of Q only up to a certain point.[27]

Earlier Freud had stressed the ego's role in fending off ideas it found incompatible, the simultaneous splitting of an idea and its affect, and the differing fates to which each was subjected, which in turn entailed different neuroses. These notions underwent no radical alteration. Rather, Freud enlarged upon the course taken by the neuropsychoses themselves. A painful experience, he wrote, did not lead to an immediate outbreak of neurosis. It led instead to a primary symptom of defense, such as conscientiousness in the case of obsessional neurosis, and that symptom was usually regarded as "successful" and "the equivalent of health." "Illness proper" occurred only when the idea (or memories) defended against—"repressed" was the term Freud shortly began to employ—returned, and when the ensuing "struggle between them and the ego" produced new symptoms of a disabling sort.[28] Freud thus characterized illness as *the return of the repressed memories*"—that is, "the failure of the defence."[29]

This failure could perhaps be attributed, Freud hoped, to something inherent in particular ideas or memories which made their taming such an arduous and even overwhelming task.

━━ ━━ ━━ ━━ ━━

If an initial painful experience had been contained by side-cathexes, why did the memory of that experience over-burden the ego? To put matters simply: sexuality offered Freud a way to explain what set pathological defense in motion.[30] (Note the conventionality of the views he still adhered to in 1895: the onset of sexuality did not occur until puberty.) Freud surmised that in this case memory provoked a greater quantity of unpleasure than the initial experience itself: the memory had a greater subsequent "releasing power" than "had been produced by the experience corresponding to it."[31] Only sexuality, or more specifically, a sexual experience in childhood remembered after puberty, fitted the postulate of an energetic discrepancy between experience and memory. By this route Freud arrived at his celebrated seduction hypothesis.

Having hit upon childhood sexual experience to account for etiology, Freud proposed linking specific sexual events with specific neuroses. His confidence, however, proved short-lived; his faith in the actuality of those events evaporated rapidly; his belief in his patients' stories of parental, largely paternal, sexual abuse crumbled.[32] But he was not led thereby to abandon sexuality. What now became imperative was the redefinition of sexuality itself.

Freud and *Libido Sexualis*

In that redefinition "instinct," as James Strachey translated Freud's *Trieb* in the *Standard Edition,* played the leading role. Whether in fact "instinct" is the correct translation for "*Trieb*" has been much debated. "Drive" is the word that critics of the *Standard Edition* most frequently prefer, since it seems to bear a closer resemblance to the German original. Yet as Strachey pointed out in his own defense, " 'drive', used in this sense, is not an English word," and this, after all, "aims at being a translation into English." Moreover, Freud employed the word *Trieb* to cover what was "from the standpoint of modern biology" a variety of different concepts, and it would require, Strachey continued, "a very brave man seriously to argue that rendering Freud's '*Trieb*' by 'drive' " would clear up the situation. "The only rational thing to do," he concluded, was "to choose an obviously vague and indeterminate word and stick to it."[33] "Instinct," he believed, fitted that description.

Freud would have liked a concept less vague and less indeterminate; yet, as he noted with regret, nothing of the sort was to be had. "No more urgent need" existed "in psychology than for a securely founded theory of the instincts on which it might then be possible to build further."[34] The working-over of psychological material called "for the application . . . of definite assumptions concerning instinctual life, and it would be a desirable thing if those assumptions could be taken from some other branch of knowledge and carried over to psychology." In the absence of a clear biological concept, Freud doubted "whether any decisive pointers for the differentiation and classification of the instincts" could be "arrived at on the basis of . . . psychological material."[35] Still he went ahead. And though he felt constrained to assert nothing that ran counter to biology, the very indefiniteness of that discipline left him wide latitude.

Even before he had explicitly abandoned the seduction hypothesis, Freud had written to Fliess that "the psychical structures which, in hysteria, are affected by repression are not in reality memories . . . but *impulses*."[36] Yet much remained to be done. Though certain key elements had already been located—and discussed with Fliess—it was not until the publication of the third edition of the *Three Essays on the Theory of Sexuality* in 1915 that the various pieces were fitted together in comprehensive fashion.[37]

━━ ━━ ━━ ━━ ━━

The theory Freud elaborated did not cover all the instincts; it was restricted to sexuality. Indeed he took pains to distinguish sexual instinctual impulses—referred to as "libido"—from instinctual forces in general. (He assumed a "special chemistry for the sexual function" whose existence would vindicate the segregation of sexuality.)[38] Why Freud came to concentrate on sex need not detain us here; it was almost as if all roads led to this particular Rome. What should be emphasized are the ways in which Freud took up concepts already at hand in the work of contemporary sexual pathologists, notably Richard von Krafft-Ebing, Albert Moll, and his own confidant, Wilhelm

Fliess, and transformed them into a wide-ranging developmental theory—and thereby transformed psychoanalysis into an evolutionary science.[39]

The general strategy adopted by Freud, and not by him alone, was to break down the notion of sexuality into distinct units and then to redeploy those units in a variety of combinations for a variety of purposes. The first such division served a largely preparatory function. Freud, like Moll in his *Libido sexualis,* distinguished between sexual aim and sexual object.[40] Drawing on studies of inversion or homosexuality, he concluded that the sexual aim was "in the first instance independent of its object" and that only later were the two "soldered together."[41] It was from aim alone that he was to derive his most versatile subconcepts.

Above all, the investigation of perversions (and here Krafft-Ebing's *Psychopathia sexualis* occupied a preeminent place) provided the necessary clinical material to unravel the matter of sexual aim.[42] Freud's definition of perversions, though hardly original, gave a clear indication of the threads of his own argument:

Perversions are sexual activities which either (a) extend, in an anatomical sense, beyond the regions of the body that are designed for sexual union, or (b) linger over the intermediate relations to the sexual object which should normally be traversed rapidly on the path towards the final sexual aim.[43]

The first notion, that of "anatomical extensions," led on to an elaboration of erotogenic zones; the second notion, of "fixations of preliminary sexual aim," opened the way for discussing component instincts. Together these two made infantile sexuality a logical deduction, and stages of libidinal development a plausible assumption.

As early as 1896, in a letter to Fliess, Freud had spoken of abandoned erotogenic zones. In childhood, so he had commented, many parts of the body could be used for sexual release.[44] Some parts of the "skin or mucous membrane" seemed predestined to play the role of erotogenic zones, and others could easily be pressed into service. In fact any part might take on that function; a "feeling of pleasure possessing a particular quality" need only be evoked from it under stimulation. Freud's interest, however, fastened on those parts that, on the ample evidence provided by sexual practices, normal and perverted, appeared "to be claiming that they should themselves be regarded and treated as genitals," that is, the mouth and anus.[45] Not only were these two bodily parts the most notably erotogenic nongenital areas; they were also to figure, along with the genitals, as markers for stages of libidinal development.

As for fixations of preliminary aim, "every external or internal factor," Freud wrote, that hindered or postponed "the attainment of the normal sexual aim" lent "support to the tendency to linger over the preparatory activities and to turn them into new sexual aims." Freud himself lingered over sadism. There was no doubt in his mind that this, along with masochism, was both abnormal and sexual. There was no doubt in his mind that it was normal as well: "the sexuality of most male human beings" contained "an element of *aggressiveness*—a desire to subjugate." It followed that in normal sexuality sadism was only one among many components, whereas in perversion sadism had "become independent and exaggerated" and had "usurped the leading position." In short, the sexual instinct was made up of "amalgamations" that were "lost to view in the uniform behaviour of normal people" but that emerged in abnormality, when the components came apart.[46]

With erotogenic zones and component instincts in place, Freud was equipped to argue that sexuality extended back to the tenderest, and supposedly innocent, years of childhood. Freud's observations were commonplace; his theoretical conclusions were not. He began with thumb sucking. (S. Lindner had already imputed to it a sexual nature.)[47] The circumstances under which pleasure was evoked from lips and mouth were not difficult to imagine: "[I]t was the child's first and most vital activity, his sucking at his mother's breast, or at substitutes for it, that must have familiarized him with this pleasure."

The need for repeating the sexual satisfaction now becomes detached from the need for taking nourishment—a separation which becomes inevitable when the teeth appear and food is no longer taken in only by sucking, but is also chewed up. The child does not make use of an extraneous body for his sucking, but prefers a part of his own skin because it is more convenient.[48]

Freud's reasoning ran like a syllogism: the mouth was an erotogenic zone; sucking involved the mouth; sucking was an erotic activity. He thus seemed to be begging the question of why the satisfaction obtained from sucking, whether nipple or thumb, should be considered sexual at all.

Component instincts offered a second line of argument, though it too smacked of special pleading. If, as Freud at least implied, it was acceptable to refer to a component as sexual, that is, to let the name of the whole stand for one of its parts, then the same name might be employed for the very first manifestation of that part. To be more concrete: no one denied that kissing as forepleasure was both a component of adult sexuality and sexual in itself. So too, Freud would have argued, was kissing at its initial appearance.[49] Above all, he refused to countenance restricting the sexual to the merely genital. One suspects that his insistence derived in part from his understanding of instinct: he could not imagine its coming into being *after* the mental apparatus had already begun to function.[50]

How, then, should one characterize sexuality before the genital had become the outstanding, if not exclusive, erotogenic zone? It was plausible to assume that a prior organization or organizations existed; after all, erotogenic zones and component instincts might be linked in a variety of ways, some more stable and more prevalent than others. In the 1915 edition of the *Three Essays* Freud was ready at last to postulate clearly demarcated stages; it was not until 1923, however, that those stages were given their final names.[51] As he remarked in a later publication:

The first of these 'pregenital' phases is known to us as the *oral* one because, in conformity with the way in which an infant in arms is nourished, the erotogenic zone of the mouth dominates what may be called the sexual activity of that period of life. At a second level the *sadistic* and *anal* impulses come to the fore, undoubtedly in connection with the appearance of teeth, the strengthening of the muscular apparatus and the control of the sphincter functions. . . . Thirdly comes the *phallic* phase in which in both sexes the male organ (and what corresponds to it in girls) attains an importance which can no longer be overlooked. We have reserved the name of *genital* phase for the definitive sexual organization which is established after puberty and in which the female genital organ for the first time meets with the recognition which the male one acquired long before.[52]

Psychoanalytic theory has not remained content with only three stages; numerous additions have been hypothesized. What is of interest here are the interpolations suggested by Karl Abraham; they were welcomed by Freud himself and became staples in the intellectual fare digested by the protagonists of this work. In "A Short Study of the Development of the Libido," which appeared in 1924, Abraham recommended dividing each of Freud's stages into two parts, making a total of six; but in fact, only with regard to the oral and anal stages did he follow his own advice. Within the oral phase Abraham distinguished between a primary level at which "the libido of the infant" was "attached to the act of sucking" and a secondary one in which the child exchanged "its sucking activity for a biting one." The first stage Abraham regarded as pre-ambivalent: the child had feelings neither of hatred nor of love. With the second stage, dominated by cannibalistic impulses and dubbed oral-sadistic, ambivalence entered upon the scene. In similar fashion, Abraham split Freud's anal-sadistic phase: in its earlier period hostile tendencies characterized by expulsion, and epitomized by defecation, emerged; in its latter period the wish to conserve and control, epitomized by retention of feces, made its appearance.[53] Note that Abraham, in placing the ambivalence of love and hate at the center of his conceptualizations, *a fortiori* reintroduced relations to specific objects: where Freud concentrated on aim, Abraham began the process of reuniting aim and object.

What was the justification for such fine-tuning of stages and substages? Granted that it was plausible to assume a developmental sequence along the road to genitality; still it was quite another matter to postulate so exact a succession. Freud was caught on the horns of a dilemma. On the one hand, he appreciated that his specific stages should not be taken literally; on the other hand, the substitution of libido theory for the seduction hypothesis in his etiological account required an adherence to the notion of such stages.

In 1896, in a letter to Fliess, Freud had enclosed a chart summing up his "solution to the aetiology of the psycho-neuroses." The left-hand column listed the neuroses in question: hysteria, obsessional neurosis, and paranoia. A horizontal row indicated chronology, the age at which the pathogenic sexual experience of each neurosis occurred. (It was not the experience itself, Freud argued, which was so fateful; rather, its mnemic residues determined the particular kind of neurotic outcome—and what happened to them was a function of age.)[54] In 1921, in a very brief comment, "Contribution to a Discussion on Tic," Abraham published a chart in four columns, two of which echoed Freud's earlier tabulation: the neuroses were the same, but age at the time of sexual experience was replaced by stage of libidinal development.[55] Abraham's tabulation was no more than a crude effort to follow Freud's injunction "to explain all neurotic and psychotic phenomena as proceeding from abnormal vicissitudes of the libido, that is, diversions from its normal employment."[56]

The critical issue this second chart raised was regression, or "a return of the sexual organization as a whole to earlier stages."[57] Regression, Freud and Abraham argued, was accompanied by fixation, or rather, it scarcely had an existence separate from its conceptual mate; for what predisposed libido to regress to an earlier stage was a fixation at that particular stage. Freud defined fixation as a lagging behind "of a part trend"; and "the stronger the fixations," the greater the likelihood of a regression:

Consider that, if a people which is in movement has left strong detachments behind at the stopping-places on its migration, it is likely that the more advanced parties will be inclined to retreat to these stopping-places if they have been defeated or have come up against a superior enemy. But they will also be in the greater danger of being defeated the more of their number they have left behind on their migration.[58]

A nice rhetorical flourish for a lay audience, particularly for an audience familiar with biological arrests of development. The descriptive value of the terms "fixation" and "regression" was incontestable; yet they offered scant explanation for neurotic phenomena.

Oedipus: A Complex Left Dangling

Was there a tension between Freud's etiological claims on behalf of libido theory and his statement that the Oedipus complex should "be regarded as the nucleus of the neuroses"?[59] On this latter point, he was unequivocal:

Every new arrival on this planet is faced by the task of mastering the Oedipus complex; anyone who fails falls a victim to neurosis. . . . The importance of the Oedipus complex . . . has become the shibboleth that distinguishes the adherents of psycho-analysis from its opponents.[60]

What was at issue here was the relation between stages of libidinal development and stages in the development of object love.

As already indicated, Freud viewed people as late arrivals on one's sexual scene; the mother's breast, or its substitute, however, was there at the start:

At a time at which the first beginnings of sexual satisfaction are still linked with the taking of nourishment, the sexual instinct has a sexual object outside the infant's own body in the shape of his mother's breast. It is only later that the instinct loses that object, just at the time, perhaps, when the child is able to form a total idea of the person to whom the organ that is giving him satisfaction belongs. As a rule the sexual instinct then becomes auto-erotic.[61]

Between the stage of autoerotism and object choice proper Freud was to interpolate a narcissistic phase—when the subject took his own person or his own body as his love object. Object love itself first appeared with the phallic stage of libidinal organization; at one and the same time, the male child found his mother as love object and discovered his genitals as a source of sexual delight.

With this convergence of what had been two separate currents, the oedipal drama began. Actually, Freud's hypothesis of such a complex predated his elaboration of libido theory; it had emerged in the course of his self-analysis, and as early as 1897 he had communicated it to Fliess:

One single thought of general value has been revealed to me. I have found, in my own case too, falling in love with the mother and jealousy of the father, and I now regard it as a universal event of early childhood. . . . If this is so, we can understand the riveting power of *Oedipus Rex*. . . . Each member of the audience was once, in germ and in phantasy, just such an Oedipus.[62]

In subsequently locating the complex at the time when two sequential developmental lines joined, Freud was making a valiant effort to set his clinical hypothesis on a biological base.

Once again fixation and regression figured as central. Recall that instincts or their components could become fixated on a pregenital aim; they could also become fixated on a pregenital object or on the object of the phallic phase. Regression thus entailed a return not only to earlier stages of sexual organization but to earlier stages of object love. It his subsequent writings Freud did no more than sketch in perfunctory fashion the development of that love. It was this very question that was to be of primary concern to his British followers.

Melanie Klein: The World of Internal Objects

At the time of the controversial discussions within the British Psycho-Analytical Society, and in the heat of debate, one question dominated: Was Melanie Klein a heretic? She herself clung to the forms of orthodoxy; so too she peppered her papers with quotations from Freud. In fact, she was far more radical than she cared to admit.[1] No doubt much of her work can be considered merely an addition to the Freudian corpus. She stretched his concepts (I will introduce or reintroduce them in due course), sometimes changing their meaning in the process, emptying them of Freud's presuppositions and filling them with hypotheses of her own. Still, until the mid-1930s, they remained recognizably his concepts. Then audacity, perhaps not fully conscious, won out: Klein called into question central psychoanalytic postulates about normal and pathological development. And though she has never won kudos for conceptual elegance, she set an agenda for future clarification. In short, Melanie Klein began by exploring terrain Freud had already staked out, and then opened up new territories he had only dimly perceived.

From Instinct to Fantasy

Klein's interest in instinct was largely instrumental. She depended upon it for one purpose alone: to account for anxiety, to give biological grounding to the phenomenon she confronted most frequently in the consulting room. Throughout the 1920s she remained within the bounds of libido theory as outlined by Freud and elaborated by her mentor, Karl Abraham. Not until 1932 did she publicly sacrifice complexity, abandon common sense, and embrace the "death instinct" that Freud had enunciated more than a decade earlier in *Beyond the Pleasure Princple*.[2] Ironically, it was the indirect effect of Freud's subsequent writings that goaded Klein on. In reworking his theory of anxiety, he himself threatened its instinctual underpinning. And in an effort to rescue what Freud had endangered, Klein latched on to the death instinct and elevated it to the status of a cardinal tenet.

In *Inhibitions, Symptoms and Anxiety*, published in 1926, Freud flatly admitted that he had changed his mind about anxiety:

It is no use denying the fact, though it is not pleasant to recall it, that I have on many occasions asserted that in repression the instinctual representative is distorted, displaced, and so on, while the libido belonging to the instinctual impulse is transformed into anxiety. . . . I can no longer maintain this view. And indeed, I found it impossible at the time to explain how a transformation of that kind was carried out.[3]

The view of anxiety Freud had just discarded had been crucial to him in the 1890s: it had provided the basis on which his concept of the actual neuroses had rested. In contrast to the neuropsychoses of defense, Freud considered neurasthenia and anxiety neurosis—the two actual neuroses he differentiated—to be of strictly somatic origin. In these maladies, *"an accumulation of physical sexual tension,"* that is, inadequate sexual satisfaction, produced neurotic anxiety.[4] (Here, one might add, Freud took his first step toward asserting the sexual etiology of neuroses in general.) Yet almost simultaneously he had adumbrated an alternative theory of anxiety. In the "Project" he had hypothesized that experiences both of pleasure and of pain left residues: wishful states and states of apprehension. These states, in turn, functioned as signals, setting in motion attempts either to repeat or to avoid the primary experience.[5] In 1926 this second formulation appeared in print. Anxiety, Freud wrote, "was reproduced as an affective state in accordance with an already existing mnemic image."[6] Before long, "anxiety as a signal announcing a situation of danger" became the new orthodoxy.[7]

Three particular situations, all of which had figured or were to figure in psychoanalytic writing, offered themselves as contestants for priority: birth, loss of one's mother, and the threat of castration. Birth, Freud argued, scarcely belonged in the competition—it had no "psychical content"; it was "not experienced subjectively as a separation from the mother, since the foetus" was "totally unaware of her existence as an object." He had more difficulty dismissing the loss of the mother herself; in his mind it seemed to occupy a position midway between the purely biological phenomenon of birth and the psychologically significant phenomenon of object loss. In contrast, in the phallic phase the child's penis had become an object par excellence. Freud went so far as to suggest that a variety of fears, including dread of death, could be "regarded as analogous to the fear of castration."[8] In short, he came close to asserting that for the male child at least the threat of castration constituted the gravest danger of all.

Taken together, his formulation of anxiety as a signal and his preference for the castration variety thereof marked a shift away from his emphasis on internal stimuli. So long as he had maintained that it was libido that was transformed into anxiety, so long as he thought that "a libidinal cathexis of the boy's mother, . . . as a result of repression, had been changed into anxiety," anxiety itself remained instinctually grounded. But once Freud had reconceptualized anxiety as a signal that set repression in operation, once he had decided that "it was anxiety that made repression," the connection between anxiety and instinct became tenuous. Being in love with one's mother appeared to the boy "as an internal danger, which he must avoid by renouncing that object" only "because it conjured up an external situation of danger." What Freud had earlier regarded as an internal instinctual threat "turned out to be a determinant and preparation for an external, real, situation of danger":

Above all, it is not a question of whether castration is really carried out; what is decisive is that the danger is one that threatens from outside and that the child believes in it. He has some ground for this, for people threaten him often enough with cutting off his penis during the phallic phase, at the time of his early masturbation, and hints at that punishment must regularly find phylogenetic reinforcement in him. It is our suspicion that during the human family's primaeval period castration used actually to be carried out by a jealous and cruel father upon growing boys, and that circumcision, which so frequently plays a part in puberty rites among primitive peoples, is a clearly recognizable relic of it.[9]

From a ubiquitous to a fortuitous external threat was a step that Freud never took. Yet he had implied such a possibility. And this was precisely what Klein was determined to deny.

At the time Freud published *Inhibitions, Symptoms and Anxiety*, Klein was in the course of a theoretical reworking of her own. By 1927, with her paper "Criminal Tendencies in Normal Children," her emphasis on aggression was amply apparent.[10] Increasingly she had come to focus on the oral-sadistic and anal sadistic stages of libidinal development, and more specifically on their sadistic components. To Klein aggression and anxiety appeared indissolubly linked: the child's primitive sadistic tendencies, directed, to be sure, against those he loved, invariably aroused his anxiety. And it was the status of these components that was particularly endangered by Freud's altered views of anxiety.

No matter how much weight Freud might give to external threats to libidinal satisfaction, there was little prospect of his severing libidinal desire itself from internal stimuli. The same could not be said of aggression: here there was a real possibility that external frustration would be called upon to explain a child's rage. The question for Klein was not whether external frustrations had an impact but whether they *produced* sadistic impulses or merely heightened impulses already in existence. Her preference for the latter formulation went without saying. By adopting Freud's hypothesis of a death instinct, she could retain anxiety as an unavoidable and omnipresent response to something internal.[11]

With the status of anxiety securely in place—at least in her own mind—Klein was free to ignore instincts themselves. The mechanics, or energetics, of anxiety scarcely interested her; its meaning or ideational content was the domain she intended to explore. "Ideational content" reminds one of Freud's beginnings, of his notion of idea and affect as separable. Was Klein doing no more than unwittingly returning psychoanalysis to the mid-1890s? That was impossible: Freud's work during the intervening years had ruled out any such "regression." In fact, libido theory left its mark on both the concept and the content of unconscious fantasy that became Klein's stock-in-trade.

Fantasy had likewise been one of Freud's staples.[12] When, in the late 1890s, he abandoned the seduction hypothesis, he latched on to it: sexual fantasies replaced sexual experiences in his revised etiological account of hysteria. Not until 1911, however, did he try to find a place for fantasy in the mental apparatus he had earlier sketched out:

In the psychology which is founded on psychoanalysis we have become accustomed to taking as our starting-point the unconscious mental processes. . . . We consider these to be the older, primary processes, the residues of a phase of development in which they were the only kind of mental process. The governing purpose obeyed by these primary processes is easy to recognize; it is described as the pleasure-unpleasure principle, or more shortly the pleasure principle. . . .

With the introduction of the reality principle one species of thought-activity was split off; it was kept free from reality-testing and remained subordinated to the pleasure principle alone. This activity is *phantasying*, which begins already in children's play, and later, continued as *day-dreaming*, abandons dependence on real objects.[13]

That fantasy itself might be unconscious posed no problem for Freud. Like an incompatible idea or a painful memory, it could be repressed. Could there, however, be a species of fantasy that had never been conscious at all?[14] Freud answered in the affirmative. Yet in his work unconscious fantasy of this sort led a shadowy existence; it held center stage in Klein's.

For her the crucial statement was simple enough: fantasy and instinctual life went hand in hand. In his early attempts to define instinct, Freud had, in fact, drawn no fixed line between it and its psychical representative; subsequently he had differentiated them, with the result that instinct had figured as "something non-psychical." (His intermediate notion of instinct as on "the frontier between the mental and the somatic" merely underlined the ambiguity of the concept itself.)[15] Susan Isaacs, who, in her contribution to the controversial discussions entitled "The Nature and Function of Phantasy," undertook to explicate Klein's views, opted for the simpler version of instinct as nonpsychical. Fantasy could then be conceptualized as "the mental corollary, the psychic representative of instinct." There was "no impulse, no instinctual urge or response," Isaacs wrote, that was "not experienced as unconscious phantasy."[16]

Although, as Isaacs claimed, fantasies expressed "primarily an internal and subjective reality," they were from the beginning "bound up with an actual, however limited and narrow, experience of objective reality":

The first bodily experiences begin to build up the first memories, and external realities are progressively woven into the texture of phantasy. Before long, the child's phantasies are able to draw upon plastic images as well as sensations—visual, auditory, kinaesthetic, touch, taste, smell images, etc. And these plastic images and dramatic representations of phantasy are progressively elaborated along with articulated perceptions of the external world.[17]

Mind was anchored in reality—or in Freudian language, the reality principle effectively operated from birth onward. In consequence, the distinction between primary and secondary processes (which corresponded to that between the pleasure principle and the reality principle) became less clear-cut—and as a developmental sequence in effect dropped out.[18]

Unconscious fantasy, then, not only transcribed instinctual drives but recorded, albeit in potentially distorted form, external reality as well. In addition unconscious fantasy served as the representative of "mental mechanisms." "Mental mechanisms" referred to the varied processes "by which impulses and feelings" were "controlled and expressed, internal equilibrium" was "maintained and adaptation to the external world achieved." Quite an assignment, the carrying out of which was "intimately related to particular sorts of phantasy."[19]

Two mechanisms (and their associated fantasies) received special attention. In the controversial discussions, with a paper entitled "Certain Functions of Introjection and Projection in Early Infancy," Paula Heimann expounded the Kleinian elaboration of these once simple concepts. (The term "introjection" had been coined in 1909 by Sándor Ferenczi to denote the opposite of projection.)[20]

When the ego receives stimuli from outside, it absorbs them and makes them part of itself, it introjects them. When it bars them off, it projects them, because the decision of their harmfulness is subsequent to a trial introjection. . . . When it discharges inner tensions, it projects something of its own. Thus projection relates to what was originally part of the self as well as to what was originally part of the outer world.[21]

Here, as in Freud, one finds the mind conceived of as existing in space. But Klein differed with the founder of psychoanalysis on how mind operated. When in the 1890s Freud had delineated the phenomenon of defense, he had initially had no clear notion of its physical referents. In subsequent speculation on a model of mind, he implied that the appropriate referent must be energy distribution within neuronic networks. In contrast, the two mechanisms Klein emphasized derived from bodily prototypes—and from Abraham's writing on oral incorporation and anal expulsion. Where Freud believed mind functioned like a machine, Klein saw it working like a digestive tract.

The rich imagery associated with mind as body, as opposed to mind as machine, discouraged any attempt to clarify clinical material in energetic terms. Though Klein might employ expressions such as "discharge of inner tension," they seemed out of place—a Freudian residue she hesitated to discard. "Mechanisms" might continue to proliferate, but there was nothing mechanical about them: they were purposive ideas in disguise.

External Objects and the Construction of Inner Worlds

Where Freud maintained a balance, albeit a shifting one, between nature and nurture, Klein has been faulted as an extremist of the naturalist variety. (In this connection, her adherence to the death instinct has offered her critics ample ammunition.) Paradoxically, however, it was Klein and not Freud who considered external objects as psychologically, and not simply biologically, significant from birth onward. She came to this major reformulation only gradually. Her attempts to make sense of the anxieties experienced by small children prompted her to push back the dates Freud had assigned to stages, complexes, and structures. And along the way, her emphasis on fantasy led her to enrich concepts that Freud had left almost without content.

Freud acknowledged the mother's presence at the start of her male infant's life, but it was her breast alone, as source of nourishment and physical gratification, that mattered. As a love object or a person in her own right, she did not make an appearance in the boy's life until he had reached the phallic stage of libidinal development. The boy's father fared no better: he too became a significant object only at the phallic stage. In short, in Freud's view external objects derived their status from the role they played in the oedipal drama.

He provided four different versions of that drama. They are worth reviewing if only to highlight the grid into which he fitted sexuality and external objects. The most familiar is undoubtedly the positive Oedipus complex in a male child. In this classic triangular situation, the boy loves mother, hates father, and finds an outlet for his incestuous attachment in masturbation. He renounces sexual activity and mother as well after mother or father threatens him with castration. Throughout, his feelings toward mother remain relatively simple: love, subsequently tinged with resentment at her "unfaithfulness" in preferring father as sexual object.[22] The sentiments toward father are more complex: the dominant emotions of hate and fear are never without a strong admixture of affection and admiration.

Castration anxiety, so prominent in the positive male oedipal drama, is likewise central in the negative male and the positive and negative female versions. In the three variants, as well as in the first enactment, it depends upon the anatomical difference between the sexes. The discovery of the female genital, or rather the discovery that women lack penises, validates a threat of castration, or, if one happens to be female, produces the conviction of having already been so mutilated.

In the negative male Oedipus complex, the boy takes his father, not his mother, as his love object: "[H]e . . . behaves like a girl and displays an affectionate feminine attitude to his father and a corresponding jealousy and hostility towards his mother."[23] When the boy realizes that to be loved by father entails not only behaving like a girl but, in a crucial sense, becoming one, he renounces the paternal object. So it had been in the case of Freud's most famous patient, the Wolfman. An anxiety dream occurring at the age of four (and remembered in adulthood), which Freud interpreted as a primal scene of parental intercourse, prompted the patient to repress his passive sexual aim:

It seems . . . as though he had identified himself with his castrated mother during the dream, and was now fighting against that fact. 'If you want to be sexually satisfied by Father', we may perhaps represent him as saying to himself, 'you must allow yourself to be castrated like Mother; but I won't have that'. In short, a clear protest on the part of his masculinity![24]

Until that fateful dream, and despite evidence to the contrary, Freud's patient had regarded women as the proud possessors of a male genital organ. Knowledge of women as castrated, which in this instance had prompted a masculine protest, could push another child—Leonardo da Vinci stood as Freud's example—in the direction of asexuality or homosexuality:

Before the child comes under the dominance of the castration complex—at a time when he still holds women at full value—he begins to display an intense desire to look, as an erotic instinctual activity. He wants to see other people's genitals, at first in all probability to compare them with his own. The erotic attraction that comes from his mother soon culminates in a longing for her genital organ, which he takes to be a penis. With the discovery, which is not made till later, that women do not have a penis, this longing often turns into its opposite and gives place to a feeling of disgust which in the years of puberty can become a cause of . . . impotence, misogyny and permanent homosexuality.[25]

Leonardo, in contrast to the Wolfman, cannot serve to illuminate the negative Oedipus complex. It is far from clear that he ever entered an oedipal, that is, triangular, situation at all; in Freud's mind the absence of Leonardo's father played a crucial role in his sexual development.[26] This very failure is what makes Freud's protagonist so interesting: it is Leonardo and not the Wolfman who behaves like the Freudian model of a little girl.

In turning to "the riddle . . . of femininity,"[27] Freud was struck by the long duration of the female child's attachment to her mother. The attachment itself came as no surprise: Freud appreciated that for all children "the primary conditions for a choice of object" were the same. But why was the little girl so slow to renounce mother and take father as her heterosexual love object? "In several cases," Freud wrote, the tie to mother "lasted well into the fourth year—in one case into the fifth year—so that it covered by far the longer part of the period of early sexual efflorescence." He noted "the possibility that a large number of women" remained "arrested in their original attachment to their mother" and never achieved "a true change-over towards men." Did they, then, fail to arrive at the Oedipus complex? Freud concluded that the female reached "the normal positive Oedipus situation" only after she had "surmounted" an earlier period "governed by the negative complex." That complex he defined as a phase during which a little girl's father was "not much else for her than a troublesome rival, although her hostility" never reached "the pitch . . . characteristic of boys."[28] In fact Freud seemed uncertain whether to call the phase in question negative oedipal or simply preoedipal.

What brings this attachment to an end? Why, Freud asked, does the little girl's tie to her mother (in contrast to the little boy's) end in hate—"a hate that . . . may last all through life"?[29] Once again castration emerges as central:

The castration complex of girls is . . . started by the sight of the genitals of the other sex. They at once notice the difference and, it must be admitted, its significance too. They feel seriously wronged, often declare that they want to 'have something like it too', and fall victim to 'envy for the penis', which will leave ineradicable traces on their development and the formation of their character and which will not be surmounted in even the most favorable cases without a severe expenditure of psychical energy.

Still more, the little girl holds her mother responsible for her lack of a penis—for her castration—and does "not forgive her for being put at a disadvantage."[30]

"*Whereas in boys,*" Freud wrote, "*the Oedipus complex is destroyed by the castration complex, in girls it is made possible and led up to by the castration complex.*" The little girl can enter the positive oedipal phase only when she has come to terms with her castrated status, only when "she gives up her wish for a penis and puts in place of it a wish for a child." The substitution of child for penis prompts the little girl to take father as love object and to change mother into an object of jealousy. In accomplishing these transformations the little girl turns herself from a little man "into a little woman." Can she go beyond being a "little woman"? The prognosis, according to Freud, is doubtful. The little girl has had difficulty getting into the oedipal phase; she has even more trouble leaving it behind. Castration anxiety, "the motive for the demolition of the Oedipus complex" in boys, has already spent its force.[31] And no other motive has equivalent power. Hence the female child remains in the oedipal configuration "for an indeterminate length of time"; if she demolishes it, she does so late and incompletely.[32]

In elaborating three variations on the positive male oedipal drama, Freud disarranged the original tidy link between the phallic stage of libidinal development and the attainment of object love. What most threatened his design was the discovery of the preoedipal (or negative oedipal) attachment of female child to mother. In regard to her mother, the girl's sexual aims were not merely phallic: they were "determined by the libidinal phases" through which the child passed, and they were "active as well as passive." Here Freud glimpsed, as he put it, "the Minoan-Mycenean civilization behind the civilization of Greece," or, more simply, a far greater richness in a child's relations to her objects than he had earlier imagined. To encompass this richness, and at the same time to retain "the universality of the thesis that the Oedipus complex" was "the nucleus of the neuroses," Freud contemplated extending the content of the complex "to include all the child's relations to both parents."[33] It was a step he never took. Yet even as he mused, Melanie Klein was putting the finishing touches on her own distinctive version of the Oedipus complex.

▬▬ ▬▬ ▬▬ ▬▬ ▬▬

As I see it, the boy's and girl's sexual and emotional development *from early infancy onwards* includes genital trends, which constitute the first stages of the inverted and positive Oedipus complex; they are experienced under the primacy of oral libido and mingle with urethral and anal desires and phantasies. The libidinal stages overlap from the earliest months of life onwards. The positive and inverted Oedipus tendencies are from their inception in close interaction. It is during the stage of genital primacy that the positive Oedipus situation reaches its climax.[34]

By stressing the ways in which libidinal trends overlapped and coincided with oedipal dramas, Klein took a major step toward refor- mulating the notion of a child's emotional ties to external objects. Where Freud retained two separate developmental lines, libido and object love, whose convergence at a fairly late date produced the Oedipus complex, Klein assumed that so clear a delineation was mis- leading rather than helpful.

One can find in Klein's writings, as in Freud's, four versions, two female and two male, of the Oedipus complex. For the girl the posi- tive course involves carrying over the "*receptive* aim . . . from the oral to the genital position." In so doing, she becomes receptive toward the penis and at the same time turns to her father as love object. In contrast, for the boy the "normal" succession entails a change of aim but not of object: when he abandons "the oral and anal positions for the genital, he passes on to the aim of *penetration* associated with posses- sion of the penis"—all the while retaining his original love object.[35] From this outline, the negatives are easy to infer: in the girl, change of aim and retention of object; in the boy, retention of aim and change of object. But just as Klein intermingled libidinal stages, so too she mixed together positive and inverted oedipal dramas. Rather than taking positive and negative elements and arranging them in a limited num- ber of fixed patterns, she was intent on transforming the Oedipus complex into a constantly fluctuating configuration.

It stood to reason that Klein differed from Freud about the little girl's tie to her mother:

Freud believes that the girl's long attachment to her mother is an exclusive one and takes place before she has entered the Oedipus situation. But my experience of analysis of small girls has convinced me that their long-drawn-out and powerful attachment is never exclusive and is bound up with Oedipus impulses.

And along with oedipal impulses come hate and anxiety:

According to my observations, it is the imaginary attacks they [the girls] have made upon the interior of their mother's body by means of destructive excrements that poison, burn and explode, which . . . give rise to their fears of pieces of stool as persecutors and of their mother as a terrifying figure.[36]

The fear the little girl experiences is not one of castration but of a retaliatory assault on her own body—and her own internal genital. (Klein claimed that even small children appreciated that the phallus and clitoris were not the only genitals, and she referred to the third stage of libidinal organization as genital rather than phallic.)[37]

And the girl expects to have those organs destroyed in the course of the attacks that will be made, principally by her mother, upon her body and its contents. Her fears concerning her genitals are especially intense, partly because her own sadistic impulses are very strongly directed towards her mother's genitals and the erotic pleasures she (the mother) gets from them, and partly because her fear of being incapable of enjoying sexual satisfaction serves in its turn to increase her fear of having had her own genital damaged.[38]

Prompted by "her dominant feminine instinctual components,"[39] indeed by vaginal sensations,[40] the little girl turns to her father and his penis. Above all she wants to incorporate his organ "as an object of oral satisfaction":

This drive to introject the father's penis, that is, the Oedipus object, and to keep it inside is much stronger in the girl than in the boy. For the genital tendencies which coincide with her oral desires have a receptive character too, so that under normal circumstances the girl's Oedipus trends are to a far greater extent under the dominance of oral impulses than those of the boy.

Eventually, if all goes well, the sexual act itself will help a woman "ascertain whether the fears which play such a dominant and fundamental role in her mind in connection with copulation are well grounded or not."[41]

What has happened to Freud's postulate of female penis envy? In Klein's account it appears as a secondary phenomenon: the girl's "feminine desire to internalize the penis and to receive a child from her father invariably precedes the wish to possess a penis of her own."[42] Where Freud portrayed the female as undergoing a metamorphosis from little man to little woman, Klein saw her as shifting back and forth between "masculine" and "feminine" positions. In Klein's mind, the outcome was not determined by how the little girl coped with a permanent sense of anatomical inferiority, but rather by how she disposed of sadistic fantasies and the anxiety they engendered.

Just as Klein had disagreed with Freud about the little girl's "preoedipal" attachment to her mother, so too she differed on the relation of son to mother—and to father as well. Again she elaborated by adding sadistic fantasies, directed initially at the mother's body and very soon thereafter at the father's penis. And from fear of a retaliatory attack in which his own body will be mutilated and dismembered, she added, the little boy advances to fear of castration:

There are good grounds for assuming that as soon as genital sensations are experienced, castration fear is activated. . . . In my view this fear is first of all experienced under the dominance of oral libido. The boy's oral-sadistic impulses towards his mother's breast are transferred to his father's penis, and in addition rivalry and hatred in the early Oedipus situation find expression in the boy's desire to bite off his father's penis. This arouses his fear that his own genital will be bitten off by his father in retaliation.[43]

In the male individual, Klein added, "fear of castration, which is only a part—though an important part—of the anxiety felt about the whole body, becomes . . . a dominating theme that overshadows all his other fears."[44]

According to Freud, castration anxiety leads the boy to abandon both positive and negative oedipal positions—to give up hetero- and homosexual love objects, repress sexuality, and enter the latency phase. Klein elaborated: if these "fears are excessive and the urge to repress genital desire is over-strong, difficulties in potency are bound to arise later."[45] If, however, sadism is adequately mastered, neither girl nor boy will flee mother permanently; the female child can return to a feminine position, and the male child can "be in touch" with a woman's "mental needs."[46]

━━━ ━━━ ━━━ ━━━ ━━━

Did the oedipal drama, after its enactment, leave a residue? For Freud, the answer had to be yes. In the "Project" he had plainly stated his belief that experiences of pain and of satisfaction were grooved into the mental appartus. On the basis of subsequent clinical practice, he specifically postulated that among "experiences" the Oedipus complex ranked as central. How, then, did oedipal relations with external objects leave their mark? Freud answered this question by formulating the concept of a superego.

In explicating it, he focused on the dissolution of the "complete Oedipus complex" (negative and positive combined) in the male child.[47] When the Oedipus complex is "demolished," he argued, the boy gives up his attachment ("object cathexes" in Freudian terminology) to his mother and to his father as well. Greatly intensified identifications with parental figures replace object ties; at the same time the completeness of the complex guarantees that such identifications derive from mother and father alike.

Identification itself is a slippery concept. In the context of superego formation Freud used it to cover both a process and its result. Identification (as process) referred to the "regressive way" in which an identification (as result) became "a substitute for a libidinal object tie." Instead of regression Freud sometimes spoke of the "introjection of the object into the ego" or "the shadow of the object" falling "on the ego"; elsewhere he admitted that he could give no "clear metapsychological representation."[48] In his view the identifications that ensued and that superseded object choices went beyond the ego's assuming the characteristics of the lost objects; rather the identifications themselves formed "*a precipitate in the ego.*" In this way a differentiation occurred within the ego, and a permanent one at that. "*The modification of the ego retains its special position; it confronts the other contents of the ego as an ego ideal or super-ego.*"[49]

How did the Kleinian superego differ from the Freudian? Klein was unlikely to find congenial the notion of the superego as a precipitate deposited as the Oedipus complex dissolved. Two modifications immediately suggested themselves: the superego was formed in tandem with oedipal experiences, and it had already undergone extraordinary vicissitudes before the oedipal phase drew to a close.

If, as Klein argued, the Oedipus complex was set in motion when oral sadism was at its height, superego formation *a fortiori* began under the same unpropitious circumstances. Sadism, and the anxiety it aroused, governed the early stages both of the Oedipus complex and of the superego:

> According to my observations, the formuation of the superego begins at the same time as the child makes its earliest oral introjection of its objects. Since the first images it thus forms are endowed with all the attributes of the intense sadism belonging to this stage of its development, and since they will once more be projected on to objects of the outer world, the small child becomes dominated by the fear of suffering unimaginable cruel attacks, both from its real objects and from its superego.[50]

For Klein the superego's punitive harshness, readily apparent in clinical material, posed no problem, whereas for Freud it remained a puzzle. In his work he offered two different, though not mutually exclusive, explanations. As Klein summarized them, "According to one, the severity of the super-ego is derived from the severity of the real father. . . . According to the other, . . . its severity is an outcome of the destructive impulses of the subject."[51] Klein did more than endorse the second view. It was she who had the right to claim priority in this matter, and Freud—who only rarely referred to her work—granted her a measure of recognition, albeit in a footnote.[52]

How could the Kleinian superego (or the Freudian for that matter) be regarded as an ego ideal? Recall that when, in *The Ego and the Id,* Freud had first used the term "super-ego" he had considered it to be synonymous with ego ideal. After close to a decade, during which "ego ideal" failed to reappear in print, he attempted, in the *New Introductory Lectures on Psycho-Analysis,* to define it once again. Simply put, the superego had at least two recognizably different tasks: as the agent of prohibition and punishment and as "the advocate of a striving towards perfection" or the "ideal."[53] Two different sets of parental images were playing these two roles: parents as terrifying figures who were hated and feared and parents as ideal figures who were loved and admired. Though Klein initially stressed the first—the superego's severity—she had no vested interest in regarding the superego as a unitary structure, indeed as a structure at all. A four year-old boy, she wrote, who "suffered from the pressure of a castrating and cannabalistic superego, in complete contrast to his kind and loving parents," had "certainly not only this one superego":

I discovered in him identifications which corresponded more closely to his real parents, though not by any means identical with them. These figures, who appeared good and helpful and ready to forgive, he called his 'fairy papa and mamma', and, when his attitude towards me was positive, he allowed me in the analysis to play the part of the 'fairy mamma' to whom everything could be confessed. At other times . . . I played the part of the wicked mamma from whom everything evil that he phantasied was anticipated. . . . A whole series of most varied identifications, which were in opposition to one another, originated in widely different strata and periods and differed fundamentally from the real objects, had in this child resulted in a super-ego which actually gave the impression of being normal and well developed.[54]

If contrasts could be accounted for by assigning to different strata and periods fantasies that stood as polar opposites, was it possible to determine to which stratum a particular fantasy belonged? Klein thought it was, but had no chronology of her own to offer—at least not in early stages of her work. Instead she reached out to classic libido theory, fastening on the distinction Abraham had drawn between oral-sucking and oral-sadistic stages of libidinal development. "Fairy mammas," she argued, derived from fixations at the oral-sucking stage. (Her use of the term *fixation* was downright confusing.) Like a dea ex machina, a kindly mother, approximating closely to the real object, was on hand at a very early age and left a positive imprint.[55] In this unheralded fashion, the "good breast," which was to become a Kleinian shibboleth, entered the scene. And in unveiling it, Klein at last made explicit the uniting of aim and object that her work on the Oedipus complex and the superego had implied.

The "object-relation" that Klein, in contrast to Freud, postulated as existing "from the beginning of post-natal life"—"a relation to the mother (although focusing primarily on her breast)" which was "imbued with . . . love, hatred, phantasies, anxieties, and defences"—was not simply a relation to an external object.[56] Recall that in her view projection and introjection too began with the first feeding:

[These] processes . . . lead to the institution inside ourselves of loved and hated objects, who are felt to be 'good' and 'bad', and who are interrelated with each other and with the self: that is to say, they constitute an inner world. This assembly of internalized objects becomes organized, together with the organization of the ego, and in the higher strata of the mind it becomes discernible as the super-ego. Thus the phenomenon which was recognized by Freud, broadly speaking, as the voices and the influence of the actual parents established in the ego is, according to my findings, a complex object-world, which is felt by the individual, in deep layers of the unconscious, to be concretely inside himself, and for which I and my colleagues therefore use the term 'internalized objects' and an 'inner world'.[57]

What were internal objects? The term "objects" was familiar enough: in psychoanalytic parlance it denoted people, and "part objects" parts of a person, such as breast or penis. The term "internal," as Alix Strachey observed in 1941, was ambiguous—and indeed ambiguity has continued to vex discussion of that word and the word for the related process, "internalization."[58] According to Strachey an obvious difficulty derived from the fact that "internal" was used to describe at least three different things:

functions, structures and constituents of the mind such as . . .
displacement, projection, introjection, ideational and imaginative
processes; objects, situations and events which are creations of the
imagination, as they appear in dreams, delusions and
phantasies; . . . [and] objects, situations and events which are
specifically imagined as being inside a person, such as a wolf
gnawing at the vitals from within or a huge penis filling the whole
of the body.[59]

This third definition alone can be considered Kleinian.

In referring, then, to internal objects, Klein meant something more than internal thoughts about external objects; she also meant something more than the way in which, under the influence of anxiety, thoughts about external objects were distorted. Klein, after all, was concentrating not on how one thought about external reality but rather on how one thought about an inner world she considered every bit as real as the world outside.

She did her best to be precise. She emphasized that she did not "interpret in terms of internal objects and relationships" until she had "explicit material showing phantasies of internalizing the object in concrete and physical terms."[60] (Elsewhere she cited a fantasy of incorporation, of taking the figure into oneself, "archaically through the mouth.")[61] Ironically, she was suspected of literal-mindedness. As Ella Sharpe queried during the controversial discussions:

Sometimes I get the impression that some analysts who deal with those beliefs [of actual objects inside: breasts, penis, parents] interpret to their patients as if they themselves believed not only their patients' beliefs, but in the actuality of concrete objects inside.

Susan Isaacs tried to lay the question to rest:

Like Miss Sharpe, we believe that the patient believes he has concrete objects and part objects inside him. And we accept the full weight of his belief, without aversion. We do not, however, ourselves believe that he has, nor give the patient reason to suppose that we believe it.[62]

Still, the compressed nature of the clinical material Klein published suggests that she was not always punctilious in following her own advice.

Could the Kleinian notion of "internal objects" be fitted to the Freudian mold? Marjorie Brierley, for one, found little trouble translating it into orthodox terms: "Artificially simplified, the concept of an 'internalized good object' is a concept of an unconscious phantasy gratifying the wish for the constant presence of the mother in the form of the belief that she is literally inside the child."[63] When, however, Klein's loose mode of expression seemed to imply that internal objects had a power of their own, she was accused of succumbing to demonology.[64] Her critics were curiously blind; they could not see that the Freudian superego was quite as much in danger of becoming a personified entity as was an internal object.

━━━ ━━━ ━━━ ━━━ ━━━

Klein's major papers "A Contribution to the Psychogenesis of Manic-Depressive States" (1935) and "Mourning and Its Relation to Manic-Depressive States" (1940), taken together, are generally regarded as having marked a new departure. In them she sought to describe the building up of an internal world and to chart the vicissitudes of object relations within that world. What emerged as central was her concept of the depressive position.

Why "position"? Klein needed a term to designate particular groupings of anxieties and different varieties of defenses. For her purposes, "phases" sounded too global; if she were to call such anxieties a phase she ran the risk of seeming to suggest that the person experiencing the anxieties in question was experiencing nothing but those anxieties. The groupings of anxieties and defenses she labeled positions were not conceived of as all-encompassing; quick change-overs or fluctuations were possible, and indeed she found them characteristic of the child.[65]

Recall the presence of good and bad objects. In the first instance such objects are not whole objects; they are part objects, and "the mother's breast is the prototype." The "badness" of the breast is not simply a function of how the mother presents it to her infant; its "badness" is not merely a consequence of frustration, though frustration certainly plays a part. Rather, because the infant "projects" his "own aggression" onto the breast, the breast that is introjected, or incorporated (Klein tended to use the two words interchangeably, a practice for which she was much rebuked), is bad. And its badness is very bad indeed: the infant conceives of it as actually dangerous—a persecutor who he fears will "devour" him, "scoop out the inside" of his body, cut him to pieces, poison him—in short, will contrive his "destruction by all the means which sadism can devise." In contrast, the breast's goodness (which Klein distinguished from a defensive idealization) appears to be dependent on external factors, on oral satisfaction. She provided no other explanation.[66] (Subsequently she postulated an inherent capacity for love, and, for good measure, added a dubious reference to phylogenetic inheritance.)[67]

It is a development of the "highest importance" when an infant (Klein later fixed the age as roughly six months)[68] takes the step from "a partial object-relation to the relation with a complete object." At this point the good object comes into its own. Wholeness heightens the likelihood that "internalized imagoes will approximate more closely to reality" and that "the ego will identify itself more fully with 'good' objects." This last phrase is obscure: "identify" once again gives trouble. Klein does not mean that the ego—"infant" would be more appropriate here—tries to be like its good external object. Rather she seems to mean that the infant becomes dependent upon it, and upon its internalized counterpart, with a new force: "From now on preservation of the good object is regarded as synonymous with the survival of the ego."[69]

Thus the infant comes to the depressive position. The word "depressive" may be misleading. As D. W. Winnicott noted, the term "seems to imply that infants . . . pass through a stage of depression or mood illness." But Klein is not, in fact, describing infants who are "depersonalized and hopeless about external contacts"; such infants lack the prerequisite, the relationship to a whole good object, for entering upon the depressive position.[70] The predominant anxiety of this position is fear that the good object will be lost: the infant feels "constantly menaced" in his "possession of internalized good objects"; he is "full of anxiety lest such objects should die." And these good objects are threatened from all sides. "It is not only the vehemence of the subject's uncontrollable hatred but that of his love too which imperils the object. For at this stage of his development loving an object and devouring it are very closely connected." A little child who believes, when his mother disappears, that he "has eaten her up and destroyed her (whether from motives of love or of hate) is tormented by anxiety."[71] In short, there seems to be no way for the child to avoid inflicting damage on his good object. No wonder, then, that anxiety alone does not dominate the picture; guilt and remorse are its constant companions.

How can these torments be assuaged? The beleaguered child has at his disposal no defenses peculiar to the depressive position. Still more, the manic and obsessional defenses he may employ can themselves miscarry and lead to a vicious circle of persecution and hate:

The very fact that manic defences . . . (defences in which dangers from various sources are in an omnipotent way denied or minimized) . . . are operating in such close connection with the obsessional ones contributes to the ego's fear that the reparation attempted by obsessional means has . . . failed. The desire to control the object, the sadistic gratification of overcoming and humiliating it, of getting the better of it, the *triumph* over it, may enter so strongly into the act of reparation . . . that the 'benign' circle started by this act becomes broken. The objects which were to be restored change again into persecutors, and in turn paranoid fears are revived.[72]

How, then, can a benign circle, as opposed to a vicious one, be reestablished? Successful reparation is the only answer Klein provided. Her notion of reparation, of the child's wish to restore an object damaged, in fantasy, by his sadism, had made its first appearance in her 1929 paper "Infantile Anxiety-Situations Reflected in a Work of

Art and in the Creative Impulse"; there, as elsewhere, she simply assumed without further ado that such wishes were intrinsic to healthy development. In stark contrast to her vivid descriptions of a haunting inner world, her efforts to depict a harmonious inner environment fell flat. Once the child began "the all-important process of bringing together more closely the various aspects of objects (external, internal, 'good' and 'bad', loved and hated),"[73] Klein seemed to lose interest. It was as if her work had now been done.

If not her work, at least the child's. In Klein's mind overcoming the depressive position ranked as the milestone of early emotional development. ("Failure to do so" might "result in depressive illness, mania or paranoia.")[74]

When the child's belief and trust in his capacity to love, in his reparative powers and in the integration and security of his good inner world increase . . . , manic omnipotence decreases and the obsessional nature of the impulses towards reparation diminishes, which means in general that the infantile neurosis has passed.[75]

What has happened to the Oedipus complex? What has become of the "infantile neurosis" par excellence? Did the depressive position usurp the place formerly occupied by what Freud regarded as the "nucleus of the neuroses"? The relation between the two was more complicated than one of simple substitution. Klein in fact had no intention of discarding the Oedipus complex. She tried to keep it in tandem with the depressive position: both, she argued, appeared at the same time, roughly midway through the infant's first year. (Initially Klein had postulated that the Oedipus complex was bound up with the "phase of maximal sadism." Subsequently she pushed back that phase and joined it to the onset of persecutory—as opposed to depressive—anxieties.)[76] In linking the two, she gave the depressive position pride of place: if the Oedipus complex became a drama of whole object relations, the depressive position provided its subtext:

The sorrow and concern about the feared loss of the 'good' objects, that is to say, the depressive position, is, in my experience, the deepest source of the painful conflicts of the Oedipus situation, as well as in the child's relations to people in general.[77]

▬▬ ▬▬ ▬▬ ▬▬ ▬▬

Above all, Klein's concept of positions—she was to postulate a "paranoid-schizoid" in addition to the depressive—represented a challenge to Freudian libido theory. How far-reaching a challenge she did not fully appreciate. To be sure, she had not abandoned the language of oral, anal, and genital—indeed interpretations in terms of orality were something of a Kleinian trademark. At the same time she had recognized, as Marjorie Brierley pointed out with approbation, that "the time for thinking of development in terms of libido alone" was "long past."[78] Such thinking had to include relations with objects, and despite her emphasis on innate aggression and sadism, Klein increasingly ascribed influence to persons in the external environment. Beyond that, her stress on "positions" made clear that in her view relations with *internal* objects had a privileged status. And it was this status that called into question the explanatory power of libido theory.

Still more, in contrast to Freud's "libidinal primacies," which drew heavily on notions current among late nineteenth-century sexual pathologists, Klein's "positions" derived from the psychoanalytic domain itself. There were some whom this display of independence made uncomfortable. Marjorie Brierley, for one, found it "easier to think of development as a progressive series of psycho-biological adaptations . . . rather than in terms of intro-psychic situations."[79] Yet it was undeniable that by the 1940s, psychoanalysis had reached a point where data observed and interpreted in clinical sessions had taken a commanding role, a point where the "intro-psychic situations" clinically disclosed had become its appropriate conceptual referents.

Children within the Clinical Domain

When in 1941 Melanie Klein undertook the treatment of the boy Richard—an account of which she later published as *Narrative of a Child Analysis*—she had already been at work with young patients for more than two decades. Richard, at age ten, ranked among the oldest; the youngest, Rita, had been merely two and three-quarters. To gather data from so small a child clearly extended the psychoanalytic domain; at the same time it required adaptations of standard psychoanalytic techniques. In her reports from the consulting room, Klein provided ample clues to how she went about analyzing children and how she read the unconscious content of the fragmentary material that her little patients brought her or that she elicited from them.

According to popular belief, child analysis began with Freud. In 1909 he published the first case history that had as its subject a child, the five-year-old Little Hans. The boy, fearful that a horse would bite him should he venture into the street, had retreated to his house. There the oedipal determinants of his phobia were unearthed—it was to illustrate the sexual development of children that the narrative was shaped—and the child gradually recovered. The therapist, however, was not Freud; it was the boy's father, who was not an analyst at all, merely a "close adherent." Indeed Freud was of the opinion that "no one" other than the father "could possibly have prevailed on the child" to avow his feelings and fantasies.[80] Though Freud did not dispute the "high theoretical interest" to which the analysis of children's neuroses might lay claim, he continued to question its feasibility:

An analysis which is conducted upon a neurotic child itself . . . cannot be very rich in material; too many words and thoughts have to be lent to the child, and even so the deepest strata may turn out to be impenetrable to consciousness.[81]

Anna Freud shared her father's skepticism. In a series of lectures delivered in 1926 and entitled *Einführung in die Technik der Kinderanalyse* (*Introduction to the Technique of Child-Analysis*), she enunciated what was to become authoritative in Vienna. H. von Hug-Hellmuth's paper "On the Technique of Child Analysis" had already appeared in 1921,[82] and where the two works overlapped, notably on the beginning of analysis, Anna Freud's indebtedness to Hug-Hellmuth seemed nearly total. Yet it was not until Freud's daughter spoke that the "orthodox" position was staked out. Meanwhile, far from Vienna, Melanie Klein was in the course of establishing herself as an authority in her own right and, indeed, had found colleagues in London eager to try out her new techniques. Their response to Anna Freud's admonitions was decidedly negative: in a "Symposium on Child-Analysis" published in 1927, the several contributors reached a consensus that Anna Freud was theoretically naive and clinically inexperienced.[83]

What was at issue? To Anna Freud the crucial matter was clear enough: could the "expedients" that made adult analysis possible be replicated with a child patient? In her mind the question seemed almost to be one of quantity. Of the three main sorts of material that provided the stuff of adult analyses—that is, interpretation of a patient's dreams and of the ideas surfacing in his free associations, as well as "the interpretation of his transference-reactions"—only dreams were readily available in the case of a child patient.[84] For Klein quantity posed no problem; she habitually cast her interpretive net so wide that dearth never threatened.

Even dreams and daydreams might be of little value without the aid of "free associations." What about such associations? Anna Freud argued that verbal associations produced according to the fundamental injunction of psychoanalysis—the suspension of conscious purposive thought—were not to be counted on in child analysis. Still more, she considered child's play, which loomed so large in Melanie Klein's procedure, an inadequate, indeed inappropriate, replacement.[85] Klein's view was more complex than Anna Freud realized; she saw play as a composite—indeed as closer to manifest dream material than to free association:

In their play children represent symbolically phantasies, wishes and experiences. Here they are employing the same language, the same archaic, phylogenetically acquired mode of expression as we are familiar with from dreams. We can only fully understand it if we approach it by the method Freud has for unravelling dreams. . . .

We soon find that children produce no fewer associations to the separate features of their games than do adults to the elements of their dreams. The details of the play point the way for an attentive observer; and, in between, the child tells all sorts of things which must be given their full weight as associations.[86]

How, in fact, did Melanie Klein proceed? The setting itself evolved only gradually. Initially the analyses had taken place in the child's own nursery, sometimes under a watchful and ambivalent maternal gaze. Klein soon realized that the child needed to be away from home and family—and to have regular sessions, fifty minutes, five times a week. The consulting room she provided was specially adapted: the floor and the walls were washable, and it contained "only simple and sturdy furniture, a small table and chair for the child, a chair for the analyst, a small couch."[87] Beyond that the child needed special equipment—though he often brought his own play materials. Toys figured prominently, small toys that is. As Klein wrote:

I found it essential to have *small* toys because their number and variety enable the child to express a wide range of phantasies and experiences. It is important for this purpose that these toys should be non-mechanical and that the human figures, varying only in colour and size, should not indicate any particular occupation. Their very simplicity enables the child to use them in many different situations, according to the material coming up in the play. . . .

Each child's playthings are kept locked in one particular drawer, and he therefore knows that his toys and his play with them . . . are only known to the analyst and himself.

Toys were "not the only requisite for a play analysis." Paper, paints, crayons, scissors were also supplied. So too was a washbasin along with "one or two small bowls, tumblers, and spoons."[88] Thus the child could draw, write, paint, cut out, and repair toys, as well as play games.

Within this setting the work of interpretation could begin. One of Anna Freud's unkindest cuts was her characterization of that work:

Melanie Klein . . . persists in translating every action that the child performs into corresponding thoughts; that is to say, she attempts to find the symbolic content underlying each single move in the play. If the child overturns a lamppost or a toy figure she interprets this action, e.g., as an aggressive impulse against the father; a deliberate collision between two cars as evidence of the child having observed intercourse between the parents.[89]

Melanie Klein took umbrage: "I should never attempt any such 'wild' symbolic interpretations of children's play."[90] On the contrary, Klein argued, "early analysis of children" had "shown again and again how many different meanings a single toy or a single bit of play" could have, and that one could "only infer and interpret their meaning" when one considered "their wider connections and the whole analytic situation" in which they were set.[91] In Klein's view there were no shortcuts to the interpretation of symbols; their meaning depended on context.

The remaining point at issue between Anna Freud and Melanie Klein, that is, the interpretation of transference reactions, was considered by both parties the one of greatest theoretical import. Sigmund Freud had begun to appreciate the therapeutic implications of what he named "transference" in analyzing "Dora," and it was in writing up the truncated treatment under the title "Fragment of an Analysis of a Case of Hysteria" that he first gave an extended account of the phenomenon:

What are transferences? They are new editions or facsimiles of the impulses and phantasies which are aroused . . . during . . . an analysis; but they have this peculiarity, which is characteristic for their species, that they replace some earlier person by the person of the physician. To put it another way: a whole series of psychological experiences are revived, not as belonging to the past, but as applying to the person of the physician at the present moment.

If friendly and hostile transferences were made conscious, Freud argued, they could be "turned into account for the progress of the analysis." He had not been fortunate in the Dora case; he had not succeeded "in mastering the transference in good time." By failing to detect it and by failing to explain it to the patient, he had forfeited the aid of what he regarded as "the most powerful ally" of psychoanalysis.[92]

For her part, Freud's daughter had difficulty detecting transference when the patient happened to be a child. The child was simply not up to the "literary" work involved; he was unready to "produce a new edition," because, in her view, the "old edition" had not yet been "exhausted":

His [the child's] original objects, the parents, are still real and present as love objects—not only in fantasy as with the adult neurotic; between them and the child exist all the relations of everyday life, and all its gratifications and disappointment in reality still depend on them. The analyst enters this situation as a new person, and will probably share with the parents the child's love or hate. But there is no necessity for the child to put the analyst fully in the parents' place.[93]

The response to her remarks bordered on incredulity. Could Anna Freud truly believe, Joan Riviere wondered, that so long as a child remained attached to his parents, he carried with him no unconscious or fantastic imagoes of them?[94] Even a three-year-old, Klein contended, had moved away from his original love objects and hence "in reference to the analyst" could "very well enter upon a new edition."[95] Anna Freud remained unconvinced.

From the outset she conceived of her task as pedagogic as well as analytic, thereby betraying a lack of confidence in analysis itself.[96] In her view, the success of such pedagogy—and, by extension, of child analysis—stood or fell "with the child's attachment to the person in charge" of him. To win over her young patients she engaged in "various means of enticement," such as "crocheting, knitting, and games." She obviously took "great pains to establish in the child" a "relationship of dependence" on her. This tie, this "positive transference" as she called it, was to her mind her most powerful ally. "Negative impulses towards the analyst" she regarded as "essentially disturbing," and to be "dealt with . . . as soon as possible."[97] In brief, given her way of proceeding, Anna Freud virtually debarred negative transference reactions from entering the analytic situation. No wonder, then, that she found transference material in short supply.

In contrast, by the mid-1920s Melanie Klein had come to consider it "impossible to combine in the person of the analyst analytical and educational work."[98] She opted for the analytic, negative transference and all. It was essential, she argued, "to enable the child to bring out his aggressiveness," even if directed toward the analyst:

I have sometimes been asked by what method I prevented physical attacks, and I think the answer is that I was very careful not to inhibit the child's aggressive *phantasies;* in fact he was given the opportunity to act them out in other ways, including verbal attacks on myself. The more I was able to interpret in time the motives of the child's aggressiveness the more the situation could be kept under control.

Throughout she defined her task as one of creating an authentic analytic situation in which the child could reexperience early emotions and fantasies and understand them "in relation to his primal objects."[99] Only then might his anxieties be diminished. Only then was one engaged in child analysis.

Reading Melanie Klein's fragmentary accounts of her early work with children, one sees that she skirted problems of interpretation by relying on undisguised fantasy to provide initial guidance. She listened to the children, particularly to her son Erich, alias Fritz, age five, and took seriously the concreteness of their fantasy lives. Quite spontaneously "Fritz" had begun to relate "longer or shorter phantastic stories, originating sometimes in ones he had been told but mostly entirely original." A few examples follow:

The stomach had a peculiar significance for this child. In spite of information and repeated correction, he clung to the conception, expressed on various occasions, that children grew in the mother's stomach . . . About this time he expressed a curiosity to see his mother quite naked. Immediately afterwards he remarked, 'I would like to see your stomach too and the picture that is in your stomach.' To her question, 'Do you mean the place inside which you were?' he replied 'Yes! I would like to look inside your stomach and see whether there isn't a child there.'

He related another phantasy . . . in which the womb figured as a completely furnished house, the stomach particularly was very fully equipped and even possessed of a bath-tub and a soap-dish. He remarked himself about this phantasy, 'I know that it isn't really like that, but I see it that way.'[100]

He pictured it [his mother's body] as a town, often as a country, and later on as the world, intersected by railway lines. He imagined this town to be provided with everything necessary for the people and animals who lived there and to be furnished with every kind of modern contrivance.

There were telegraphs and telephones, different sorts of railways, lifts and merry-go-rounds, advertisements, etc. . . . There were two kinds of trains on the rails: one was the 'Pipi'-train, conducted by a 'Pipi'-drop, while the other was a 'Kaki'-train, which was driven by a 'Kaki'.[101]

But if the dream or daydream material was disguised, interpretation became more problematic—even with the aid of play. And Klein became famous, possibly notorious, for complicated interpretations of internalized part objects. How did she arrive at them?

In reporting the case of "Dick," she came close to answering this question. The patient was only four years old, and psychotic. His behavior was markedly different from that of the neurotic children she had previously analyzed:

He had let his nurse go without manifesting any emotion, and had followed me into the room with complete indifference. There he ran to and fro in an aimless, purposeless way, and several times he also ran round me, just as if I were a piece of furniture, but he showed no interest in any of the objects in the room. His movements as he ran to and fro seemed to be without co-ordination. The expression of his eyes and face was fixed, far-away and lacking in interest.

His defective capacity for speech was a serious obstacle; far more serious, however, was his defective capacity for symbolism:

In Dick symbolism had not developed. This was partly because of the lack of any affective relation to the things around him, to which he was almost entirely indifferent. . . . Since no affective or symbolic relation to them existed in his mind, any chance actions of his in relation to them were not coloured by phantasy, and it was thus impossible to regard them as having the character of symbolic representation.

Klein did succeed, however, in creating something resembling an analytic situation:

It has been possible to get into contact with him with the help of . . . a few words, to activate anxiety in a child in whom interest and affect were wholly lacking, and it has further been possible gradually to resolve it and to regulate the anxiety released. . . . I found myself obliged to make my interpretations on the basis of my general knowledge, the representations in Dick's behavior being relatively vague.

With material so scanty and disguised as Dick's, Klein could not wait to interpret until a particular fantasy or anxiety had found expression in multiple representations. She dealt with this extreme case by what she recognized as a modification of her usual technique.[102]

The modification consisted of relying on her "general knowledge," and that knowledge in fact was far from unproblematic. Much of it derived from Freud. To the Freudian primal scene as phylogenetic heritage, rephrased in terms of an innate knowledge of parental intercourse,[103] Klein added the mother's body as the focal point of children's fantasies—after all, Fritz had pictured it as the whole world:

The child expects to find within the mother (a) the father's penis, (b) excrement, and (c) children, and these things it equates with edible substances. According to the child's earliest phantasies (or 'sexual theories') of parental intercourse, the father's penis (or his whole body) becomes incorporated in the mother during the act.[104]

What Klein failed to do was to adduce independent evidence that children had *sexual* fantasies of this sort. In following Freud along the slippery path of phylogenetic inheritance, she simply begged the question. Still more, this initial misstep encouraged her to attribute to infants fantasy contents in excess of their mental abilities, to ignore the issue of cognitive capacity. In sum, when Klein modified her technique, she endangered her interpretive enterprise.

Yet such danger was always lurking. Klein, like every other analyst, necessarily worked with the impedimenta of "general knowledge." What mattered was whether or not that knowledge induced complacency and led to a closure that was premature.

When are we to begin making our communications to the patient? When is the moment for disclosing to him the hidden meaning of the ideas that occur to him? . . . It is not difficult for a skilled analyst to read the patient's secret wishes plainly between the lines of his complaints . . . ; but what a measure of self-complacency and thoughtlessness must be possessed by anyone who can, on the shortest acquaintance, inform a stranger who is entirely ignorant of all the tenets of analysis that he is attached to his mother by incestuous ties, that he harbours wishes for the death of his wife whom he appears to love, that he conceals an intention of betraying his superior, and so on![105]

According to Freud—whose strictures have just been quoted— the moment for "disclosing . . . hidden meaning" was unlikely to come early in an analysis. Melanie Klein thought otherwise. In treating her child patients she found herself departing from the line Freud had marked out for adults.[106] Her interpretations came early, and they were "deep." What considerations informed her choice of tactics?

Her new method had been unpremeditated; it had been her natural response to the intense anxieties of her son and first patient. She had simply gone ahead and interpreted what she thought most urgent in the material he presented:

The anxieties I encountered when analyzing this first case were very acute, and although I was strengthened in the belief that I was working on the right lines by observing the alleviation of anxiety again and again produced by my interpretations, I was at times perturbed by the intensity of the fresh anxieties which were being brought into the open. . . . As it happened, in the next few days the child's anxiety, which had come to a head, greatly diminished, leading to further improvement. The conviction gained in this analysis influenced the whole course of my analytic work.[107]

Thereafter Klein never lost sight of anxiety.[108] Time and again an anxious state would prevent either the establishment or the maintenance of contact. "Only by *interpreting* and so *allaying* the child's anxiety" could the analyst gain or regain "access to his Ucs and get him to *phantasy*." Anxiety might be alleviated, but not eradicated: it was a recurring phenomenon.[109] As the case of "Dick" suggested, anxiety and its vicissitudes ensured that the analysis would keep moving.

Klein's handling of "Peter" shows her in action. The analysis of this boy, age three years and nine months, began in 1924 and lasted for 278 sessions. At the outset the child

was very difficult to manage. He was strongly fixated upon his mother and very ambivalent. He was unable to tolerate frustration, was totally inhibited in play and gave the impression of being an extremely timid, plaintive and unboyish child. At times his behaviour would be aggressive and sneering, and he got on badly with other children, especially with his younger brother.

When treatment ended, "he had lost not only his morbid fears but his general timidity, and had become a happy and lively child. He had overcome his inhibition in play and had begun to get on well with other children, in particular with his little brother."[110]

In this case Klein attributed crucial significance to the primal scene—but not on the basis of "general knowledge." She had independent evidence that the scene had actually been witnessed by the boy. According to the mother:

Peter had greatly changed for the worse after a summer holiday during which at the age of eighteen months he shared his parents' bedroom and had opportunity of observing their sexual intercourse. On that holiday he . . . slept badly and relapsed into soiling his bed at night, which he had not done for some months. He had been playing freely until then, but from that summer onwards he stopped playing and became very destructive towards his toys; he would do nothing with them but break them. Shortly afterwards his brother was born, and this increased all his difficulties.[111]

During the first two analytic sessions Klein made a number of interpretive interventions, all the while paying close attention to context. Peter began by playing with the toy carriages and cars Klein provided. One sequence stood out: "[H]e took two horse-drawn carriages and bumped one into another, so that the horses' feet knocked together." In so doing he commented that he had "a new little brother called Fritz. . . . Then he knocked two toy horses together in the same way." Klein interpreted: "Look here," she said, "the horses are two people bumping together." After an initial demurral Peter accepted this equivalence of horses and people. He returned to the knocking play in the next session, extending the range of toys to include engines and swings as well as horses and carriages. His manipulation of swings—putting two side by side and pointing out how they dangled and bumped—prompted Klein to interpret further: the two engines, carriages, horses, and "dangling" swings were in each case "two people—Daddy and Mummy—bumping their 'thingummies' (his word for genitals) together."[112] Peter again objected, then agreed that not only did horses symbolize people but bumping symbolized intercourse. In concurring, Peter repeated the information about his brother. This remark, taken by Klein as confirmation, led her to continue her interpretation:

'You thought to yourself that Daddy and Mummy bumped their thingummies together and that is how your little brother Fritz came.' He now took another small cart and made all three collide together. I interpreted: 'That's your own thingummy. You wanted to bump your thingummy along with Daddy's and Mummy's thingummies.' He thereupon added a fourth cart and said: 'That's Fritz.' . . . After this he repeatedly hit the two small carts together and told me how he and his little brother let two chickens into their bedroom so that they could calm down but that they had knocked about and spat in there. 'He and Fritz', he added, 'were not rude gutter boys and did not spit.' When I told him that the chickens were his and Fritz's thingummies bumping into one another and spitting—that is masturbating—he agreed with me after a little resistance.[113]

Certainly Melanie Klein could not have read Peter's "secret wishes plainly between the lines of his complaints." Rather than "a premature communication" bringing "the treatment to an untimely end," as Freud had feared,[114] Klein's intervention seemed to set free her patient's fantasies and to widen the scope of his play. Yet the question of timing, and even of depth, could not be settled in the abstract. Fidelity to her own guiding principle entailed allowing anxiety rather than dogma to set the pace.

━━ ━━ ━━ ━━ ━━

Melanie Klein was still going through the proofs and index of *Narrative of a Child Analysis* at her death in 1960. In so doing she was carrying out a long-cherished intention: "to write a full case study of a child's analysis, based on daily detailed notes."[115] Why did she settle on Richard, who had been in treatment with her almost twenty years earlier? When he had come to her in 1941 as a boy of ten, she and he had both known that the analysis would have to be brief—ninety-three sessions in all as it turned out. Its brevity, imposed by wartime circumstances, alone made possible the daily account Klein wanted to write. Hence from the outset she determined to keep a record that would subsequently allow her to write up the case. Her detailed notes were not verbatim reports of each session; she agreed with Freud, who had warned that note taking during a session diverted "the analyst's attention from the course of the analysis."[116] (She also decided against introducing a tape recorder on the grounds that if the patient "had any reason to suspect that a machine was being used," he "would not speak and behave" as he would were he "alone with the analyst.") So she took her extensive notes after each session; hence she could not be absolutely "sure of the sequence," nor could she "quote literally the patient's associations" or her own interpretations.[117] If her non-verbatim reports sometimes left a blurred image of the child's material, they brought into focus the work she did as analyst. After all, she wanted her case history to elucidate technique.

When one reads Klein's *Narrative*, it quickly becomes apparent that her title is a misnomer: there is no story whatsoever. She merely strung together session notes in which her interpretations came thick and fast—not surprising in view of the fact that she frequently "brought together . . . several interpretations separated by some play or comment of the child."[118] As one Kleinian analyst remarked, "These interpretations seem rather staccato descriptions of separate phantasies, often overlapping, sometimes seeming mutually exclusive," all, in Klein's view, "existing at the same time at different levels."[119] She herself expressed the hope that "if such interpretations" were "to some extent understood by the patient, . . . the analysis" would not have been "without value."[120]

The technique might have been more or less her usual one; the setting was not. At the time, Klein was staying in a Scottish village and was renting a playroom, since her lodgings were unsuitable for child patients. The playroom, "though a large place with two doors and an adjoining kitchen and lavatory," had drawbacks. It was used by Girl Guides, and Klein had to leave in place a number of their books, pictures, and maps. "The absence of a waiting room and the fact that there was nobody to answer the door" meant that the analyst had to fetch the key, unlock the room, and lock up again, before and after each session. Thus some conversation with Richard outside the playroom was unavoidable. The setting was ususual for Richard as well. He and his family had settled for the duration of the war in a place not too far from Klein's Scottish village. "For the purposes of the analysis, arrangements were made for Richard and his mother to stay in a hotel" in that village. On Saturdays he was to go home for the weekend. These arrangements imposed a strain on the boy; and it was compounded first by a brief illness of his mother's and then by a heart attack his father suffered. Despite the difficulties due to time and place, Klein believed that she had reached the troubled child and enabled him "to become conscious of some of his anxieties and defences"—though an "adequate working-through was not possible."[121]

What was the matter with Richard? Klein gave no precise answer in terms of the then-current notions of psychopathology. She did, however, furnish a description of this severely incapacitated child. Since about the age of four or five, Richard had suffered from a "progressive inhibition of his faculties and interests," accompanied by hypochondriacal symptoms and depressed moods. By the age of eight he had become so frightened of other children that he had to stop attending school. His fears gradually increased to the point where he was scarcely able to go out by himself. The war, quite naturally, exacerbated his difficulties.[122] In this light the fact that he managed to cope with his stressful living arrangements suggested his commitment to analytic treatment.

Although Richard was terrified of children, he could get on with adults, particularly with women. "He tried to impress them with his conversational gifts and to ingratiate himself in a rather precocious way."[123] Certainly his behavior differed from what Klein regarded as typical of the latency period: he lacked that "general attitude of reserve and distrust" which made children of his age "deeply averse to anything" that savored of "search and interrogation."[124] One might be tempted to dismiss his ease with Klein as part of his symptomology were it not for the depth of the communications he was able to make. "He could verbalize his feelings, memories, and anxieties to her, and was also very open in his disagreements as well as agreements."[125] Richard, desperate for help, and Klein, eager to offer it, lost no time in setting down to work together.

The first session illustrates how that work was done. (Since it is the first, it is easier to describe than its successors; there is as yet no quantity of material to keep in mind from previous sessions.) Richard readily agreed to "talk about his worries." He ticked off his fear of going out into the street, his school phobia, and his anxiety about the war. The war was his dominant concern: he hoped that Hitler would be beaten; he spoke of the cruel treatment of conquered countries, Austria among them; he gave a dramatic account of how the family cook had been frightened when a bomb had fallen near their former house. "After that he tried to remember whether he had any worries he had not yet mentioned. Oh yes, he often wondered what he was like inside and what other people's insides were like." Klein interposed a question: she asked "whether he also worried about his mother sometimes." This query opened up a new vein. Richard talked about his night terrors and how these terrors centered on his mother: "In the evenings he often feared that a nasty man—a kind of tramp— would come and kidnap Mummy during the night."[126]

At this point Klein began to interpret:

Mrs K. suggested that the tramp who would hurt Mummy at night seemed to him very much like Hitler who frightened Cook in the air-raid and ill-treated the Austrians. Richard knew that Mrs K. was Austrian, and so too she would be ill-treated. At night he might have been afraid that when his parents went to bed something could happen between them with their genitals that would injure Mummy.

Richard did not fully understand. He had not learned the word "genital"; he had no conception of sexual intercourse; he had only vague notions about eggs, fluids, babies, and mothers' insides. Klein explained the term and continued:

Mrs K. interpreted that he might have contradictory thoughts about Daddy. Although Richard knew that Daddy was a kind man, at night when he was frightened, he might fear that Daddy was doing some harm to Mummy. When he thought of the tramp, he did not remember that Daddy, who was in the bedroom with Mummy, would protect her; and that was, Mrs K. suggested, because he felt it was Daddy himself who might hurt Mummy. (At that moment

Richard looked impressed and evidently accepted the
interpretation.) In day-time he thought Daddy was nice, but at
night when he, Richard, could not see his parents and did not
know what they were doing in bed, he might have felt that Daddy
was bad and dangerous and that all the terrible things which
happened to Cook . . . were happening to Mummy. . . . Just now he
had spoken of the terrible things that the Austrian Hitler did to the
Austrians. By this he meant that Hitler was in a way ill-treating his
own people, including Mrs K., just as the bad Daddy would ill-treat
Mummy.[127]

Klein had gone straight to the depths, all the while tying together scattered bits of material. She had begun to analyze an oedipal configuration—the bad Hitler-tramp father attacking Richard's
mother at night. She would continue to analyze it; the Oedipus complex, after all, was intrinsic to the theoretical understanding she had
brought to the therapy. And the case history she subsequently wrote
was designed not only to elucidate technique, but to clarify concepts
as well.

In illustrating what kinds of clinical material might be subsumed under specific concepts, Melanie Klein's *Narrative* (and Freud's case histories) could be likened to the standard examples shared by a scientific
community. And yet in contrast to such examples, they remain essentially unfinished. (It is not even clear what the genre consists in, so
diverse have been the contributions to it.) They provide no immediate
solutions to concrete problems; the "problems" are difficult to formulate; the "solutions" do not fit all the particulars. Were it otherwise,
there would scarcely be any reason to return again and again to the
full texts. What cannot or could not be tidily subsumed under the
theories demonstrated exerts as much fascination as the demonstra-
tions themselves.

Klein had already used material from Richard's analysis in a paper entitled "The Oedipus Complex in the Light of Early Anxieties"
(1945). Her aim had been to pull together her work on that complex
and on the depressive position and to illuminate the relation between
the two. Indeed, it was in this paper alone that she provided a clear
indication of what concepts she thought the case served to illustrate.
The commentary she later appended to the notes of each session
allowed her to discuss technique and beyond that to tack on to her

original interpretations ideas about psychic processes that she arrived at only after 1941. Yet she seemed unwilling to rethink her earlier formulations. She failed to suggest how her later work might help turn to account material left unexploited by the theory with which she had first approached the case.

In her exposition Klein concentrated on a series of Richard's drawings, patterned in four differently colored sections. Though superficially similar, they "varied greatly in detail"—in fact no two were exactly alike. "The way he made these drawings . . . was significant. He did not start out with any deliberate plan and was often surprised to see the finished picture."

In one of the first drawings in which these four colours were used he introduced black and red by marching the pencils towards the drawing with accompanying noises. He explained that black was his father, and accompanied the movement of the pencil by imitating the sound of marching soldiers. Red came next, and Richard said it was himself and sang a cheerful tune as he moved up the pencil. When colouring the blue sections he said this was his mother, and when filling in the purple sections he said his brother was nice and was helping him.[128]

Part way through the forty-first session the boy began another such drawing, chatting all the while:

Suddenly Richard pointed out to Mrs K. the long red section 'which goes all through Mummy's empire'. He at once tried to take this back by saying, 'It is not Mummy's empire, it is just an empire where all of us have some countries.'

Mrs K. interpreted that he was afraid to realize that he meant it to be his mother's empire because this would mean that the red section pierced her inside.

Richard, looking at the drawing again, suggested that this red section looked 'like a genital'.

Mrs K. interpreted that he felt that with such a long genital he could take everything good which Mummy had received from Daddy out of her. . . . But he was afraid of injuring and robbing her, and that was why he did not wish to realize that the long red genital was going 'all through Mummy's empire'. . . .

Richard had become more alive and interested after this interpretation. He looked at the drawing again and pointed out that the red section (which he had called a genital) divided the empire into two; in the west there were countries belonging to everybody; the part in the east did not contain anything of Mummy but only himself, Daddy, and Paul [Richard's brother]. . . .

Mrs K. pointed out that Richard's genital, the long red section, dominated the whole empire and was thrust into Mummy from top to bottom. The division of the empire also expressed his wish to keep the dangerous Daddy away from Mummy and to protect her against him; but it also meant that Mummy was divided into a bad Mother, the east, full of dangerous male genitals, and into a good and peaceful Mother. . . .

Richard replied to Mrs K.'s interpretation about the drawing that Mummy in the west was preparing to fight against the people in the east and would regain her countries there.[129]

It was the "sharp and elongated section which Richard interpreted as a genital" that he himself considered particularly "piercing and dangerous." It looked "like a long sharp tooth or like a dagger, the former," in Klein's view, "symbolizing the danger to the loved object from the oral-sadistic impulses, the latter the danger pertaining. . . to the genital function as such because of its penetrating nature."[130]

Richard's "potency," Klein claimed, "was bound up with a . . . hope that his mother could be preserved"—a hope he only fleetingly entertained. With such hope in short supply, he took "flight to the 'breast' mother"; along with that flight went an "*idealization* of the mother-and-baby relationship." Above all, he wished "to turn himself into an infant free from aggression" of any sort.[131] Klein, for her part, wanted to bring Richard's depressive anxieties to full consciousness and therewith pursue the analysis of his Oedipus complex.

She did not succeed. A revelation of paranoid fears had already cut across the track of depressive anxiety that Klein was following, and it was to do so again. The material had emerged, taking Klein by surprise, in the twenty-seventh session. Not for the first time, Richard had asked his analyst whether she and her son spoke Austrian—he refused to refer to the language as German:

Mrs K. interpreted that he had . . . shown how much he distrusted her and her son as foreigners and potential spies. They also stood for the unknown Mummy and Daddy, the parents who had secrets, particularly sexual ones, and he felt he could not know whether

Mummy contained the Hitler-Daddy. When he was not with his parents, he often distrusted them and he thought that Mummy would give him away to Daddy. . . .

Suddenly and with determination he said that he wanted to tell Mrs K. something which was worrying him very much. He was afraid of being poisoned by Cook or Bessie. They would do this because he was often horrid or cheeky to them. From time to time he had a good look at the food to find out whether it was poisoned. He looked into bottles in the kitchen to see what they contained; they might have poison in them which Cook would mix with his food. Sometimes he thought that Bessie, the maid, was a German spy. He occasionally listened at the key-hole to find out whether Cook and Bessie were speaking German together. (Both Cook and Bessie were British and did not know a word of German, as I subsequently ascertained.) He obviously forced himself to tell all this, looking tortured and worried. . . . He said that these fears made him very unhappy and asked if Mrs K. could help him with them. . . .

Mrs K. interpreted that he distrusted not only Cook and Bessie but also his parents because he wished to blow them up with his 'big job' as well as to poison them with his urine, both of which were felt to be poisonous when he hated his parents. . . . His main fear and guilt came from his unconscious desires to attack them with urine and faeces, to devour and kill them.[132]

In Richard's case Klein dealt sporadically with material of this sort; she failed to treat it as central. Yet as her interpretation indicated, she did have a theoretical framework for coping with paranoid fears. Simply put, *lex talionis* ruled: Richard's sadistic impulses toward his mother, impulses to attack her breasts as part objects by biting and scooping, with the intention of stealing their food, and to attack the mother as a whole object to rob her of her beauty, babies, and internal penises, provoked a dread of retaliation. Klein was not to rest content with that law. In her work after the Second World War, she shifted her emphasis from depressive anxieties and oedipal conflict to more primitive paranoid processes. Had that shift occurred earlier, Richard's paranoid fears might have come to the fore in her own interpretations.

What was striking, however, indeed poignant, about the episode was Richard's confidence in Klein, his ability to confess to her a fear that he felt "particularly badly about . . . because he thought of it as irrational and abnormal."[133] Had he viewed her as a schoolmistress whose good opinion he needed to win, he scarcely would have made such an admission. Klein's abjuration of the role of pedagogue allowed him, albeit only gradually, to forgo efforts at ingratiating himself and to unfreeze his emotions instead. Because she had created a genuine analytic situation, Richard could express a wide range of feelings and fantasies. And such material from a child in turn widened the range of the psychoanalytic domain itself.

The Paranoid-Schizoid Position

Now, the direct observer of infants must be prepared to allow the analyst to formulate ideas about very early infancy, ideas which may be psychically true and yet which cannot be demonstrated; indeed it may be possible sometimes by direct observation to prove that what had been found in analysis could not in fact exist at the time claimed because of the limitations imposed by immaturity. What is found repeatedly in analysis is not annulled by being proved wrong through direct observation. Direct observation only proves that the patients have been antedating certain phenomena and therefore giving the analyst the impression that things were happening at an age when they could not have happened.[134]

Winnicott failed to reckon with the analyst's own penchant for antedating; Klein's propensity in that regard, her linking of infantile and psychotic, are notorious. Yet it was Freud, after all, who had first advanced the etiological claims of regression to fixation points:

It is very remarkable that in the case of all the narcissistic neuroses we have to assume fixation points for the libido going back to far earlier phases of development than in hysteria or obsessional neurosis.[135]

Klein simply carried on:

If persecutory fears are very strong, and for this reason (among others) the infant cannot work through the paranoid-schizoid position, the working through of the depressive position is in turn impeded. This failure may lead to a regressive reinforcing of persecutory fears and strengthen the fixation-points for severe psychoses (that is to say, the group of schizophrenias).[136]

Though incomplete, Melanie Klein's effort to map what she came to call the paranoid-schizoid position once again broadened the psychoanalytic domain—this time to include very ill patients. Klein had long ago questioned, at least by implication, Freud's dictum that "sufferers from narcissistic neuroses" had "no capacity for transference" and hence lacked the prerequisite for analytic treatment.[137] She had, after all, rejected Freud's concept of autoerotic and narcissistic stages as prior to object love, and in so doing had cast aside the theoretical rationale on which his judgment had rested. Her conviction that there was "no instinctual urge, no anxiety situation, no mental process" that did "not involve objects, external or internal," led her to deny to no one the capacity for transference. It was postwar work on the "mechanisms, anxieties and defences operative in earliest infancy" that prompted her followers to open their consulting rooms to psychotics.[138]

Psychotic, paranoid, schizophrenic, narcissistic, schizoid—a babel of terms that defied and continues to defy tidy discrimination. Each has its own history, and each entered psychiatric parlance with differing theoretical baggage and etiological pretensions. Freud himself suggested that paranoia and dementia praecox "be brought together under the common designation 'paraphrenia.' "[139] No one heeded his advice: paranoia remained in both its neurotic and its psychotic guises, while psychiatrists followed Eugen Bleuler in separating schizophrenia from dementias as a disease entity. In the case of narcissism, however, Freud's work stood at the beginning of a process that culminated in its inclusion in the latest diagnostic manual—as a personality rather than a psychotic disorder.[140] Klein has no such nosological category to her credit. In linking "schizoid" with paranoid, she was borrowing from W. R. D. Fairbairn.[141]

━━━ ━━━ ━━━ ━━━ ━━━

"In the course of working out my concept of the infantile depressive position," Klein wrote, "the problems of the phase preceding it again forced themselves on my attention."[142] Persecutory anxiety and manic and obsessional defenses against it had been merely a beginning. In going beyond her earlier formulations, Klein landed in difficult terrain; she found herself grappling, albeit gingerly, with problems that heretofore she had managed to avoid: problems of structure. Ill at ease in this realm, she latched onto Fairbairn's term "schizoid" while simultaneously rejecting much of the content he had packed into it.

Above all, she felt obliged to look hard at the ego. (Up to this point, among Freud's structural triad, only the superego had figured prominently in her work; as for the id, it never made more than fleeting appearances.) Freud had already shown the way. In his "Notes on a Case of Paranoia," based on Dr. Daniel Schreber's autobiographical account of his severe psychotic illness, Freud had remarked that paranoia was linked with "abnormal changes in the ego."[143] It had been merely a suggestion, carrying with it, however, the implication that such changes ought to be explained in energetic terms. Klein did not entirely ignore energy, but her references to it were little more than addenda.

Once again her interest focused on fantasy, in this case on Schreber's fantasy of world catastrophe:

At the climax of his illness, under the influence of visions which were 'partly of a terrifying character, but partly, too, of an indescribable grandeur', Schreber became convinced of the imminence of a great catastrophe, of the end of the world. Voices told him that the work of the past 14,000 years had now come to nothing, and that the earth's allotted span was only 212 years more; and during the last part of his stay in Flechsig's clinic he believed that that period had already elapsed. He himself was 'the only real man left alive', and the few human shapes that he still saw—the doctor, the attendants, the other patients—he explained as being 'miracled up, cursorily improvised men'.[144]

Freud and Klein agreed that Schreber's "end of the world" delusion represented "the projection of . . . [an] internal catastrophe"; she described it in terms of "anxieties and phantasies about inner destruction and ego-disintegration."[145] (Even more than Freud, Klein slid between "ego" as some sort of psychical agency and "ego" as self.) The question that concerned her was what "abnormal changes in the ego" brought about paranoid hallucinations such as Schreber's.

Two ideas emerged as crucial in her paper "Notes on Some Schizoid Mechanisms" (1946): splitting (hence "schizoid") and projective identification. Klein had long before claimed that the ego projected sadism onto objects or part objects and then split them into good and bad—and that this splitting took place in relation not only to external objects but to internal ones as well. Now she flatly stated that the ego was "incapable of splitting the object—internal and external—without a corresponding splitting taking place within the ego" itself.[146] What is of interest, however, is not so much the notion of the ego as fissionable but the picture of the ego in relation to its external and its internal objects that the notion prompted.

Klein referred to that complicated picture as a mechanism and called it "projective identification." (The term "identification" simply indicated that it was the subject's self that was projected.) This newly designated process differed from projection in two ways—both tending toward an image of mind still more spatial and concrete. First, projective identification operated not on qualities or properties like love or anger, as did projection, but on "things or bits of things—more specifically, split-off parts of the self." Second, projective identification, unlike projection, did not aim at transposing a property from the subject to another; rather it aimed at ridding the subject "not merely of the offending substance but also of the thought of it." If one then asked where the thought or substance was, the answer would be that it was "now lodged inside an external thing—initially the mother or the mother's breast." Henceforth that object would be regarded as containing what had been expelled.[147]

Just as Klein always coupled projection with introjection, so too she gave this new mechanism a suitable introjective partner—without, however, naming it. The introjective process again hinged on incorporation, but the object now incorporated contained what had previously been gotten rid of, and its reincorporation thus entailed the failure of projective identification. This failure further entailed the reinstatement with a vengeance of the persecuting thought or substance.[148]

Actually, schizoid patients might experience little anxiety; after all, their defensive strategies aimed precisely at that result. Nonetheless, Klein claimed, tracking anxiety remained central to the analytic work:

The schizoid mechanisms imply a dispersal of emotions including anxiety, but these dispersed elements still exist in the patient. Such patients have a certain form of latent anxiety. . . . The feeling of being disintegrated, of being unable to experience emotions, of losing one's objects, is in fact the equivalent of anxiety. This becomes clearer when advances in synthesis have been made. The great relief which a patient then experiences derives from a feeling that his inner and outer worlds have not only come more together but back to life again. At such moments it appears in retrospect that when emotions were lacking, relations were vague and uncertain and parts of the personality were felt to be lost, everything seemed to be dead.[149]

Had it been thus with Richard? Klein did not say; she did not return to Richard's paranoid anxieties. Had she done so, she might have realized that what had once appeared a simple matter of retaliation now looked vastly more complicated. Projective identification raised the possibility that such anxieties might not be repayment in kind for fantasized biting, scratching, or urinating on an object. It raised the possibility that they might derive from an attack of one part of the ego (lodged in someone else) on another part.[150]

Klein's discussion of schizoid mechanisms was plagued by a persistent (and familiar) ambiguity. Were "mechanisms" processes or fantasies? Klein would have answered that they were both. Quite simply she saw no point in trying to disentangle them:

The processes I have described are, of course, bound up with the infant's phantasy-life; and the anxieties which stimulate the mechanism of splitting are also of a phantastic nature. It is in phantasy that the infant splits the object and the self, but the effect of this phantasy is a very real one.[151]

On the subject of splitting, Freud had left behind only a few brief remarks, set down late in life. His emphasis fell on the splitting off of ideas or the disavowing of pieces of reality: the persistence of "two attitudes . . . side by side throughout their lives without influencing each other" might "rightly be called a splitting of the ego."[152] Elsewhere, "two contrary reactions" to instinctual conflict—the first, continuance of satisfaction, the second, compliance with a prohibition against such satisfaction—persisted "as the centre-point of a splitting of the ego."[153] Klein's notions were far more concrete. "Splitting the ego," she wrote, resulted in the feeling that the ego was "in bits"; splitting was tantamount to a fantasy of fragmentation. At the same time she claimed that it amounted "to a state of disintegration."[154] But what had disintegrated—a fantasy or a structure? In Klein's mind fantasy and mechanism were enmeshed; so too were fantasy and structure.

Klein's last major work, entitled *Envy and Gratitude,* appeared in 1957. Her stress on envy derived from clinical material and proved useful to her followers in the consulting room. The notion itself bore a family resemblance to sadism (and the death instinct), which Klein was quick to underline:

I have often described the sadistic attacks on the mother's breast as determined by destructive impulses. Here I wish to add that envy gives particular impetus to these attacks. This means that when I wrote about the greedy scooping out of the breast and of the mother's body, and the destruction of her babies, as well as putting bad excrements into the mother, this adumbrated what I later came to recognize as the envious spoiling of the object.[155]

In the late 1920s she had insisted that anxiety was rooted in inborn sadism; similarly, half a century later she insisted that "the infant's difficulties in building up his good object" were grounded in innate envy.[156] Yet the two were not identical. What distinguished envy from sadism was that envy constituted an attack upon the good *because it was good;* it attacked the goodness of the object.

The matter of innateness landed Klein in disputed terrain. What opened new vistas was her "good object" and, more generally, the world of internal objects.

W. R. D. Fairbairn: Object Relations and Ego Structures

During the same year, 1943–1944, in which the British Psycho-Analytical Society held its controversial discussions, W. R. D. Fairbairn was ruminating on his own about the issues being hotly debated in London. In a preface to the single volume of Fairbairn's papers collected in book form, Ernest Jones commented on this isolation. He tactfully balanced its advantages and disadvantages: originality stood as a decided plus, but along with it came the risk of developing a "train of thought" unmodified by the constructive criticism of co-workers, in short, of being "one-sided."[1] Beyond that, Jones refused to go; he hesitated to make any detailed assessment. What may strike others is Fairbairn's neatness: his was an orderly and economical mind; his style was spare almost to the point of ellipsis. His writing was not without contradiction and obscurity, but it never suffered from the downright sloppiness that plagued the work of Melanie Klein.

Problems of structure fascinated Fairbairn; so too did problems of development. In both realms he initiated far-reaching attempts to reshape the psychoanalytic domain. He challenged Freud's structural hypothesis, the division of the mental apparatus into id, ego, and superego, offering his own theory of endopsychic structure as a replacement. He also challenged Freud's libido theory and, once again, suggested a major reformulation. Of the three protagonists of the present study, he alone made fully explicit his departures from Freud.

Freud's Structural Hypothesis: A Flawed Synthesis

Freud's "Project" had constituted his first effort to elaborate something resembling structural theory. He had adopted a strategy—the only one available to him—of progressing from mind to brain, that is, from the intentional realm of clinical phenomena to the cerebral phenomena of neurophysiology. Simple reduction of mind to matter was not the issue; rather, Freud had hoped that postulates about clinical phenomena might gain in credibility if proved congruent with a mechanical model. In fact he did not succeed in finding a place in his model for pathological defense, and he abandoned his attempt to give a mechanical account of that phenomenon. He did not abandon modeling, nor did he fully abandon the "Project" itself. Yet never again would he so clearly state his dependence on neurophysiology.

The Ego and the Id represented a stark contrast. Here, in outlining what is reputed to have become the "central paradigm of psychoanalysis,"[2] Freud followed no consistent strategy: he did not seek in a systematic fashion to sort out the relations of psychoanalysis with neighboring disciplines. Instead he plundered and exploited them. To put it another way, they served a rhetorical rather than a corroborative function; above all, Freud was after analogy, whether from biology or from mythology. And in arguing from analogy, he jumbled the hierarchy of complexity that gave a natural order to the sciences.

Does Freud's admitted speculative bent alone account for his blurring of boundaries? Perhaps. Yet he had implicitly assigned himself a daunting task that would have sorely taxed even a more rigorous thinker: to introduce into his new structural theory the major lines of argument he had developed since the "Project." Two in particular stood out. The first was libido theory, which had, after the publication of *Three Essays on Sexuality*, enjoyed more than fifteen years of luxuriant growth, culminating in the dual-instinct theory—the hypothesis of a polarity between life and death—of *Beyond the Pleasure Principle*.[3] The second was the theory of the Oedipus complex, which in its positive and negative variants had come to dominate the clinical scene.[4] How to solder a family drama onto an evolutionary biological base was the problem Freud confronted in *The Ego and the Id*. To solve it, he transformed the disparate theoretical components into structural entities and then, by implication, tried to assemble these entities into a mental apparatus that recalled the "Project" itself. The result was seriously flawed, and in subsequent years Freud's attempted synthesis fractured along fault lines that his work of transformation had merely papered over.[5]

Already in the late 1930s Heinz Hartmann was making a name for himself in Vienna as the founder of psychoanalytic ego psychology. His reading of the Freudian ego and his elaboration of its autonomous functions remained untranslated for the better part of two decades and were unknown to Fairbairn. Unlike Hartmann, Fairbairn interpreted Freud's ego in object relational terms and, as a consequence, directed his attention to areas the Viennese overlooked. The id-ego axis absorbed Hartmann; that of the superego-ego caught Fairbairn. Hartmann showed little interest in the superego; Fairbairn made a strong case against allowing the id a separate existence. Freud's structural theory had invited such a bifurcation.

What precisely was the "id"? The term "id" was James Strachey's rendering of "das Es": he chose the Latin word rather than the English "it," "so as to be parallel with the long-established 'ego'."[6] The term "das Es" was not of Freud's invention; he borrowed it from Georg Groddeck, who had tried to capture therewith the passive quality of existence, the experience of being " 'lived' by unknown and uncontrollable forces."[7] In adopting so open-ended a concept, Freud had ample opportunity to complete it as he wished:

It is the dark, inaccessible part of our personality. . . . We approach the id with analogies: we call it a chaos, a cauldron full of seething excitations. . . . It is filled with energy reaching it from the instincts, but it has no organization, produces no collective will, but only a striving to bring about the satisfaction of the instinctual needs.[8]

Above all, Freud commented, the "impersonal pronoun" seemed "particularly suited for expressing the main characteristic of this province of the mind—the fact of its being alien to the ego."[9] For Freud to set id against ego was merely to pursue a train of thought which ran throughout his work; at the same time it created difficulties for his "ego."

The id with its "seething excitations" stood in direct line of descent from the endogenous stimuli of the "Project"; the ego of the structural hypothesis similarly descended from the "Project." In that unpublished work Freud had depicted it as the extreme form of the impermeable system of neurons, constantly cathected, and hence serving as a storehouse of Q.[10] In subsequently attributing all energy to the id, Freud ran the risk of so depleting the ego as to leave it no supplies for fulfilling the tasks he assigned it—or rather, to make an energetic account of its functioning *a fortiori* impossible. To resolve this conundrum (of his own making) Freud gave the ego a developmental history—something it had lacked in the "Project."

This developmental account, though a bare outline, was a confusing mix of mechanistic and purposive, or quantitative and cognitive. (Freud's discussion of the id betrayed the same confusion: even that powerhouse he frequently described in intentional language.) In the beginning ego and id were undifferentiated; the ego was the portion of the id which had "been expediently modified by the proximity of the external world with its threat of danger."[11] The modification may have been expedient, but it remained unexplained. It followed nonetheless that the ego had to extract energy from the id; it could do so only by subterfuge. Freud wrote a number of scenarios for the ego to enact, ascribing to it a cunning and sophistication that belied its weakness. Beyond that he allotted to it functions that echoed those specified in the "Project." In *An Outline of Psycho-Analysis* he wrote:

It has the task of self-preservation. As regards *external* events, it performs that task by becoming aware of stimuli, by storing up experiences about them (in memory), by avoiding excessively strong stimuli (through flight), by dealing with moderate stimuli (through adaptation) and finally by learning to bring about expedient changes in the external world to its own advantage (through activity). As regards *internal* events, in relation to the id, it performs that task by gaining control over the demands of the instincts, by deciding whether they are to be allowed satisfaction, by postponing that satisfaction to times and circumstances favourable in the external world or by suppressing their excitations entirely.[12]

Clearly there was a job of clarification to be done, and Hartmann set out to do it. Two objectives dominated this enterprise: to spell out a mechanical account of the ego's sources of energy and to describe its functions in detail. To attain the first, Hartmann deployed the concept of the neutralization of energy, a notion already adumbrated in *The Ego and the Id*. There Freud had briefly referred to displaceable or neutral energy active in the ego—energy which could be no other than desexualized libido.[13] Hartmann broadened this hypothesis to include "deaggressivized" as well as desexualized energy.[14] In his view each should be given equal billing in the "build-up of the ego."[15] Still more, he now felt confident in asserting that the ego disposed of "independent . . . energy."[16]

Besides depicting the ego as engaged in conflict, struggling to wrest energy from the id and to neutralize it, Hartmann delineated the ego's functions and, in so doing, attributed to it a conflict-free sphere.[17] That sphere covered a range of learning and motivational processes, such as perception, thinking, memory, and motor development. These constituted the primary autonomous functions of the ego, and they were not dependent on the neutralization of instinctual energy. (On what energy such primary autonomy drew, Hartmann did not specify; here "energy" defeated even him.)[18] "Secondary autonomy," however, *was* dependent, and it in turn was linked with "ego strength": the relative distance, Hartmann claimed, of "ego function from id pressure" determined mental health.[19] In this convoluted fashion he elaborated Freud's pithy dictum "Where id was, there shall ego be."[20]

Hartmann's attempted clarification was nothing if not ambitious. On the one hand he remained intent on preserving psychoanalysis as a biological discipline, and in his mind that preservation required the full array of Freudian mechanistic terminology. On the other hand he aspired to include academic psychology within the psychoanalytic domain: as he put it, psychoanalysis had "the potentiality to become a general theory of mental development, broader, both in its assumptions and scope, than any other psychological theory."[21] Neither claim could be sustained. Energy theory degenerated into pseudo-explanation, a mere tautological renaming.[22] Its continued vogue in the United States, where Hartmann had arrived as an émigré from Hitler's Europe, hindered the reckoning with newer neurophysiological data.[23] In contrast, the claim to the status of general psychology, pretentious though it may have been, did less harm. It did not trap psychoanalysts in a blind alley; rather it alerted them to the possibilities afforded by neighboring psychological disciplines of providing indirect evidential support.

▬▬ ▬▬ ▬▬ ▬▬ ▬▬

The id and the ego could trace their lineage back to the "Project." In a less direct fashion, so too could the superego: it could claim memory as its ancestor. In that early work, memories grooved into the mental apparatus acted as a normal motive force. Beyond that, Freud had pointed to specific memories, those of childhood sexual experiences, as pathogenic. Against such memories the ego struggled to defend itself—and failure, which permitted the return of repressed memories, brought on illness. In focusing on the Oedipus complex, Freud reiterated his notion of a permanent change in the mental apparatus: he insisted "that the hypothesis of the super-ego really describes a structural relation and is not merely a personification."[24]

At the same time Freud claimed that the superego reached

down into the id.[25] His account of that relation, however, was obscure; first one, then the other, of the id's dual instincts dominated the scene. When discussing the formation of the superego—the precipitate of abandoned primal ties—Freud concentrated on the id as the source of libidinal object choices. (Insofar as the superego also represented "an energetic reaction-formation against those choices," the obscurity increased.)[26] When discussing the clinical phenomenon of melancholia—the result of an "excessively strong super-ego" raging "against the ego with merciless violence"—Freud gave pride of place to the death instinct: "a pure culture of the death instinct" was now "holding sway in the super-ego."[27] Examples of muddled presentation could be multiplied—but to no purpose. Once again a job of clarification needed to be undertaken.

Melanie Klein sidestepped this task. To be sure, she had drawn on the contents of Freud's structural triad—cannibalized them so to speak—but with scant regard for conceptual niceties. The death instinct and phylogenetic legacies figured prominently in her work; the id as a structural entity did not concern her. At first glance she seems to have shown greater respect for the superego; yet she never considered it a unitary structure, and in fact she transformed it into a complex world of internal objects whose structural properties remained unclear. Even the ego Klein left poorly defined; it lacked the limits that would serve to demarcate it from other psychic agencies. Yet for Klein to have ignored such limits was fully appropriate: Freud's tripartite division could not help her to elucidate relations between the ego and its objects. And this was the enterprise that had gripped her imagination.

Fairbairn attacked the assignment directly, while continuing to stress the axis running from superego to ego and internal objects that Klein had already charted. With the ego as the central focus, Fairbairn made a concerted attempt to disentangle the levels of reference in Freud's structural theory. That work of extrication entailed rethinking the boundaries of the psychoanalytic domain, and here the contrast between Fairbairn and Hartmann emerged in striking fashion. Fairbairn rejected the notion that psychoanalysis ranked as a biological discipline. (He also abandoned Freud's speculative physiology.) Biology, Fairbairn implied, rather than being intrinsic to the domain, formed part of that domain's background knowledge and hence lost none of its relevance. Still more, Fairbairn never showed the slightest inclination to install general psychology under a ballooning psychoanalytic tent; in his mind, psychology, like biology, remained crucial yet distinct. In short, he performed an operation of pruning that was urgently required.

Above all, such pruning was called for if structural theory was to be clinically anchored. Freud had never forgotten clinical data; a nugget from the consulting room—the unconscious sense of guilt discussed in *The Ego and the Id* is a case in point—provided him a springboard for a speculative leap. Yet he jumped so high that the clinical material figured minimally in the final product. Fairbairn took fewer leaps. His focus did not waver from what gave psychoanalysis its claim to being an empirical discipline: the purposive activities of single subjects.[28]

"A Revised Psychopathology"

In Fairbairn's earliest paper one can already detect a note of dissatisfaction with classic libido theory.[29] Still it was not until the mid-1930s, not until he read Melanie Klein's work on manic-depressive states, that he ceased thinking along fairly conventional lines.[30] He quickly appreciated that Klein's concept of positions, by granting relations with internal objects a privileged status, called into question the explanatory power of libido theory. He also realized that Klein "failed to push her views to their logical conlusion."[31] For Fairbairn to push matters to their logical conclusions was his stock-in-trade, and what could be more logical than to reassess Freud's libido in the light of Klein's internal objects?

The operation that began as a mere tidying-up turned into a major revision of libido theory. In Fairbairn's view what mattered was not libidinal aims but object relations; what needed investigation was not infantile sexuality atomized into component instincts and erotogenic zones but the relationship between child and caretakers in both external and internal reality.

━━━ ━━━ ━━━ ━━━ ━━━

" 'You're always talking about my wanting this and that desire satisfied; but what I really want is a father,' " a patient protested. It was reflection upon such clinical phenomena that prompted Fairbairn to voice his own protest: the ultimate goal of libido was not pleasure; rather, *"the ultimate goal of libido"* was *"the object."*

The real libidinal aim is the establishment of satisfactory relationships with objects; and it is, accordingly, the object that constitutes the true libidinal goal.[32]

Fairbairn's "libido" differed markedly from Freud's original notion of grossly sexual desire. Over the course of time the Freudian version had "developed into a properly mannered, barely sexual, almost mythical, hazy conception."[33] Fairbairn tried to dissipate the haze, and in the process, distanced himself from Freud. In his hands "libido" became *the object-seeking principle.*"[34]

Much more than semantics was involved. Fairbairn proposed a radical move: to replace libidinal development understood as sexuality by libidinal development understood as dependency. In Freud's view sexual pleasure ranked as primary, and objects acquired importance only insofar as they provided gratification. In Fairbairn's opinion pleasure seeking figured as a "secondary and deteriorative . . . principle of behaviour":

Explicit pleasure-seeking, [that is], . . . the relieving of . . . tension . . . for the mere sake of relieving this tension, . . . does, of course, occur commonly enough; but, since libidinal need is object-need, simple tension-relieving implies some failure of object-relationships. The fact is that simple tension-relieving is really a safety-valve process. It is thus, not a means of achieving libidinal aims, but a means of mitigating the failure of these aims.[35]

Like Freud, Fairbairn chose thumb sucking as a concrete example. Freud considered such activity as evidence of a "need for repeating sexual satisfaction," a need that had gotten "detached from the need for taking nourishment";[36] Fairbairn argued that Freud had missed the point. He had failed to ask the crucial question: Why the thumb? The answer was obvious: because there was "no breast to suck. Even the baby," Fairbairn claimed, "must have a libidinal object; and, if he is deprived of his natural object (the breast), he is driven to provide an object for himself. Thumb-sucking thus represents a technique for dealing with an unsatisfactory object-relationship; and the same may be said for masturbation."[37]

Fairbairn was on the verge of formulating his radical proposal when, as visiting psychiatrist at Carstairs Hospital, a psychoneurosis unit in the Emergency Medical Service, he "began to see military cases in large numbers." During the early years of the Second World War, he treated something of an epidemic, a situation stressful to the therapist yet potentially illuminating to the scientist. Fairbairn quickly realized that the size of the patient population might lend credence to hypotheses derived from the intensive study of a very few. Beyond that, the nature of the epidemic—Fairbairn described it as "homesickness"— was ideally suited to his interests: the patients he saw had been, as he put it,

suddenly removed from their normal environment, separated from their love-objects and isolated from all the accustomed props and supports upon which a dependent person would ordinarily rely. It was almost as if a laboratory experiment under controlled conditions had been gratuitously provided for the testing of my conclusions.[38]

Here, surely, dependency could be observed.

Observe it he did, and even though Fairbairn made no detailed statistical analysis, he came away convinced that his hypothesis had survived a preliminary trial. His civilian patient had wanted a father; the soldiers he encountered wanted their mothers or wives. One example stood out as paradigmatic, that of a twenty-four-year-old gunner who had been hospitalized three months after entering military service:

He had felt 'depressed' from the day he entered the Army; and, in the absence of his wife, he felt completely 'alone'. It seemed to him that everything was against him; and he felt that his only hold on life resided in the hope of seeing his wife again—a fact in explanation of which he volunteered the remarks, 'She is like a mother to me', and 'She is all I have'.

Fairbairn's soldier had earlier been utterly dependent upon his maternal grandmother, with whom he had lived after his mother's premature death. He could scarcely be separated from her; he could venture out alone only if a speedy return was possible. What had saved him when his grandmother's health began to fail was meeting the young woman who eventually became his wife. Marriage, however, did not "provide an adequate solution to his problems."[39] Only after he had so arranged his affairs that his wife could remain constantly at his side was his separation anxiety allayed. And just at the point when those arrangements were complete, he was summoned for military service.

Why had this patient's infantile dependency persisted? What accounted for individual variation? Fairbairn confronted these questions; he did not answer them. With the data at his disposal, that is, clinical material from adult patients, he could merely discern the sketch of an answer. Nor for that matter could similar questions about

infantile sexuality be resolved. Yet given a choice between Freud's
sexual libido and the object-seeking variety, Fairbairn had grounds
for preferring his own formulation. Still more, it had proved reasonable to pursue the revision of libido theory—an enterprise based more
on logic than on new facts.

To replace libidinal development understood as sexuality with libidinal development understood as dependence required grappling with
Abraham's elaboration of Freudian oral, anal, and phallic stages. Criticism was crucial, yet by itself insufficient. Fairbairn did not expect
either theoreticians or clinicians to cast aside what they regarded as a
mainstay unless he offered them something in return. And he was
intent on providing such an alternative sequence.

Recall that Freud's stages had derived in large part from the
notion of erotogenic zones. Fairbairn demurred: instead of recogniz-
ing "that the function of libidinal pleasure" was "to provide a sign-
post" to the object, Freud had made the object the "sign-post to libidinal pleasure."[40] What would happen to the stages if the object should
be given precedence? At the very least the nomenclature would have
to be altered: "oral" would give way to "breast"; "anal" would give way
to "feces." It was at this point that a severe lack of comparability
became apparent: the breast was a functioning biological object; feces
were not. Anality seemed spurious; it could be reckoned an artifact.
Yet deleting anality meant subverting Freud's sequence.

Fairbairn's alternative was simplicity itself. The earliest stage,
which he called infantile dependence, contained within it Abraham's
earlier and later oral phases; in similar fashion, "the stage of mature
dependence" corresponded "to Abraham's 'final genital phase' ":

Between these two stages of infantile and mature dependence is a
transition stage characterized by an increasing tendency to abandon
the attitude of infantile dependence and an increasing tendency to
adopt the attitude of mature dependence. This transition stage
corresponds to three of Abraham's phases—the two anal phases
and the early genital (phallic) phase.[41]

"In infancy," Fairbairn noted, "owing to the constitution of the
human organism, the path of least resistance to the object" happened
"to lie almost exclusively through the mouth; and the mouth accordingly" became "the dominant libidinal organ." This dominant mouth

shaped Fairbairn's conceptualization of infantile dependence: in his view such dependence and the "incorporation of the object" were "intimately associated." It followed, then, that the course taken by object-seeking turned on *"the extent to which objects are incorporated and the nature of the techniques which are employed to deal with incorporated objects."*[42]

But not only did the infant incorporate the object; he also identified with it. Infantile dependence, oral incorporation, and a third notion, that of primary identification, formed a cluster of linked concepts. "Oral incorporation" echoed the work of Melanie Klein. (So too did the notion of object relations from birth onward.) "Primary identification" harked back to Freud.[43] Fairbairn spelled out more clearly than Freud what primary identification meant: non-differentiation of subject from object. In his words, *"[T]he abandonment of infantile dependence"* involved *"an abandonment of relationships based upon primary identification in favour of relationships with differentiated objects."*[44] How was such differentiation to be accomplished? At this point the significance of equating primary identification with oral incorporation became apparent: differentiation *a fortiori* entailed explusion.

By the time the child entered the transition stage, Fairbairn argued, he was no longer dealing with a solitary incorporated object. In line with Abraham, Fairbairn stressed the onset of ambivalence in the later oral phase: the original object had by now been replaced by two—*"an accepted object,* towards which love" was "directed, and *a rejected object,* towards which hate" was "directed."[45] (Fairbairn subsequently modified his views and wrote instead of an accepted object on the one hand and of exciting and rejecting objects on the other.) Acceptance and rejection—or retention and expulsion—furnished Fairbairn the requisite flexibility for reassessing the standard account of psychopathology. The variations he played on these themes, however, were less important than his having sketched an object-relational version.

Was Fairbairn's sequence of infantile to mature dependence sturdy enough to replace orthodox libido theory? Clearly Abraham's stages had been found wanting. Even Freud's allegiance to a libidinal explanation of neurotic phenomena had been far from exclusive: he preferred the Oedipus complex, which, after all, emphasized object relations. To test the matter of his own theory, Fairbairn could not postpone confronting that complex.

For Freud the Oedipus complex and libido theory were not alternative or incompatible accounts of neurosogenesis. On the contrary, the Oedipus complex and the phallic stage went hand in hand: in his view, the incestuous wishes that characterized the complex acquired their imperative force from instinctual drives. For Melanie Klein too, the Oedipus complex was fueled by sexual (and aggressive) instincts. Her departure from Freud concerned the question of dating. To make room for object relations, internal and external, from the moment of birth, without challenging the centrality of the Oedipus complex, she had simply pushed back both oedipal relations and the phallic stage (her term was "genital") to the first year of life. In so doing she had tried to pour new wine into old bottles.

Fairbairn would have none of this:

> The Oedipus situation . . . is not . . . basic . . . , but the derivative of a situation which has priority over it not only in the logical, but also in the temporal sense. This prior situation is one which issues directly out of the physical and emotional dependence of the infant upon his mother, and which declares itself in the relationship of the infant to his mother long before his father becomes a significant object.[46]

For Fairbairn, with his understanding of development in terms of dependence, Freud's dictum that "every new arrival on this planet" was fated to become a little Oedipus obviously required emendation.

In emphasizing the mother-infant relationship, Fairbairn was once again following Melanie Klein. Yet he soon went beyond her. Not only did he deprive the father of his crucial status in the oedipal triangle; he relegated him to a derivative position:

> The chief novelty introduced into the child's world by the Oedipus situation, as this materializes in outer reality, is that he is now confronted with two distinct parental objects instead of . . . only one. . . . His relationship with his new object, viz., his father, is, of course, inevitably fraught with vicissitudes similar to those which he previously experienced in his relationship with his mother—and in particular, the vicissitudes of need, frustration and rejection. In view of these vicissitudes, his father becomes an ambivalent object to him, whilst at the same time he himself becomes ambivalent toward his father. In his relationship with his father he is thus faced with the same problem of adjustment as that with which he was originally faced in his relationship with his mother. The original

situation is reinstated, albeit this time in relation to a fresh object; and, very naturally, he seeks to meet the difficulties of the reinstated situation by means of the same series of techniques which he learned to adopt in meeting the difficulties of the original situation.[47]

In the triangle the child appeared to be doing most of the work; indeed, Fairbairn argued, he *"constitutes the Oedipus situation for himself."* The child confronted with a maternal object that had turned ambivalent—a situation he found intolerable—had responded by dividing it into an accepted object and a rejected object. To be called upon to deal with two ambivalent objects was still worse. In order to simplify the situation, and to make it more bearable, the child designated one parent the accepted object, and the other he rejected.[48]

What had happened to sexuality in Fairbairn's version of the oedipal drama? He assigned it a secondary role. The child's initial understanding of the difference between his parents had to do with breasts, not genitals: father was different from mother because he lacked breasts. (Unlike Melanie Klein, Fairbairn did not traffic in phylogenetically inherited knowledge of male and female organs.)

When the child comes to appreciate, in some measure at least, the genital difference between his parents, and as, in the course of his own development, his physical need tends to flow increasingly (albeit in varying degrees) through genital channels, his need for his mother comes to include a need for her vagina. At the same time, his need for his father comes to include a need for his father's penis.[49]

Here Fairbairn introduced an important caveat: "The strength of these physical needs for his parents' genitals varies . . . in inverse proportion to the satisfaction of his emotional needs. Thus, the more satisfactory his emotional relations with his parents, the less urgent are his physical needs for their genitals."[50]

This last point Fairbairn illuminated by a clinical vignette drawn from the case of a female patient:

Owing to disagreements between her parents they occupied separate bedrooms. Between these bedrooms lay an interconnecting dressing-room; and, to protect herself from her husband, my patient's mother made her sleep in this dressing-room. She obtained little display of affection from either parent. . . . Her father was of a detached and unapproachable personality; and she experienced greater difficulty in making emotional contact with him than with her mother. After her mother's death, which occurred in her teens, she made desperate attempts to establish contact with her father, but all in vain. It was then that the thought suddenly occurred to her one day: 'Surely it would appeal to him if I offered to go to bed with him!' Her incestuous wish thus represented a desperate attempt to make an emotional contact with her object—and, in so doing, both to elicit love and to prove that her own love was acceptable. . . . In the case of my patient the incestuous wish was, of course, renounced; and, as might be expected, it was followed by an intense guilt reaction.[51]

Fairbairn's own conclusions followed relentlessly:

I venture to suggest that the deep analysis of a positive Oedipus situation may be regarded as taking place at three main levels. At the first level the picture is dominated by the Oedipus situation itself. At the next level it is dominated by ambivalence towards the heterosexual parent; and at the deepest level it is dominated by ambivalence towards the mother.[52]

Fairbairn did not discard the Oedipus complex; he did not reject outright Freud's "nucleus of the neuroses." He *did* transform it. And in the work of transformation his fundamental concept of libido as object-seeking emerged as a vigorous rival to the orthodox version.

Once again Fairbairn had insisted that psychopathology sprang from the infant's dependence on the maternal object. It remained for him to delineate what stemmed from that earliest stage.

When Melanie Klein had taken up what she had initially called the paranoid position, she found that her concerns intersected with those of Fairbairn's. They were both attempting to chart the psycho-pathology that in their view—and Abraham's as well—germinated in the first year of life. Though their work overlapped, Klein took care to point out the differences in how she and Fairbairn conceived their enterprises: her approach, she noted, "was predominantly from the angle of anxieties and their vicissitudes," whereas Fairbairn's "was largely from the angle of ego-development in relation to objects."[53] What she failed to elucidate was the divergent conception of objects that prompted their respective approaches.

The point at issue was the status of external objects. In her early writings, when she had focused on aggression, Klein had suggested that "the first objects of the drives" were "created out of the drives themselves; their content" was "derived from the content of the child's own impulses which" were "experienced as directed towards him by the external object." With her papers on the depressive position, after she had shifted her attention to good objects, "the theory of the internal origins of early objects" receded "into the background"; instead Klein argued that "the real others in the infant's external world" were "constantly internalized, established as internal objects, and projected out onto external figures once again." This historical development resulted in a curious asymmetry: Klein had "a tendency to see bad objects as . . . derived from the child's own drives, and good objects as derived largely from external others."[54] In contrast, Fairbairn's views remained constant. As he saw it, the badness of an object was not a projection of the child's sadism; it was a reflection of a mother's unavailability. In short, the real mother, not some fantasy, now emerged as central to psychopathology.

What ranked as crucial for the child was the establishment of "a satisfactory object-relationship during the period of infantile dependence. . . . The traumatic situation," according to Fairbairn, was "one in which the child" felt he was "not really loved as a person, and that his own love" was "not accepted." (The critical nature of unsatisfactory object relationships, Fairbairn conceded, in part depended upon their continuing into "the succeeding years of early childhood.") That traumatic situation, and the ensuing psychopathology, he further differentiated in terms of whether it arose during the early or the late oral phase. His discussion of the latter amounted to a reiteration of Melanie Klein's depressive position.

> If . . . the phase in which infantile object-relationships have been pre-eminently unsatisfactory is the late oral phase, the reaction provoked in the child conforms to the idea that he is not loved because of the badness and destructiveness of his hate; and this reaction provides the basis for a subsequent depressive tendency. . . . Where [such] a . . . tendency is present, . . . the ultimate psychopathological disaster . . . follows from loss of the object.[55]

It was when Fairbairn got to the schizoid position that the difference between his approach and that of Melanie Klein began to tell. (It should be recalled that her work on schizoid mechanisms appeared after his.) Fairbairn concentrated on the child's first and failed love relationship with an external object: deprivation during the pre-ambivalent oral phase provoked "in the child a reaction conforming to the idea that he" was "not loved because his own love" was "bad and destructive." ("Bad" in this context may be more than usually obscure.) Faced, then, with the dilemma of whether to love or not—an infinitely less tolerable choice than the one characteristic of the late oral phase between loving and hating—the child might forsake object-seeking entirely. Given the child's unconditional dependence on his object, to renounce object-seeking would be tantamount to psychic suicide. Hence Fairbairn's summary statement, "Loss of the ego" was "the ultimate psychopathological disaster" for those with a schizoid tendency.[56]

What became of such people? Fairbairn sketched out the consequences of a chronic traumatic situation:

(a) The child comes to regard his mother as a bad object in so far as she does not seem to love him.
(b) The child comes to regard outward expression of his own love as bad, with the result that . . . he tends to retain his love inside himself.
(c) The child comes to feel that love relationships with external objects in general are bad, or at least precarious.
    The net result is that the child tends to transfer his relationships with his objects to the realm of inner reality. . . . In the case of individuals with a schizoid component in their personality, accordingly, there is a great tendency for the outer world to derive its meaning too exclusively from the inner world. . . . Not only do their objects tend to belong to the inner rather than to the outer world, but they tend to identify themselves very strongly with their internal objects. This fact contributes materially to the difficulty which they experience in giving emotionally.

The unloved child—unloved as a person in his own right, though perhaps valued as his mother's possession—"remained profoundly fixated" upon that mother as an internal object.[57] Once again Fairbairn had returned to the phenomenon of extreme dependence, as the paradoxical result of withdrawal from the external world.

Fairbairn appreciated full well that no child enjoyed "a perfect object-relationship during the impressionable period of infantile dependence, or for that matter during the transition period" that succeeded it. Maternal failure undoubtedly came in all shapes and sizes. It could be inferred (and this was Fairbairn's central point) that there was "present in every one either an underlying schizoid or an underlying depressive tendency."[58] What figured as decisive (and here Fairbairn returned to orthodox libido theory) was the relative strength of fixations and the degree of regression. Taken together, they would determine the mix of tendencies which might predominate.

In subsequent papers Fairbairn slighted the depressive position; the schizoid emerged as truly fundamental. It was this that he came to regard as the basis of all psychopathological development. And it soon came to serve as the basis of a unified structural model that brought together incorporated objects and ego splitting—the primary schizoid phenomenon, after all, for both him and Klein.

▬▬ ▬▬ ▬▬ ▬▬ ▬▬

In pushing to its logical conclusion Melanie Klein's argument about object relations from birth onward, had Fairbairn abandoned "instinct"? In revising libido theory, had he severed the connection between biology and psychoanalysis?

Implicit in all Fairbairn's work was an appreciation of man as animal. (He was conversant with ethology and liked to point out comparisons between animal and human behaviors.) As one commentator notes, he considered object-seeking to be "as primary and . . . biological as the sexual and aggressive drives of instinct theory."[59] But he never would have referred to object-seeking as an instinct: "the conception of separate 'instincts' " he dismissed as "hypostatisation" (perhaps it would have been more accurate for him to say "reification"). What he did regard as meaningful was the description of "basic behaviour as 'instinctive.' "[60]

Equally implicit in all Fairbairn's work was his realization that biology and psychoanalysis constituted separate scientific domains. Where Freud felt free to exploit and appropriate imprecise biological concepts, Fairbairn looked to biology—recognized as existing in its own right—to lend support to concepts that derived from the clinical material of psychoanalysis itself.

"The Most Formidable Resistance": Harry Guntrip's Analysis

What impact did Fairbairn's revision of libido theory have on his clinical practice? Analysts often claim that theory is of little importance—or intrudes little into their exchanges with their patients. Interpretations may rarely be framed in technical terms, yet it is naive to suppose that those interpretations are not informed by theory. Fairbairn was far from naive. His analysis of Harry Guntrip represented a not altogether successful attempt to bring his theory to bear on an individual case.

Guntrip was an unusual analytic patient. By the time he sought out Fairbairn—in 1949, at the age of forty-eight—he had already established himself as a psychotherapist in Leeds. He chose Fairbairn with great deliberation: he had made a study of his articles (which had not yet appeared in book form) and had determined that "philosophically" he and Fairbairn stood "on the same ground and no actual intellectual disagreements would interfere with the analysis."[61] With equal deliberation he kept track of the analysis itself:

Immediately after a session I would go straight to my rooms and write up my dreams (which I always pencilled down on getting up) and all that I remembered of my 'Free Associations' and Fairbairn's comments and interpretations. Fortunately for years I had a photographic memory for this kind of material. . . . I did not keep on refreshing my memory of my analysis notes, once made, but left them to accumulate and kept them with the vague idea that sometime I might find it interesting to look back over them. To have studied them en route would have risked the danger of 'intellectualizing' and disguising my 'resistance'.[62]

Shortly before his death Guntrip went back over those notes and, extracting from them, wrote an account (never published) of his analysis with Fairbairn. (In that document his "intellectualizing" is amply apparent.)

In addition, Guntrip drafted a psychoanalytic autobiography, basing it, in part, on records of dreams he had meticulously kept for more than a dozen years prior to starting analysis with Fairbairn. Here, as well as in a brief published assessment, Guntrip dramatizes and simplifies the story. He presents himself as having lived on top of a buried traumatic event:

At the age of 3½ years I went into our sitting room and there was confronted with the sight of my brother of 2 years lying naked and dead on my mother's lap. The effect of that shock on me was, so mother told me, so great that very quickly I was thought to be dying. I was revived, but all memory of that event was totally gone. I was left with an infantile traumatic amnesia for the rest of my life, which, from time to time (greatly to my mystification), when anything faintly comparable to it occurred in real life, would reinstate the original illness. Sometimes this outbreak was short-lived and not too severe and disappeared as suddenly as it had erupted. Once or twice, its eruption landed me with serious exhaustion illness, which lasted longer but would again fade out.[63]

Neither of Guntrip's two analyses (the second with D. W. Winnicott), which together took close to twenty years, succeeded in breaking through his amnesia. (His expectations in this regard harked back to Breuer's treatment of Anna O., wherein the undoing of a repression, that is, the patient's remembering the circumstances surrounding the formation of a symptom, had led to the disappearance of the symptom in question.) Guntrip's dreams eventually broke through. At the age of seventy, roughly two years after the end of his second analysis, he had a compelling dream sequence, of several months' duration, which he claimed led him so far back in time that he was able to summon up his dead brother and his aloof, unresponsive mother. With his dream-apparition of his mother as "a woman who had no face, arms or breasts," he thought he had reached bedrock.[64] He had found at last what he regarded as proof positive that his mother had failed to relate to him. (Guntrip construed manifest content as a reliable rendering of the historical past!) With that he seemed ready to renounce his lifelong quest for maternal recognition—by the crushing verdict that he had had no mother at all.

The previous seventy years had in fact been dominated not by his brother's death but by this quest. (The one obviously contributed to the other.) What was the matter with the mother? According to Guntrip she simply had no desire to be one. As the eldest daughter among eleven children she had borne heavy maternal responsibilities long before she bore children of her own; by the time she married "she had had her fill of mothering . . . and did not want any more." She preferred business to babies; she was far more interested in her clothing shop than in her children. In her old age, living with Guntrip and his wife—she spent her last nine years in their house—she remarked: "I ought never to have married and had children. Nature did not make me to be a wife and mother, but a business woman" and "I don't think I ever understood children. I could never be bothered with them."[65]

In fact she did bother with her son—at least with his body. Two items stand out in his account. First, his mother tried to remake him into a girl. As a very small child he wore his hair long and dressed in female attire; in that garb he served as model in his mother's shop, until customers suggested that it was improper to display him in this fashion. Second, she fussed over his health. Until the age of five he had suffered from a series of minor maladies that evoked maternal solicitude. After undergoing a painful circumcision (at his mother's insistence), he managed to stay well and tried to stay out of his mother's way. He did not succeed: he endured her temper and her beatings until the age of eight, when her business began at last to thrive and he began to grow away from her.

His brother's death may have left Guntrip his mother's sole child, but he did not have only her; the household included his mother's sister and his father. It was his aunt's responsibility to look after him, and from Guntrip's account she emerges as gentle and kindly—yet a pallid invalid, which, in fact, she was, having been born with a defective heart and having been seriously ill when Guntrip was a child. His mother, he commented, adhered to "the neurotic pattern of identifying masculinity with strength and aggressiveness and femininity with weakness and passivity. Aunt Mary, who adored her, was her ideal female." She was Guntrip's as well. It was something neither mother nor son wanted to be.[66]

As for Guntrip's father, under his wife's ministrations "he slowly but inevitably lost his active self" and gradually became wedded to an "unvarying routine":

He came home from the City, lay on his black horse-hair sofa and read the paper . . . for half an hour, had his evening meal, and then went into the shop desk to spend the rest of the evening making up the books and giving change. At week-ends, which then meant only Sundays, he went to Church in the morning, in the afternoon chaired a Men's Brotherhood meeting associated with the local Congregational Church, the one remaining relic of his active days, and went to Church again in the evening.[67]

This father deferred to his wife without a murmur, just as he had earlier deferred to his authoritarian mother. Notwithstanding his inability to oppose his wife or to shield his boy, his son insisted on his steadfast benevolence. In all his years of dreaming, Guntrip asserted, his father "never appeared as other than a supportive figure *vis-à-vis* mother, and in actual fact she *never* lost her temper in his presence."[68] The son might not want to be like the father, but he did not want to hit a man when he was down.

The son was determined to resist the mother, notably to resist her interference with his sex life. Her dislike of sex, as well as her puritanical views on the subject, had early been impressed upon Guntrip. Indeed his mother had been quite explicit:

In one of her, to me, rather strange and at first somewhat embarrassing moments of confidential talking, she told me that she had once . . . gone . . . to have a long talk with an older female friend, who had told her that a man's health would suffer if he did not have a regular relationship. . . . I was in my late teens when she told me that and she must have felt uneasy for she added, seeking to shift responsibility off herself: "I don't know how we ever had any babies for often your father couldn't get in." I inferred that this was not true for the first three years, and after that was determined by herself. I several times heard her make the general remark "I don't like being touched" and she never showed any physical tenderness to me as a child.

Yet for Guntrip potency does not seem to have posed a major difficulty. "Variations," he commented, occurred during "periods of physical and mental strain and fatigue, or sinus attacks; and normal energy for sex . . . would return . . . after a good holiday or a rest." The one prolonged stretch of impotence he recorded, lasting two months, coincided with his mother's taking up permanent residence in his house.[69] Still, the problem of keeping her out of his bedroom, metaphorically that is, did not entirely vanish.

Guntrip's impotence may have been mild; his sinus attacks were not. Beginning in the mid-1930s, after his sinuses had become badly infected and sugical intervention had been required, he suffered from repeated attacks. In 1943 he submitted again to surgery, this time of a drastic kind:

It was the time when the medical men were obsessed with the idea of 'focal infections'. This surgeon decided that I had a focal infection in the soft alveolar tissue of my upper jaw, and ordered a 'radical alveolectomy'. . . . All my top teeth were removed and the soft alveolar bone removed and the skin sewn back over the hard bone. Ever since I have had dentures which it is impossible to eat with, or even to wear for long, for the denture rapidly cuts through the skin on the hard bone, and my mouth becomes full of sores. The operation was a total failure, for my sinus attacks recurred each winter as usual, as soon as fogs or winter cold arrived. . . . It was in a social sense a 'castration' for I have never since been able to eat a meal in company with other people with comfort.[70]

Even after the advent of penicillin, Guntrip continued to be laid low by his sinuses. In the course of his analysis these attacks faded out. So too did his insomnia. At the very least, analytic therapy notably improved his health.

It also, according to his own account, made him more appreciative of and open with his wife. From the start his marriage had stood in marked contrast to that of his parents: he and his wife, whom he had met in his early twenties, adhered to the conventions of gender stereotyping. He was a model of masculine drive and she of feminine self-sacrifice; he was constantly pushing himself; she smoothed the way and supported his morale. Her devoted nursing of his mother, who was tyrannical, critical, and bad tempered, allowed Guntrip to remain at a safe distance during the old woman's final years. More than that, it freed him to travel to Edinburgh for analysis with Fairbairn.

It was not until 1946, when Guntrip was in his mid-forties, that he finally determined what he wanted to be and settled into a psychotherapeutic career. Before that he had been occupied with religion—first, in last adolescence, as an officer in the Salvation Army, and then, during the following two decades, as a Congregational minister. In both cases, as he put it, he "grew away from" the surrogate family that failed to nourish him (intellectually) and threatened to confine him. He did not grow away from psychotherapy. He did, however, grow away from his analyst: his own theoretical work, he claimed, took him "right beyond Fairbairn's halting point," and Fairbairn "with great courage . . . accepted that."[71]

━━ ━━ ━━ ━━ ━━

According to Guntrip, by the time he began commuting to Edinburgh (two nights, four sessions per week), Fairbairn was already past his prime. With regard to his analyst's emotional and physical vigor, Guntrip's assessment was undoubtedly correct. Fairbairn's wife, after years of alcoholism, died in 1952, and though he remarried in 1959, it is clear that the intervening period had been difficult. (At one point he admitted as much to Guntrip.)[72] In that same decade, Fairbairn's own health began to deteriorate. In 1950 he suffered a first attack of viral influenza; such attacks became more and more severe as the years wore on. By the late 1950s Fairbairn's health, or rather Guntrip's concern about it, became a central issue in the analysis—and crucial to the latter's decision to terminate.

In Guntrip's view, Fairbairn was past his prime intellectually as well. "After his experimental creative 1940s," the analysand commented, "his conservatism slowly pushed through into his work."[73] By "conservatism" Guntrip meant, above all, interpretations framed in terms of castration anxiety and/or incestuous wishes—or more generally, the penis. During the 300th session (May 23, 1951), the following exchange occurred. Guntrip led off: "Maybe as a small boy I felt I could never grow as big as father. He's a being of a different order." Fairbairn interpreted: "You felt forbidden to have a penis of your own. It's not for little boys to have a penis and be sexual." Guntrip subsequently added for his own benefit:

This is one of the points at which I now feel that Fairbairn's constant reiteration of interpretations in terms of penises, was a survival of classic Freudian sexology that his theory had moved beyond. I feel that kept me stationary, whereas interpretations in terms of the penis ultimately standing for the 'whole personality' which mother did her best to restrict and dominate would have felt to me much more realistic. In effect, his analysis was a 'penis-analysis', not an 'ego-analysis'.

In session 512 (January 13, 1953), however, the analyst behaved as if he were heeding the analysand's retrospective advice. "*Castration,*" Fairbairn remarked, was "*really symbolic of a total personality situation, feeling stopped from being oneself, fear of loss of individuality and personality.*"[74] With this pithy statement Guntrip had no quarrel.

In 1953 "penis-analysis, not . . . ego-analysis" may actually have been on target. Fairbairn was hard at work on his article "Observations on the Nature of Hysterical States," in which he summarized his revision of structural theory, illustrating that revision with clinical material. Guntrip, disguised as "Jack," was one of the patients pressed into service. Fairbairn quoted a dream of Jack's—of a leopard sprawled out on the floor, kept down by the dreamer's hand on his head—and interpreted. Jack himself had understood the dream in terms of holding down his vital, energetic side and adopting a passive attitude vis-à-vis his mother. What he had not seen was how "keeping the leopard down" might represent "keeping his penis down and preventing it erecting."[75] Guntrip was not convinced, or at least not in retrospect:

At a time when my life was overclouded with the gathering prospect of mother's death and real cause for anxiety about the strain that had been growing on my wife, . . . it was a question, not of sexual potency, but of survival, a life or death matter. . . . In holding the leopard down I am in no doubt that I am keeping a tight hold by repression on my lifelong accumulated rage against her [i.e., his mother].[76]

At this point, with his mother on the verge of death, Guntrip felt the need to mobilize that rage.

Two years later, when Fairbairn was writing "Considerations Arising Out of the Schreber Case," the primal scene came to the fore. (Fairbairn was intent on substituting for Freud's libidinal explanation of paranoia an explanation phrased in terms of object relations.)[77] Guntrip protested; he claimed—on what grounds remain unclear— that he was simply being fitted into his analyst's "new twist of . . . theory." What *is* clear, however, is that Guntrip, not Fairbairn, was doing the fitting:

I re-examined every activity of my life in terms of its being an unconscious expression of primal scene involvement; playing father's role in cricket, in preaching, in starting psychotherapy . . . , in writing and doing intellectual research, and much more detail to that effect, including psychosomatic symptoms as mother's role of sexual suffering. . . . I certainly did my best to co-operate and tried to find out what truth there was in this approach.[78]

A less methodical patient would have sloughed off an inaccurate interpretation more readily.

Analyst and analysand alike were using the analysis to try out "new twists of theory." They also pursued these interests in extra-analytic sessions—infrequently, it would seem, possibly no more than ten times over the course of a decade. (In his article "Analysis with Fairbairn and Winnicott" Guntrip gives the impression that such sessions were regular occurrences.) That Guntrip found the discussions gratifying is clear: in talking "face to face," he claimed he found "the human Fairbairn," a Fairbairn who "realistically" became an "understanding good father."[79] What gratification a lonely and intellectually isolated Fairbairn derived from discussions with an obviously gifted analysand can only be surmised. So too the impact of this technical deviation, which was left unanalyzed, can only be guessed at. One suspects that, at the very least, it reinforced Guntrip's tendency to tidy up and pigeonhole feelings aroused in the analysis. In short, in indulging Guntrip, and possibly himself, in extra-analytic sessions, Fairbairn made his analytic task all the more difficult.

━━━ ━━━ ━━━ ━━━ ━━━

"The Oedipus complex is central for therapy, but not for theory." With this dictum, Fairbairn answered Guntrip's query about that complex—or so Guntrip claimed in his published account of his analysis.[80] If accurate, it would have been an extraordinary statement for his analyst to have made, all the more so since it is belied by the analysand's unpublished account. (Guntrip may have misrepresented Fairbairn because of how he himself used the term "oedipal." He extended it to cover *all* internalized bad-object relations, and then, rather illogically, complained that "oedipal" problems bulked too large.) To be sure, the unpublished document cannot be considered complete: it is not a verbatim transcript. Yet it provides evidence that at the end of his life Guntrip was still struggling with transference and that that struggle interfered with his full appreciation of what had gone on in the analysis.

The consulting room itself contributed to "the clear negative transference" that emerged at the start. Here is Guntrip's description of the setting:

I entered a large drawing room as waiting room, furnished with beautiful valuable antiques, and proceeded to the study as consulting room, also large with a big antique bookcase filling most of one wall. Fairbairn sat behind a large flat-topped desk, I used to think 'in state' in a high-backed plush-covered armchair. The patient's couch had its head to the front of the desk. At times I thought he could reach over the desk and hit me on the head. . . . Not for a long time did I realize that I had 'chosen' that couch position, and there was a small settee at the side of his desk at which I could sit if I wished and ultimately I did.[81]

"Before a word was spoken," Guntrip had cast Fairbairn "in the role of the mother who dominated" his "personality and crushed any initiative."[82]

Fairbairn consistently interpreted the negative transference. A few examples from early in the analysis follow:

You feel a struggle for power, for potency. A fundamental assumption is involved. You automatically, from a deep level, treat yourself as a little child, and automatically treat anyone like me as big, powerful, authoritative. You've never lost that assumption since childhood. Everyone else is a great big authority, in both sex and anti-sex and all matters.

You always feel a child vis-à-vis parent figures, a child over against a big dominating authoritative mother in both discipline and sex. Then you have to reverse that and be the big dominating man making the woman the child. But it's always a parent-child relationship, not two people 'on a level'. 'Being a man' came to mean to you 'dominating', 'turning the tables', not being grown up in the sense of being equal, but of being 'bigger'.

Your inner system demands that I take this role of the mother who is down on you. You justify it, or her, by making me do it.[83]

What was this "inner system"? Fairbairn was intent on finding out. (Keeping track of the transference, of Guntrip's oscillations between openness and reserve, of course, remained crucial.) The initial step was obvious—to explore Guntrip's attachment to his mother. Fairbairn interpreted:

You changed yourself from your natural desires into something else, to meet with approval from the puritanical crushing down self. *You changed into mother imposing restrictions on the child, on yourself.* When you were a child and mother imposed restrictions on you, you were helpless. When you identified with mother and imposed the restrictions, you were powerful, you exercized mastery.[84]

Guntrip was quite ready to acknowledge his identification with his mother and, still more, his perpetual struggle against it; he found it painful to recognize his continued longing for her:

She's not an attractive person now but I am conscious of wishing she were so that it could be a pleasure to come home and chat with her. It's harder to give up a bad mother than I realized. . . . I'm still unconsciously tied to the mother I hate and resent and regard as bad and a failure: depressing. She early roused a deep need and longing for her which she has never met.[85]

Guntrip remained tied, though he became more and more conscious of it. Four years into the analysis the following exchange took place. Guntrip asked:

When should I finish analysis? Why does it concern me? . . . I've made definite progress. Compared with five years ago, I was then depressed . . . , not sleeping too well, working feverishly, tense. Now I'm far better in health and freer in mind, and much more creative in my work and in writing. But *I'm up against a hidden core which I can't penetrate.* . . . I can't go on with analysis indefinitely, but must secure some further changes in myself. I still feel mother interferes with my freedom.

Fairbairn commented, "Tied to her by your needs." Guntrip replied:

Yes. Ultimately I feel *I need mother deep down, it underlies my preoccupation with persisting anger and hate.* Some part of me can't give her up, so I keep hammering at her in my secret feelings to make her see how she neglects me, and make her change, I must settle accounts with mother. It's her I want love from and not make do with Aunt Mary. I feel I can't yet get out of this deep down dilemma.[86]

In his analysis with Fairbairn, Guntrip never did. A few months later the mother died at last; the son obtained little relief thereby. He was still hammering at her on the first anniversary of her death, or rather, he was hammering at his analyst:

Towards the world outside me I'm feeling a sort of lifeless despair and rejection of it and fall back withdrawn into myself. I feel just now as if I've given up the outer world as hopeless, no one will ever understand. The child in me has only two choices, to create an internal fantasy world of fighting and suffering, . . . it's that or nothing, and I feel I don't understand what that means. On last Sunday morning I felt like a child of 1 year old and can't get them [adults] to understand what it is I need. I'm lonely, cut off, out of touch, because they are inaccessible and they don't understand. I'm puzzled, hopeless and helpless, can't find a way of opening their eyes to the fact and they haven't got the human intuition to see it. I don't even know what it is I need. If mother had been a real mother she would have met that need without my needing to know what it was.[87]

In Guntrip's eyes, Fairbairn was in the course of taking over the role of the parent who did not understand his needs as "child."

A graphic (albeit disguised) image of that child emerged in a dream whose clarity surprised the dreamer himself:

I was going home from Edinburgh by train and had a lifesize dummy of a man left with me, made of flesh, human but no bones in it. I put it in the Guard's van to get rid of it, and propped it up as it slumped limp. I hurried away so the Guard wouldn't know it was mine. Not that I was doing anything wrong but I didn't want him to know I had any connection with it. I met the Guard in the corridor and suddenly heard it shambling up after me, calling out. I felt a queer horror as if it was a sort of fleshly ghost, and said to the guard, 'Quick, let's get away. It's alive. It'll get us.'

Guntrip gave the following associations:

This is my passive self that I am afraid will emerge into consciousness. I want to bring it to you. You are the guard. I want you to see it because I fear it. It's the part of me I've spent a lifetime trying to keep repressed. It would undermine me.

Fairbairn replied: "It's a good thing this is being uncovered and coming out now. That's what we're working for. A very interesting important dream."[88]

At this point the "passive self" became crucial. Fairbairn understood it in terms of "repression of the self mother crushed." Guntrip demurred: he insisted that it was the self that had never been evoked. Retrospectively he composed the lines he would have liked his analyst to utter:

There was no mother there. That's the part of you mother never saw, never related to, never called into life. Because she didn't you have now brought him to me so that I can recognize this inner you and call you to life.

If, according to Guntrip, Fairbairn had seen that it was "not being crushed, but being not noticed at all as a person" that was the problem, he would thereby have given his patient the relationship the mother had failed to provide.[89] From his demand that Fairbairn be a "good mother" to him in place of his "bad mother" Guntrip never retreated.

The analysis had reached a stalemate. By this time (March 1955) Guntrip had been in treatment for just under six years; he had had 777 sessions with Fairbairn. He was to keep at it for another five years, though with the frequency much reduced; in all he had 1,014 sessions. His account of those last five years is thin; he complained repeatedly of ringing changes on old themes and of Fairbairn's continued off-the-mark interpretations. Yet he seemed tied to his analyst, no less than to his mother—as he himself appreciated full well: "I realize that my feeling unable either to go on or to stop analysis must involve a real transference of my rebellious bondage to mother. . . . Now I'm working hard at analysis and wanting to break free of it, from you."[90]

What brought the analysis to an end? By the seventh year it seemed destined to be interminable, with Guntrip oscillating between an effort to force his analyst to be the mother he wanted and anger at his own failure to control him. (Fairbairn at last confronted his patient with his compulsive and coercive note taking, but to no avail.)[91] All the while Guntrip was toying with the idea of phasing out. Still it was not until Fairbairn's health began to fail that his patient became serious about ending the analysis.[92] Rather than deal with the fears—fear of abandonment among them—that his analyst's ill health aroused, Guntrip abandoned Fairbairn, and he did so without a regular termination and without resolving his "rebellious bondage" to his analyst.

━━ ━━ ━━ ━━ ━━

[The aim of] maintaining relationships with objects in the inner world at the expense of a realistic and therapeutic relationship with the analyst, viz., a movement having the aim of preserving internal reality as a closed system, . . . seems . . . to constitute the most formidable resistance encountered in psycho-analytical treatment.

Fairbairn wrote these words at a point when Guntrip's analysis had stalled. He had not succeeded in breaching his patient's "closed system"; he had not succeeded in inducing him "to accept the open system of outer reality."[93] At least he possessed the theoretical equipment for understanding his own lack of success.

"Back to Hysteria"

Fairbairn had elaborated his model of endopsychic structure before Guntrip began analysis with him, and Guntrip frequently referred to it in the course of treatment, using Fairbairn's terms as a kind of shorthand for communicating with his analyst. Still, it is ironic that he should have figured as Fairbairn's chief proselytizer, for he consistently failed to appreciate that Fairbairn's model had as its empirical referent a case such as his own.[94]

Beyond classifying and sorting clinical material, Fairbairn aimed at classifying and sorting higher-level psychoanalytic concepts. More particularly he wanted to provide a cross-sectional or compositional model that dovetailed with his version of libido theory. The result possessed a clarity and coherence that Freud's model had notably lacked. It was also far more modest.

The ego, the key to every effort to depict structure, has proved a protean notion. It would be tempting to claim that of the two poles of Freud's concept, psychical agency and person, Hartmann gravitated to the former and Fairbairn to the latter. It would, however, be misleading. Where Hartmann refused to deny personhood to *his* ego, even if it required postulating a separate "grade" within it which he called self,[95] Fairbairn insisted that *his* ego retain its directing role. The British analyst chose to allow an interplay of meanings, and to facilitate it he unwittingly took a leaf out of Freud's "Project"—a text that was unknown to him at the time. Like the ego of the "Project," Fairbairn's figured as the repository of energy and memory alike.

In attributing energy to the ego, Fairbairn thought he was departing dramatically from Freudian orthodoxy, and he was in fact radically revising the structural hypothesis of *The Ego and the Id*. As usual he arrived at his conclusion from two directions at once. From the standpoint of clinical practice, Fairbairn contended that it was impossible to consider impulses apart from objects, and since "it was only ego structures" that could "seek relationships with objects," it followed that it was equally impossible to consider impulses apart from ego structures. From the standpoint of conceptual coherence, he argued that the prevailing view (energy detached from ego) produced a psychoanalytic theory "permeated by . . . hypothetical 'impulses' and 'instincts' " that bombarded "passive structures, much as if an air-raid were in progress." Impulse was not, he maintained, while shifting metaphors, "a kick in the pants administered out of the blue to a surprised, and perhaps somewhat pained, ego." Impulse, he insisted, should be conceived of "as inseparable from structure and as representing simply the dynamic aspect of structure" itself.[96]

The implications for the id were clear: if it should "be true that no 'impulses' " could "be regarded as existing in the absence of an ego structure," it would "no longer be possible to preserve any psychological distinction between the id and the ego."[97] In Fairbairn's mind, the id, or rather its contents, had not ceased to exist; it simply no longer led a separate existence. But with that "cauldron of seething excitations" now absorbed into the ego, doubts about the ego itself would follow fast.

More particularly its ontological status prompted questioning. On this matter the contrast between the ego of the "Project" and that of the structural hypothesis had been marked. Working within an energetic framework, Freud, in his unpublished essay, had thought of the ego as more or less there from the beginning. Within the same framework, but with the id as an all-encompassing energy source, the Freud of *The Ego and the Id* had found himself obliged to account for the differentiation of the two. That accounting was neither detailed nor convincing. Fairbairn, unwittingly, harked back to Freud's earlier position: what Fairbairn called the central ego was not "conceived as originating out of something else (the 'id'), or as constituting a passive structure dependent for its activity upon impulses proceeding from the matrix out of which it originated. On the contrary, the 'central ego' was conceived as a primary and dynamic structure."[98]

It was at this point that the two meanings of the ego threatened to get in each other's way. Insofar as it appeared in the guise of directing agency, it had to be there from the beginning. Indeed insofar as it answered to that description, it was unclear whether the ego could be endowed with a history at all. Yet insofar as it stood for person or self, a history was very much in order. (And Fairbairn has been accused— wrongly—of misconstruing that history: he has been faulted for suggesting that man is born whole, for failing to appreciate that "acutal wholeness is a life-long integrative achievement.")[99] In the first meaning of ego, primary unity figured as a logical necessity; in the second, it figured as a convenient fiction. This much ambiguity Fairbairn proved quite willing to tolerate.

If in the beginning all was ego, how could intrapsychic conflict be expressed, or as Fairbairn put it, what became of "Freud's conception of repression as a function exercised by the ego in its dealings with impuses originating in the id?" Fairbairn's seemingly paradoxical answer was that the ego repressed itself. Ego splitting dissolved the paradox. It surely was not inconceivable, Fairbairn argued, "that one part of the 'ego' with a dynamic charge should repress another part of the 'ego' with a dynamic charge":

The correctness of this assumption is confirmed by the phenomena of multiple personality, in which the linkage of repressed 'impulses' with a submerged ego structure is beyond question; but such a linkage may also be detected in the less extensive forms of dissociation, which are so characteristic of the hysterical individual.[100]

By this route Fairbairn arrived at his slogan "Back to hysteria."

━━━ ━━━ ━━━ ━━━ ━━━

The analysis of a female patient's dream, Fairbairn wrote, "provided the occasion" for his "chief step" in the direction of a "revised conception of psychical structure." (In his view dreams were not wish fulfillments; they were "dramatizations or 'shorts' . . . of situations existing in inner reality.")

The (manifest) dream . . . consisted in a brief scene in which the dreamer saw the figure of herself being viciously attacked by a well-known actress. . . . Her husband was looking on; but he seemed quite helpless and quite incapable of protecting her. After delivering the attack the actress turned away and resumed playing a stage part, which, as seemed to be implied, she had momentarily set aside in order to deliver the attack by way of interlude. The dreamer then found herself gazing at the figure of herself lying bleeding on the floor; but, as she gazed, she noticed that this figure turned for an instant into that of a man until eventually she awoke in a state of acute anxiety.[101]

The dramatis personae in the manifest dream consisted of four figures; (1) the attacking actress, (2) the male onlooker, (3) the dreamer as victim, and (4) the male victim. The victim had been a composite, and Fairbairn, on the basis of the patient's associations and previously analyzed material, inferred that the attacking actress was a composite as well, representing both the patient and her mother. The presence of a sixth figure was readily apparent: the one witness to the dream, that is, the dreamer herself as observer. It was the six figures of the latent content that prompted Fairbairn's reflections on endopsychic structure.

The six naturally fell into two groups of three each—object structures and ego structures. The object structures were (1) the observing object, representing the patient's husband, (2) the attacked object, representing the patient's father, and (3) the attacking object, representing the patient's mother. The ego structures were "(1) the observing ego or 'I', (2) the attacked ego, and (3) the attacking ego." In turn,

Fairbairn argued, the dreamer's "ego" could be regarded as split into three, "a central ego and the two subsidiary egos, . . . both, relatively speaking, cut off from the central ego. . . . Since the ego" which was "attacked" was "closely related to the dreamer's father (and by transference to her husband)," it was "safe to infer that this ego was highly endowed with libido"; hence Fairbairn called it "libidinal." "Since the attacking ego" was "closely related to the dreamer's mother as a repressive figure," he described it as an "internal saboteur" and subsequently labeled it "anti-libidinal." Fairbairn completed his nomenclature by providing terms for the objects linked to the subsidiary egos: the "exciting object" went along with the libidinal ego, and the "rejecting object" went along with the anti-libidinal ego.[102]

What of the relationships among these structures? How did Fairbairn handle repression? All the elements were now in place for giving an account of intrapsychic conflict:

In terms of the line of thought so far developed, repression is a process originating in a rejection of both the exciting object and the rejecting object on the part of the undivided ego. This primary process of repression is accompanied by a secondary process of repression whereby the ego splits off and rejects two parts of itself, which remain attached respectively to one and the other of the repressed internal objects. The resulting situation is one in which the central ego (the residue of the undivided ego) adopts an attitude of rejection, not only towards the exciting object and the rejecting object, but also towards the split off and subsidiary egos attached to these respective objects, i.e. the libidinal ego and the internal saboteur. This attitude of rejection adopted by the central ego constitutes repression.[103]

But that was not all. Fairbairn went on to postulate an indirect form of repression, that is, the attacks of the internal saboteur on the libidinal ego and the exciting object. In launching its assaults, he claimed, the internal saboteur (or anti-libidinal ego) acted as a co-belligerent alongside the central ego, reinforcing and facilitating its repression of these structures. The libidinal ego and the internal saboteur might share the common fate of repression; only the libidinal ego, however, was treated to the indirect variety. In this fashion Fairbairn accounted for both the fact that the attacking (or aggressive) component of the psyche was subject to repression and the fact that the libidinal component was subject to a greater measure thereof.

Fairbairn's Endopsychic Structure

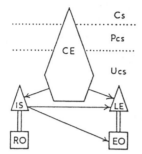

CE, Central Ego; IS, Internal Saboteur; LE, Libidinal Ego; RO, Rejecting Object; EO, Exciting Object. Cs, Conscious; Pcs, Preconscious; Ucs, Unconscious. →, Aggression; =, Libido.

Source: Fairbairn, *Psychoanalytic Studies of the Personality,* p. 105.

The "uncompromisingly aggressive attitude" adopted by the internal saboteur toward the object of the libidinal ego might have aided repression; it did nothing to loosen the tie between that subsidiary and its object. On the contrary, the constant threat served merely to perpetuate the attachment—still more, to strengthen it. Here the quintessence of infantile dependence was encoded. By the same token, here, in Fairbairn's view, lay the key to psychopathology: there could "be no room for doubt that the obstinate attachment of the libidinal ego to the exciting object and its reluctance to renounce this object" constituted "a particularly formidable source of resistance"—perhaps even the "most formidable."[104]

━━ ━━ ━━ ━━ ━━

What was the origin of the endopsychic structure that had found "classic expression" in the dream of Fairbairn's patient? Why did Fairbairn ask this question? Why did he feel obliged to formulate an answer? The answer was necessary for comparing his model to Freud's structural hypothesis. Fairbairn described their respective positions in terms of levels: "[T]he level at which split off parts of the ego" found "themselves confronted with internal objects . . . devoid of moral significance" was "beneath the level at which a "central ego" found "itself confronted with the super-ego as an internal object of moral significance."[105] Given the psychoanalytic equation of deep and early, the next step was logical enough: Fairbairn claimed temporal priority for his model of endopsychic structure. In so doing he relied on the postulate that developments in the first year were crucial; and along with it he ran the danger of attributing to infantile minds excessive cognitive sophistication.

In taking up the matter of origin, Fairbairn bypassed the depressive position: structuralization, he argued, derived from the first oral phase, and correspondingly, from the schizoid position alone. (He insisted that hysteria, the basis of his structural model, was essentially a schizoid phenomenon and that dissociation was tantamount to splitting.) Abraham had thought of the first oral phase as pre-ambivalent. Fairbairn followed him and explicitly distanced himself from Melanie Klein, who, in line with her acceptance of the death instinct, found sadism operating from the very beginning:

At this point I must explain that, whilst I regard aggression as a primary dynamic factor in that it does not appear capable of being resolved into libido . . . , at the same time I regard it as ultimately subordinate to libido, not only metaphysically, but also psychologically. Thus I do not consider that the infant directs aggression spontaneously towards his libidinal object in the absence of some kind of frustration; and my observation of the behavior of animals confirms me in this view.

In short, Fairbairn concluded, "under theoretically perfect conditions the libidinal relationship of the infant to his mother would be so satisfactory that a state of libidinal frustration could hardly arise; and . . . there would consequently be no ambivalence on the part of the infant towards his object."[106]

Initially Fairbairn had claimed that the infant finding himself with a mother who had become an ambivalent object split the figure into two and internalized the bad:

In my opinion it is always the 'bad' object (i.e. at this stage, the unsatisfying object) that is internalized in the first instance; for . . . I find it difficult to attach any meaning to the primary internalization of a "good object" which is both satisfying and amenable from the infant's point of view. . . . Internalization of objects is essentially a measure of coercion and it is not the satisfying object, but the unsatisfying object that the infant seeks to coerce.[107]

Subsequently Fairbairn changed his mind. He argued that the object originally internalized was "pre-ambivalent" rather than exclusively "bad." (Therewith he let the motive for internalization slip away from him.)

On this assumption ambivalence will be a state first arising in the original unsplit ego in relation, not to the external object, but to an internalized pre-ambivalent object. The resulting situation will then be one in which the unsplit ego is confronted with an internal ambivalent object. . . . Since both the *over-exciting* and the *over-frustrating* elements in the internal (ambivalent) object are unacceptable to the ego, these elements are both split off from the main body of the object and repressed in such a way as to give rise to "the exciting object" and "the rejecting object". . . . It will be noticed, however, that, after the over-exciting and over-frustrating elements have been split off from the internal ambivalent object, there remains a nucleus of the object shorn of its over-exciting and over-frustrating elements. This nucleus will then assume the status of an "accepted object" in eyes of the central ego.[108]

In the foregoing, Fairbairn implicitly suggested that internalization might not have structural consequences and then again it might. When the fate of an "accepted" object was at issue, internalization had no structural consequences. The accepted object was not repressed; it could be integrated into the central ego. When the destiny of a "bad" object, or of the "bad" aspects of an ambivalent object, was at stake, internalization led to structural differentiation.[109]

Under "theoretically perfect conditions" structural differentiation would not occur; by the same token such differentiation was virtually unavoidable. It was thus both pathological and normal: to varying extents it diminished the functioning of all human beings. Could it be altered? What, in brief, was the nature of therapeutic change? Fairbairn never suggested that a return to a purely theoretical primary unity was possible; he did not pin his hopes on exorcising internal objects. On the contrary he argued that some decrease in splitting and increase in the "sphere of influence of the central ego" might occur in analysis; yet he remained skeptical about the magnitude of the alterations.[110]

Fairbairn had shown himself eager to abandon the id and with it the notion of a reservoir of instinctual impulses; he was not, however, prepared to abandon the superego and with it the hope of a "satisfactory psychological explanation of guilt."[111] Instead of forsaking the superego, he followed Melanie Klein's lead in splitting it along its natural fault lines into an advocate of the ideal and an agent of punishment.

Fairbairn's concern with the ideal predated his elaboration of endopsychic structure. In an earlier paper he had presented a picture of the child trafficking in bad and good objects, the superego (as ideal) among them:

The bad objects which the child internalizes are unconditionally bad; for they are simply persecutors. In so far as the child is identified with such internal persecutors . . . he too is unconditionally bad. To redress this state of unconditional badness he takes what is really a very obvious step. He internalizes his good objects, which thereupon assume a super-ego role. Once this situation has been established, we are confronted with the phenomena of conditional badness and conditional goodness. In so far as the child leans towards his internalized bad objects, he becomes conditionally (i.e. morally) bad vis-à-vis his internalized good objects (i.e. his super-ego); and in so far as he resists the appeal of his internalized bad objects, he becomes conditionally (i.e. morally) good vis-à-vis his super-ego.

When Fairbairn subsequently worked out his structural model, the former superego figured as the "accepted object," that is, the "*nucleus of the original object* shorn of its over-exciting and over-frustrating elements," which had assumed "the status of a desexualized and idealized object . . . retained for itself by the central ego. . . . In view of its nature," Fairbairn thought "it would be appropriate to revive the term 'ego-ideal' for its designation."[112]

Within his structural model Fairbairn's internal saboteur bore an obvious resemblance to the superego as agent of punishment. Like the primitive Kleinian variety, it was "unquestionably a prolific source of anxiety." But in contrast to both its Freudian and its Kleinian forebears, Fairbairn's internal saboteur was "in no sense conceived as an internal object." It was an ego structure, though "very closely associated with an internal object." Ego structure and object, taken together, came near, Fairbairn admitted, to replicating the punitive superego.[113]

With endopsychic structure secure, the superego thus fell into place. So too, Fairbairn claimed, would clinical material. In this respect, he continued, his model provided greater flexibility than the

Freudian triad. The latter allowed for the operation of only two structures, the ego and the superego—the id, a mere source of energy, lacked structure. "The possibilities left open by Freud's theory in the abstract" were "still further limited by his conception of the function of the superego . . . as characteristically anti-libidinal. . . . The endopsychic drama" thus largely resolved "itself into a conflict between the ego in a libidinal capacity and the super-ego in an anti-libidinal capacity." In contrast, Fairbairn's theory enlarged the number of structural factors to five—five rather than six: the "ego-ideal," since it had been accepted by the central ego, did not rank as a structure. "Psychopathology and characterological phenomena of all kinds" could thus be described "in terms of the patterns assumed by a complex of relationships" among "a variety of structures."[114] In short, Fairbairn offered the clinician a schema for clarifying and sorting that came closer than Freud's to the stuff of analysis itself.

CHAPTER 5

D. W. Winnicott: Facilitating Environments, Maternal and Analytic

During the early 1940s, while the Kleinians and Anna Freudians were struggling within the British Society, D. W. Winnicott was only an occasional participant. War work claimed his attention. During those years he was officially serving as a consultant psychiatrist to the Government Education Scheme in an English reception area; in practice this entailed supervising, through weekly visits, close to three hundred delinquent children who were being housed in a group of five hostels.[1] Though Winnicott had not previously worked with delinquents, his clinical experience had never been confined to the psychoanalytic consulting room. He had begun his career as a pediatrician, and, as he put it, "never cut loose" from the pediatric practice that had been his starting point.[2] Over a period of several decades—that is, before, during, and after his war service—he saw several thousand mothers and children as pediatrician in an outpatient clinic at the Paddington Green Children's Hospital. The result was an uninterrupted dialogue in his own mind between two kinds of clinical experience and two kinds of clinical data.

What relationship between the two realms did he discern? His claims, at least initially, were quite orthodox; he echoed both Freud and Klein in arguing that "the study of the transference in the analytic setting" made it "possible to gain a clear view of what" took place "in infancy itself."[3] Elsewhere, and in a similar vein, he asserted that "dependent or deeply regressed patients" could "teach the analyst more about early infancy than" could "be learned from direct observation." Still, such observation, he believed, did teach something— something he prized greatly: "Clinical contact with the normal and the abnormal experiences of the mother-infant relationship," he wrote, alerted the analyst to what went on "in the transference (in the regressed phases of certain of his patients)."[4] The relationship, then, was reciprocal and complex, and because of this reciprocity, Winnicott felt under no obligation to specify what was influencing what at any given moment.

With mothers and children always before him, Winnicott charted his way within the psychoanalytic realm. Though he frequently quoted Freud and Klein, though he tried to link his work to theirs (often having misread it), such attempts were acts of filial piety that obscured rather than clarified his own project. Had reckoning with forebears or peers been crucial to his intellectual development, he would have been obliged to pay closer attention to Fairbairn: time and again he landed right in "the territory of Fairbairn"—something he appreciated only rarely.[5] Instead he followed his own muse, and by straddling disciplines, the pediatrician-analyst succeeded in notably reshaping one of them—the psychoanalytic domain.

The Good-Enough Mother

Toward the end of his life Winnicott was spending an increasing proportion of his time conducting what he called therapeutic consultations in child psychiatry. (A number of the resulting reports were published in book form in 1971, the year he died.)[6] Such consultations appeared deceptively simple. He and the child spent much of the interview playing "the squiggle game": initially he drew a squiggle, asking the child to make it into something; then the child took the lead, and Winnicott finished the picture. And so the session went, as analyst and child talked in a free and easy manner, with an occasional dream being elicited. All the while Winnicott was getting in touch with the child in a profound way. He appreciated and took advantage of the special circumstances of the first interview, of the fact that the child arrived with a "preconceived notion" of Winnicott as someone "supposed to be helpful." This notion rarely outlasted the first few sessions—but frequently therapeutic consultations consisted of no more than one interview. When all went well, he managed to turn the child's confidence to account, and in so doing strengthened "the child's belief in being understood":

There will be those cases in which deep work . . . and the resulting changes in the child can be made use of by the parents . . . so that whereas a child was caught up in a knot in regard to . . . emotional development, the interview has resulted in a loosening of the knot and a forward movement of the developmental process.[7]

The nub of the matter lay in utilizing the child's multifarious communications. To do so, Winnicott wrote, one needed to "have in one's bones a theory of the emotional development of the child and of the relationship of the child to the environmental factors."[8]

Of all his cases, that of "Bob" brought into sharpest focus the theory Winnicott had in his bones. The six-year-old boy communicated readily, but his language was distorted. In the course of the consultation Winnicott concluded that the proper diagnosis was not mental retardation (it turned out that Bob had an IQ of ninety-three) but "infantile schizophrenia, with the patient tending to make a spontaneous recovery." The boy's residual defensive isolation, protecting him against unbearable anxiety, confusion, and disorientation, had resulted in a severe learning difficulty. His mother was also emotionally disturbed (and had been undergoing psychotherapy, with considerable success): she had begun to suffer from serious depression and panic attacks when Bob was fourteen to sixteen months of age. In this regard, one item proved crucial—which Winnicott discovered only after the consultation: "I [Winnicott] asked: 'How did you first become ill? . . . In what way did your depression show itself?' She answered: 'I kept finding myself going to sleep while I was engaged in doing something.' "[9]

Shortly into the second phase of the consultation—the first had been marked by caution and conformity—Bob began to open up: he put eyes on Winnicott's squiggle (no. 6) and called it Humpty Dumpty. "The theme of Humpty Dumpty," Winnicott noted, alerted him "to the idea of disintegration." But he said nothing, and at that point also failed to appreciate the significance of the eyes. A bit later Bob made a wavy squiggle (no. 9) which he called a "puzzle-place" and then rapidly and anxiously recalled a "horrid" visit to a maze. Here, Winnicott thought, was a representation of the boy's "threatened confusional state, his potential disorientation"—and hence a deepening of the Humpty Dumpty theme. Then Bob simply drew a picture (no. 11) of a jet airplane. When asked if he would like to ride in such a plane, he replied, "No, because they may go upside down." Winnicott took this answer as Bob's way of letting him know "of his experience of environmental unreliability during the period of his own near-absolute dependence."[10] Thus Humpty Dumpty began to acquire a past.

After a period in the "doldrums," the consultation entered a third phase: one of Bob's squiggles (no. 21), a confused squiggle with wavy lines called "a mountain: you walk all around and get lost," prepared Winnicott for "a new version of environmental failure." When the boy drew another picture of a mountain (no. 23), this time in a representational style, and remarked in so doing, "You climb up there and you slip; it's all ice," Winnicott felt convinced that he was being told about "being held, and about being affected by someone's withdrawal" of attention. Still he made no comment; instead he asked Bob about his dreams. The boy remembered a dreadful dream of a witch who made one disappear; he drew an extremely disordered illustration of horror, and then one of himself in bed upstairs having the nightmare. He told Winnicott that these drawings were about a real incident—a nice, not a horrid one—as well as about the nightmare: "He really fell downstairs, and there was Daddy at the bottom of the stairs, and he cried, and Daddy carried him to Mummy, and she took him and made him well." By now Winnicott felt confident that he had grasped Humpty Dumpty's history: despite a serious lapse, "the environmental provision . . . had been 'good' in a general way."[11]

He also felt that the boy was ready to be more explicit about the mother's lapse. Winnicott proceeded to draw a mother holding a baby (no. 26) and then "scribbled out the baby." As he started "to put into words the baby's danger of being dropped, Bob took the paper and *smudged in the woman's eyes. As he smudged in the eyes he said: 'She goes to sleep.'* " And later, as he was leaving, he commented to Winnicott, "Did you see how I rubbed in the lady's eyes?"[12] In this way the boy illustrated his mother's withdrawal of attention.

Winnicott did not stop here. He wondered how Bob would deal with the anxiety associated with falling, so he finished the picture by drawing a baby at the bottom, on the floor. Bob responded with a fantasy:

No, the witch came when the mother shut her eyes. I just
screamed. I saw the witch. Mummy saw the witch. I shouted: 'My
mummy will get you!' Mummy saw the witch. Daddy was downstairs
and he took his penknife and stuck it into the witch's tummy so it
got killed for ever.[13]

Obviously the recovery from trauma had depended on father's help; at the same time that recovery had left the boy in the precarious position of Humpty Dumpty.

Bob's testimony about his mother's sleepiness while tending him—and, by implication, her depression as well—had been the high point of the consultation. The boy, Winnicott concluded, had "retained a clear idea of the beginning of his illness, or of the organisation of his defences into a personality pattern. He was able to communicate this, and he did so with some urgency once he had felt" that Winnicott "might possibly understand and therefore make his communication effective."[14] And effective it was: the follow-up report indicated that Bob was making steady progress at school and managing well at home.

The boy's communication also effectively exemplified Winnicott's understanding of the relationship between "environmental provision" and emotional development. By environmental provision Winnicott meant much more than the physical sustenance a child needed to stay alive; indeed he was determined to rescue the needs of infant and child from a purely biological understanding. Environmental provision, as he used the phrase, referred to mothers and fathers, to their psychological ability or inability to tend their children. But ability and inability he conceived of as in no sense absolutes or polar opposites. What interested Winnicott was temporary and/or specific failure. In similar vein, for him emotional development was not an either/or proposition. Again what interested him were particular configurations of anxieties and defenses and how much of the personality was affected. If his understanding of environmental provision and emotional development hardly ranked as original—after all, Fairbairn could claim priority in matters of infantile dependence—Winnicott took up these questions with an imaginative exploration of mother-infant relations that was absent in the work of the schematic Scot.

━━━ ━━━ ━━━ ━━━ ━━━

I suppose that every one has a paramount interest, a deep, driving propulsion towards something. If one's life lasts long enough, so that looking back becomes allowable, one discerns an urgent tendency that has integrated all the various and varied activities of one's private life, and one's professional career.

As for me, I can already see what a big part has been played in my work by the urge to find and then appreciate the ordinary good mother. Fathers, I know, are just as important, and indeed an interest in mothering includes an interest in fathers, and in the vital part they play in child care. But for me it has been to mothers that I have so deeply needed to speak.[15]

In his first book, *Clinical Notes on Disorders of Childhood,* published in 1931, Winnicott had shown little appreciation for the ordinary good mother, or the bad one, for that matter. The influence of the early Melanie Klein, of the pre-good breast Melanie Klein, had been much in evidence: "[A]nxiety, delinquency, conversion hysteria," Winnicott wrote, were "produced and kept up chiefly by emotional causes in a child"; environment, in his opinion, was of only indirect importance.[16] Within a decade, Winnicott had altered his view dramatically. So too had Melanie Klein, but Winnicott regarded her revision as inadequate. A few years after her death he commented:

I am longing for the day when one of the Kleinian group will be able to say that the dependability of the internal mother has a history in the . . . dependability [of the mother] at the beginning, but Melanie Klein would not allow this. She would only say: "Of course I have always said that environment is important"—and imply thereby that she would be giving away something vital if she were to say what I have just put down in words.[17]

Winnicott faulted Klein for failing to see that there was "a stage at the beginning of the development of the individual when the environment" came "into its own" and had "its proper place and that a statement of its importance" could not "be avoided."[18] For "environment," read "mother." Klein may have written about whole breasts, good and bad; Winnicott wrote about whole mothers.

He took as his starting point the mother's mental state during the last stages of pregnancy. (Insofar as he considered the mother's mental state prior to conception, he simply echoed Kleinian themes of internalized objects and how a baby was linked up to them in unconscious fantasy.) Her condition, a very special one in his view, deserved a name: he dubbed it "primary maternal preoccupation." About this condition he made the following epigrammatic remarks:

It gradually develops and becomes a state of heightened sensitivity during, and especially towards the end of, the pregnancy.
It lasts only a few weeks after the birth of the child.
It is not easily remembered by mothers once they have recovered from it.
I would go further and say that the memory mothers have of this state tends to become repressed.[19]

"Heightened sensitivity" hardly indicated all that Winnicott was driving at: "normal illness" came closer. "Withdrawn," "dissociated," "fugue"—terms usually connoting serious disturbance—were all used by Winnicott to describe the mother's state. And this normal illness, he added, was an achievement, one that would be compromised by a precipitate "flight to sanity." The mother who was healthy enough to be "ill" withdrew her interest from the outside world and became exclusively preoccupied with the infant she was carrying first in her womb and then in her arms. Only in this state could "she feel herself into her infant's place, and so meet the infant's needs."[20] Only in this state did she reach the heightened sensitivity required by the infant at the start:

The important thing, in my view, is that the mother through identification of herself with her infant knows what the infant feels like and so is able to provide almost exactly what the infant needs at the beginning, which is a *live adaptation to the infant's needs.*[21]

Just as it was an achievement to get into a preoccupied state, so too was it an accomplishment to get out of it in time—roughly within a few weeks of the baby's birth. A mother might provide "good initial care, but . . . fail to complete the process through an inability to let it come to an end." Instead of relinquishing her identification with her infant, she remained merged with him. Here Winnicott discerned an important, if subtle, distinction in a mother's management of her baby, a distinction between her "understanding of her infant's needs based on empathy" and her understanding based on her ability to read "a signal" given by the infant and to be "guided" by it to his needs. A mother's empathy might be short-lived; her answering to her child's signals was lifelong. Above all, Winnicott insisted that this range of response came naturally to mothers:

It seems to be usual that mothers who are not disturbed by ill-health or by present-day environmental stress do tend on the whole to know accurately enough what their infants need, and further, they like to provide what is needed.

This was "the essence of maternal care."[22] This was the essence of good-enough mothering.

I once risked the remark, 'There is no such thing as a baby'— meaning that if you set out to describe a baby, you will find you are describing a *baby and someone.* A baby cannot exist alone, but is essentially part of a relationship.[23]

What Winnicott was trying to elucidate, he added, had been hinted at by Freud: he appealed to a phrase Freud had consigned to a footnote in "Two Principles of Mental Functioning": "the infant—provided one includes with it the care it receives from its mother."[24] (Winnicott's elaboration of that phrase was so extensive that he would have been amply justified in claiming priority.) To differentiate the mother of this mother-infant system from the traditional psychoanalytic mother as sexual object, he coined the term "environment mother":

It seems possible to use these words 'object-mother' and 'environment-mother' . . . to describe the vast difference that there is for the infant between two aspects of infant-care, the mother as object, or owner of the part object that may satisfy the infant's urgent needs, and the mother as the person who wards off the unpredictable and who actively provides care in handling and in general management.[25]

A cluster of Winnicottian expressions became associated with the latter: "reliability" and "reliably present," "protection from impingement," "the capacity to be alone." The first two were self-evident. "Impingement" required refinement. Like Freud's stimuli, impingements came in two varieties: endogenous and exogenous. The environment mother, Winnicott claimed, had as her "main function the reduction to a minimum of impingements to which the infant must react." Where Freud wrote of pain as quantity, Winnicott wrote of unthinkable anxiety; where Freud postulated a mental apparatus engaging in pathological defensive operations, Winnicott hypothesized the "annihilation" of the infant's "personal being."[26]

The capacity to be alone he regarded as "either a highly sophisticated phenomenon . . . or . . . a phenomenon of early life" on which "sophisticated aloneness" was "built":

There is one [experience] that is basic, and without a sufficiency of it the capacity to be alone does not come about; *this experience is that of being alone, as an infant and small child, in the presence of mother.* Thus the basis of the capacity to be alone is a paradox; it is the experience of being alone while someone else is present.

At this point Winnicott introduced the notion of a relationship into the evolving mother-infant system. What was crucial was that the "*ego immaturity*" of the infant be "*balanced by ego support* from the mother":

Here is implied a rather special type of relationship, that between the infant or small child who is alone, and the mother or mother-substitute who is in fact reliably present. . . . I would like to suggest a name for this special type of relationship.

The term he proposed was "ego-relatedness."[27]

It was when Winnicott turned to object mother that he leaned on Freud and Klein. This mother allowed him to incorporate into his developmental hypotheses what he wanted of instinct theory, explicitly excluding the death instinct and Klein's version of envy. Still more, the object mother gave him a chance to reinterpret the depressive position. Where Klein had pictured the crucial issue as the integration of the "good breast" with the "bad breast," Winnicott depicted it as the integration of the "child-care environment and exciting environment":

Let us now think in terms of a day, with the mother holding the situation, assuming that at some point early in the day the baby has an instinctual experience. For simplicity's sake I think of a feed, for this is really at the basis of the whole matter. There appears a cannibalistic ruthless attack. . . . The baby puts one and one together and begins to see that the answer is one, and not two. The mother of the dependent relationship . . . is also the object of instinctual love. . . .

The mother is holding the situation and the day proceeds, and the infant realizes that the 'quiet' mother was involved in the full tide of instinctual experience, and has survived.[28]

Clearly Winnicott gave the environment mother a privileged position. In so doing he charted, albeit using a different vocabulary, the territory Fairbairn had already staked out.

What happened when mother did not "hold the situation"? What happened when she did not provide a "facilitating environment"? Winnicott expressed the gravity of the consequences epigrammatically: "psychosis," in his view, was "an environmental deficiency disease."[29] Beyond such sloganeering he suggested that the impact of environmental failure be conceptualized in structural terms. What he offered, however, was in the nature of *aperçus* rather than a thoroughgoing discussion. These *aperçus* fell into two groups: the one reckoned in gingerly fashion with Freud; the other aligned Winnicott with

Fairbairn. Both, he admitted, derived from the analytic setting and not from mother-infant observation.[30]

Where Freud pictured ego and id as originally undifferentiated, with the ego being that portion of the id "expediently modified by proximity to the external world,"[31] Winnicott seemed to reverse the sequence. In pithy fashion he claimed that there was "no id before ego." What figured as crucial was the "imaginative elaboration of pure body-functioning." In Winnicott's view the Freudian dichotomy between ego and id served to highlight the psychological risk of splits between mind and body: "psycho-somatic indwelling or cohesion" was a complex achievement with a vast potential for distortion.[32]

Among possible distortions, "over-activity of the mental function" took pride of place. Winnicott tried to distinguish between normal maturational processes and what he referred to as an "overgrowth":[33]

The mental activity of the infant turns a *good-enough* environment into a perfect environment, that is to say, turns relative failure of adaptation into adaptive success. What releases the mother from her need to be near-perfect is the infant's understanding. In the ordinary course of events the mother tries not to introduce complications beyond those which the infant can understand and allow for.

When mothering was erratic or tantalizing, the infant's intellect was foiled, so to speak, in its attempt at comprehension. Instead of making use of a relative environmental failure, it usurped the environment's function: "[T]he thinking of the individual" began "to take over and organize the caring. . . . *Mental functioning*" became "a *thing in itself*"; the individual in effect was " 'seduced' away into this mind," with intellectual activity becoming dissociated from psycho-somatic existence.[34]

Hypertrophy of the intellect linked up with Winnicott's second set of structural *aperçus*, that is, the dichotomy between false and true self. In the beginning, as he conceptualized it, there was no self at all; there was no unity; there was simply "unintegration." (Where Fairbairn postulated primary unity as a convenient fiction, Winnicott started with an equally fictional state of unintegration.) Here Winnicott, echoing the case of "Bob," cited Humpty Dumpty to illustrate the changes that then took place:

He has just achieved integration into one whole thing, and has emerged from the environment-individual set-up so that he is perched on a wall, no longer devotedly held. He is notoriously in a precarious position in his emotional development, especially liable to irreversible disintegration.[35]

Where did Winnicott's "true self" fit into this sequence? His writings provide at best a fragmentary answer. He appreciated that "true self" was a loose concept. There was "but little point," he wrote, "in formulating a True Self idea except for the purpose of trying to understand the False Self," because it did "no more than collect together the details of the experience of aliveness."[36] In fact the "true self," and along with it a notion of the individual as *an isolate, permanently noncommunicating, permanently unknown, . . . unfound,*" functioned as a theoretical stopgap.[37]

Winnicott's notion of "false self"—a structure built on reactions to environmental demands and compliance with them—has (wrongly) been likened to Fairbairn's central ego.[38] A point-by-point comparison would not be worthwhile here. What does, however, deserve underlining is that for both Fairbairn and Winnicott structure was a way to talk about pathology.[39] Above all, for Winnicott it was a congenial way to talk about a patient's sense of unreality:

In psychoanalytic work it is possible to see analyses going on indefinitely because they are done on the basis of work with the False Self. In one case, [that of] a man patient who had had a considerable amount of analysis before coming to me, my work really started . . . when I made it clear to him that I recognized his non-existence. He made the remark that over the years all the good work done with him had been futile because it had been done on the basis that he existed, whereas he had only existed falsely. When I had said that I recognized his non-existence he felt that he had been communicated with for the first time.[40]

The Good-Enough Analyst

The case of "Cecil," Winnicott wrote, concerned a boy with "a capacity to regress to dependence in his home setting." The parents, he continued, proved able to turn his regressions "into positive therapeutic experiences."[41]

When Cecil was twenty-one months of age, his father consulted Winnicott about him. There was already a second son in the family, now one month old, and Cecil's difficulties had begun with his mother's pregnancy and were exacerbated by the birth of this sibling. As his father put it, the boy "began to go back." He again displayed the sleeplessness that had plagued him during his earliest months: "[E]ach night he would wake several times and . . . when he woke, he woke screaming." At the time of his brother's birth "Cecil's symptomatology had got worse, especially in the matter of his difficulty in going to sleep and his waking screaming, and he had started to resist going to bed." The father also reported that "play had . . . almost ceased. Water and sand were neglected, and toys had become unimportant. At times he would mope and sit sucking his thumb."[42]

During the next fourteen years, as Winnicott periodically saw Cecil's parents and the boy himself—not much more than a dozen interviews in all—he became clearer about the "mother's tendency towards depression." She "worked very hard at giving the children the setting" they needed, "this often being difficult because of her mood disorder." As she herself remarked when Cecil was eight:

You do understand, Doctor, don't you, that with Cecil I was never outgoing; not even at the beginning. I realise this through my relationship with his brother with whom I have been easy from the start, and he has been easy with me.

Fortunately the father proved "an absolutely stabilising factor in the whole situation."[43]

Following the initial interview with the father Winnicott made a tentative assessment. In his view the parents were "not failing the child" and they might be able to bring him "through the present illness."[44] He encouraged them to make the attempt. In concrete terms he recommended that they stick with the one practice that they had hit upon to soothe the boy's crying, that is, allowing him to sleep in their bed.

After a month's interval the father reported to Winnicott as follows:

For the last 3–4 weeks he [Cecil] has been happier much of the time—but with some days when he is miserable. Eating, playing, sleeping and generally co-operating, these all improve or deteriorate together. I sleep in bed with him. He only wakes up in the night once or twice now, sometimes getting out of bed and crying, but for a shorter time than previously. In the morning and after a mid-day sleep with my wife he now wakes nearly always without crying. But he does not use his bed normally, but likes to get in and out of bed several times, often going to sleep on the floor.

A year and a half later Winnicott wrote to the medical colleague who had referred Cecil to him:

The main trouble is at night, although the nights are very much better than they were. He can now stand the parents' being together and he has no trouble about his father going off to work. On the other hand he needs to sleep in his parents' bed with his father turned towards him all the time. This means that the parents can never get together and the mother finds this a terrible frustration. They are willing to put up with this for another few months if assured that the sacrifice is worth while.

After a further half year had elapsed, the mother told Winnicott of "an immense change":

Not only had Cecil grown, but also he was happier. Nevertheless he would not stay in his own bed. She and her husband had not had a single night without him. They had to make the best of the fact that Cecil is now in his own cot from bedtime till 2 a.m. in order to have a sexual life at all. "Cecil feels he has a right to be in his parents' bed and he talks about it. We tell him," she said, "that we are fed up, and he says: 'When I grow bigger.' " He was sleeping next to his father or across the bottom of the bed. The mother said that she loved him very much but she occasionally got exasperated.[45]

Such was the last report Winnicott made of Cecil's unusual sleeping habits.

At this point Cecil was three and a half years old. The main residual symptom, that is, the boy's "continued need to be in his parents' bed," was being handled simply "by allowing it"; any other course would have produced "a good deal of evidence of emotional disturbance." "Allowing it" summed up how the mother and father had met the boy's "regression"—and, in Winnicott's estimation, met it "beautifully": the parents had permitted themselves to "spoil" their troubled son, and now he had "nearly emerged from his state of dependence."[46]

A gap of four and a half years intervened: Winnicott next heard from the parents shortly after the boy's eighth birthday. According to the mother, Cecil "had got better but . . . had never become an easy child to manage." Now his "junior" school wanted Winnicott to see the boy "because he had been stealing." He had started to do so, not only there but at home as well, after advancing from nursery school to the junior level. That stealing should have turned up did not come as a surprise to Winnicott. He recalled items of behavior from previous interviews in which Cecil had sucked his thumb and claimed "a right to his mother's mouth, then . . . used his mother's bag and its contents (including money) instead."[47] Notwithstanding Winnicott's insight, he appreciated that the nub of the matter remained communication with the boy himself.

In the squiggle game that ensued, two drawings proved crucial, number 9—Cecil turned Winnicott's squiggle into two apples—and number 10—Winnicott simply declared that the boy's squiggle represented three apples. But at that moment Winnicott made no further comment. As the game continued, Cecil provided the analyst with an opportunity to ask him about growing up. The boy answered simply, "I don't want to grow up; it's a pity to leave the younger ages." At this point Winnicott came in with an interpretation: "I referred here to the apples and said they could stand for breasts and for his need to keep in touch with his own infancy and breast-feeding." The interpretation, Winnicott wrote, seemed natural to the boy; so too did "wanting to be held and treated like a baby." With these wishes now verbalized, Winnicott asked Cecil directly about stealing. The boy answered with factual and dream material and, still more significantly, a purported memory: "When my brother was 2 years old he stole 1s. from me."[48]

In what relation did stealing and apples stand to each other? Winnicott did not specify; he did not wrap up the interview with Cecil into a neat package. "His brother's usurpation of his rights," "deprivation related to the mother's . . . becoming pregnant," as well as the boy's claim for restitution—all these themes came to light. Above all, what impressed Winnicott was that Cecil had remained aware of his dependency needs; he had not been forced to wall them off and, in the process, disown them. "A bridge into the past and into the unconscious" had been preserved, and parents and analyst alike could make use of it to correct previous "inadequate adaptation-to-need."[49]

After this session Cecil did not steal again. Certain symptoms, nevertheless, remained, one of which was tiredness. The mother knew that she must accept her son's weariness and "let him go to bed at 5 o'clock if necessary." Implicit in "this tiredness and early going to bed," Winnicott concluded, was depression, Cecil's own and that of his mother.[50]

Winnicott seems to have had the mother in mind when writing his paper "Primary Maternal Preoccupation," that is, when writing of mothers who were unable "to become preoccupied with their own infant to the exclusion of other interests, in the way" that was "normal and temporary." Still, he had entrusted her and the boy's father with their son's therapy. And therapy it had been. Again with Cecil's mother possibly in mind, he wrote:

In practice the result is that such women, having produced a child, but having missed the boat at the earliest stage, are faced with the task of making up for what has been missed. They have a long period in which they must closely adapt to their growing child's needs, and it is not certain that they can succeed in mending the early distortion. Instead of taking for granted the good effect of an early and temporary preoccupation they are caught up in the child's need for therapy. . . . They do therapy instead of being parents.[51]

If Winnicott likened mothers such as Cecil's to therapists, he was equally ready to compare analysts to mothers, to describe what happened in "regressed" phases of an analysis as a "form of infant-mother relationship."[52] He meant the comparisons to be suggestive rather than exact. They prompted him to make use of a functioning family setting; at the same time they prompted him to explore what in the analytic setting itself figured as therapeutic.

When Winnicott wrote about regression to dependence, whether in a setting provided by family or by analyst, his distinction between environment and object mothers stood him in good stead: mother as environment highlighted what the analytic setting had to offer.

What of the physical surroundings? Winnicott included them in his itemization of the clinical milieu created by Freud—but as only seventh on the list:

This work was to be done in a room, not a passage, a room that was quiet and not liable to sudden unpredictable sounds, yet not dead quiet and not free from ordinary house noises. This room would be lit properly, but not by a light staring in the face, and not by a variable light. The room would certainly not be dark and it would be comfortably warm. The patient would be lying on a couch, that is to say, comfortable, if able to be comfortable, and probably a rug and some water would be available.[53]

"If able to be comfortable" should be underlined. Freud had appreciated that the couch position might well be an imposition on the analysand: the patient, he noted, usually regarded "being made to adopt this position as a hardship" and rebelled "against it."[54] Fairbairn agreed:

It seems to me beyond question that the couch technique has the effect of imposing quite arbitrarily upon the patient a positively traumatic situation calculated inevitably to reproduce such traumatic situations of childhood as that imposed upon the infant who is left to cry in his pram alone, or that imposed upon the child who finds himself isolated in his cot during the primal scene.

Thus, late in his life, Fairbairn abandoned the couch technique:

In actual practice I sit at a desk, and the patient sits in a comfortable chair placed to the side of the desk, almost parallel to mine, but slightly inclined towards me. In terms of this arrangement, patient and analyst are not ordinarily looking at one another; but either may look at the other if he so wishes.[55]

According to Harry Guntrip, Winnicott (his second analyst) carefully planned surroundings conducive to enabling the analysand "to be comfortable":

His consulting room was simple, restful in colours and furniture, unostentatious. . . . I would knock and walk in, and presently Winnicott would stroll in with a cup of tea in his hand and a cheery 'Hallo,' and sit on a small wooden chair by the couch. I would sit on the couch sideways or lie down as I felt inclined, and change position freely according to how I felt or what I was saying. Always at the end, as I departed he held out his hand for a friendly handshake.[56]

In Guntrip's mind the inanimate and the animate obviously blended. When Winnicott himself characterized the setting, he was concerned above all with the person of the analyst—and his reliability: he "would be reliably there, on time, alive, breathing"; he "would keep awake and become preoccupied with the patient"; he would remain "free from temper tantrums, free from compulsive falling in love"; and "an absence of the talion reaction" could be "counted on." Reliability and being reliably present served to link analyst and mother, and

Winnicott insisted that he was not alone in appreciating this resemblance. Freud, he claimed, took "for granted the early mothering situation . . . and . . . *it turned up in his provision of a setting for his work,* almost without his being aware of what he was doing."[57]

Elsewhere Winnicott spoke for himself. His descriptions of mothering and of analysis resonated with each other: protection from impingement, provision of ego support, and, more generally, "holding" figured alike in his discussions of mother and analyst. Just as the mother kept to a minimum the number of impingements to which her infant must react, so too the analyst should keep to a minimum the number of interpretations. It was bad practice, Winnicott argued, "to interpret whatever one" understood, "acting according to one's own needs, thus spoiling the patient's attempt to cope," which could best be done "by dealing with one thing at a time":[58]

My interpretations are economical, I hope. One interpretation per session satisfies me if it has referred to the material produced by the patient's unconscious co-operation. I say one thing, or say one thing in two or three parts. I never use long sentences unless I am very tired. If I am near exhaustion point I begin teaching. Moreover, in my view an interpretation containing the word "moreover" is a teaching session.[59]

If an interpretation could be likened to an impingement, it could also be viewed as a kind of ego support. In this connection Winnicott told of a young woman who had just begun analysis as he was about to go abroad for a month. Already, in her dreams at least, she was becoming extremely dependent. "In one dream she had a tortoise, but its shell was soft so that the animal was unprotected and would therefore certainly suffer. So in the dream she killed the tortoise to save it the intolerable pain that was coming." Winnicott understood the patient's suicidal dream as a reaction to his impending departure. It was, he wrote, as if he had been "holding her and then became preoccupied with some other matter so that she felt *annihilated.*" "Annihilated" was in fact her word. And so Winnicott interpreted the dream to her. "The patient became able to cope" with his absence because "she felt (at one level) that she was now not being annihilated, but in a positive way" had acquired "reality as the object" of his concern.[60] From the experience, Winnicott concluded:

Whenever we understand a patient in a deep way and show that we do so by a correct and well-timed interpretation we are in fact holding the patient, and taking part in a relationship in which the patient is in some degree regressed and dependent.[61]

▬▬ ▬▬ ▬▬ ▬▬ ▬▬

What then of regression itself? Here Winnicott's maternal model came into its own. And in bringing it to bear on regression, he made explicit a concept of analysis as development, or better still, as evolution.

When Winnicott wrote of regression, he was not referring to something that, along with fixation, happened to libido. Rather he was referring to something that happened to the analysand in the consulting room, something that Freud had touched on only in passing.[62] This something was more than mere childishness. Though Winnicott appreciated full well that "one of the difficulties of . . . psycho-analytic technique" was knowing "at any one moment how old a patient" was "in the transference relationship," he did not think it appropriate "to use the word regression whenever infantile behaviour" appeared.[63] In this connection he set down in schematic order what regression entailed:

A failure of adaptation on the part of the environment. . . .
A belief in the possibility of a correction of the original failure represented by a latent capacity for regression. . . .
Specialized environmental provision, followed by actual regression.
New forward emotional development.[64]

What ranked as crucial was going back to the early failure in adaptation, which, in Winnicott's view, had become frozen. (He argued that it was normal for the individual "to defend the self against specific environmental failure by a *freezing of the failure situation*"— and, further, that this notion was related to the concept of fixation point.)[65] An environment "making adequate adaptation," that is, the analytic setting, would allow the patient to unfreeze and reexperience that failure situation.[66] The patient, for his part, was in a regressed state: he had managed to relinquish pathological defenses and hence was extremely vulnerable—like a tortoise with a very soft shell.

Regression itself came in all sizes and shapes. It could be, Winnicott wrote, "of any degree, localized and momentary, or total and involving a patient's whole life over a phase." Was it, then, encountered in every analysis? Here Winnicott hesitated, while emphatically denying that he encouraged his patients to regress.[67] He did, however, encourage his colleagues to examine less severe regressions and to make a scientific study of the analyst's "environmental" adaptation.

In this vein he described how he himself had handled such a case. The patient had had a brief period of analysis with Winnicott as a late adolescent, but war conditions had imposed an interruption. More than a decade later,

> he broke down at work (as a doctor in a hospital) and was admitted into an institution . . . because of unreality feelings and a general inability to cope with work and with life. He was not aware at that time that he was seeking out his former analyst, and was quite incapable of asking . . . for analysis, although as it turned out later, this is what he was precisely doing and nothing else would have been of value.[68]

That Winnicott had conducted the first analysis turned out to be vital to the patient: he could present himself only in bits, and both he and his analyst appreciated that so long as he did not feel integrated, it was up to Winnicott to hold those bits together and perceive a human being.

"On important but rare occasions," Winnicott wrote, this patient became "withdrawn," that is, momentarily detached "from a waking relationship with external reality, this detachment being something of the nature of a brief sleep." In that withdrawn state unexpected things happened which the patient sometimes recounted—and it was then that the analyst had a chance to transform the withdrawn state into a therapeutic regression. Winnicott reported the following episode:

> He [the patient] had said it would be a waste of time to go on talking in his ordinary way, and then said that he had become withdrawn and felt this as a flight from something. He could not remember any dream belonging to this moment of sleep. . . . He just managed to tell me that he had . . . had the idea of being *curled up*, although in actual fact he was lying on his back as usual, with his hands together across his chest. . . . When he spoke of being curled up, he made movements with his hands to show that his curled-up position was somewhere in front of his face and that he was moving around in the curled-up position.

Winnicott made an interpretation that, he claimed, he would not have been able to formulate twenty years earlier:

> I immediately said to him: 'In speaking of yourself as curled up and moving round, you are at the same time implying something

which naturally you are not describing since you are not aware of it; you imply the *existence of a medium*.' After a while I asked him if he understood what I meant and I found that he had immediately understood; he said, 'Like the oil in which wheels move.' Having now received the idea of the medium holding him, he went on to describe in words what he had shown with his hands.[69]

Winnicott later commented:

I have the impression that if I had delayed the interpretation it would have been of no use. I had to put a medium around the revolving infant immediately or else all that had happened was that the man had had an unexplained and unuseful hallucination. I had made myself responsible for the environmental factor just in time before the man came right out of touch with the regressive experience that he had had.[70]

The patient felt the session to have been momentous. Why momentous? Winnicott conjectured: thanks to the provision of a "medium," the patient surrendered symbolically—without acting out—to the curled-up state and from there, he began to come to "grips with his reality situation."[71]

It was very noticeable that the man's concern about his environment started from this point. He became aware of an attitude towards me. . . . He became able to express dissatisfaction with me for the first time and also hopes.[72]

In due course recognition of the "limits of the analyst's capacity for adaptation to the patient's needs" would also come.[73] Winnicott was insistent that over time that capacity would indeed prove limited. Still more, the analyst's failures, he argued, were themselves potentially therapeutic:

The corrective provision is never enough. What is it that may be enough for some of our patients to get well? In the end the patient uses the analyst's failures, often quite small ones, perhaps maneuvered by the patient. . . . The operative factor is that the patient now hates the analyst for the failure that originally came in as an environmental factor, . . . but that is *now* staged in the transference.

So in the end we succeed by failing—failing the patient's way. This is a long distance from the simple theory of cure by corrective experience. In this way, regression can be in the service of the ego if it is met by the analyst, and turned into a new dependence in which the patient brings the bad external factor into the area of his or her . . . control.[74]

Just as the good-enough mother—in contrast to the "bad external factor"—could fail in adaptation as the infant's intellectual processes became able to account for and allow for such failures, so too the analyst could begin to fail his patient.

What followed the return to the early failure situation? Did progress thereafter occur in a straight line according to some preordained sequence? Far from it. Here the model of mother as environment paid off. The very "environmental" adaptation that allowed a therapeutic regression, Winnicott commented, opened up before the patient "the prospect of gradually evolving in his own way in the analytic situation."[75] Choices made earlier—defenses selected and rigidly maintained—could be undone. What happened subsequently, Winnicott did not specify; he left it up to the patient.

——— ——— ——— ——— ———

Where did fathers fit in? Winnicott suggested an answer in his *Holding and Interpretation*—a report of six months in the treatment of the man for whom he had already provided a "medium." This account began when the analysis had been underway for roughly a year and a half, and oedipal themes had started to appear in the material.

What appeared in Winnicott's reconstruction of his patient's childhood was a father who had come into his son's life "deliberately at a very early stage and established himself as an alternative mother."[76] Fathers might, in Winnicott's view, compensate for the relative failures of their depressed wives—and so it had been in the cases of Bob and Cecil; yet these fathers had not been alternative mothers. It might be, Winnicott wrote elsewhere, that "there are some fathers who really would make better mothers than their wives, but still they cannot be mothers"; mothers cannot "simply fade out of the picture."[77]

Winnicott's strictures highlighted his belief that a child needed two parents—above all, to allow him to sort out ambivalent emotions: "One parent can be felt to remain loving while the other is being hated, and this in itself has a stabilizing influence."

Every now and again the child is going to hate someone, and if father is not there to tell him where to get off, he will hate his mother, and this will make him confused, because it is his mother that he loves most fundamentally.[78]

The father of Winnicott's patient had refused to play the role that in retrospect the analyst designated as his. He had "avoided the ordinary clashes that belong to the father-son relationship." As a result, Winnicott explained to his patient, "[y]ou were not able to get the relief that the triangular situation brings when a child is in a clash with father; relief from the struggle with mother alone."[79]

None of the above suggested why the second parent need be male. On this point Winnicott was explicit: fathers were crucial to their children's sexual development. For a son it was necessary that the male parent say no—and thus Winnicott remarked (in his analytic shorthand) to his patient:

If I go to your adolescent dream of intercourse with mother, or to your early childhood, I can say that you needed father to say 'I know you love mother and want intercourse with her, but I love her and I do not allow it.' In that way father would have freed you to love other women.[80]

The patient stopped the analysis with these themes scarcely explored. In the very last session he was reflecting on the views he had earlier held about Freud and psychoanalysis, in particular his objection to Freud's having "dabbled in anthropology." But he could not recall the title of Freud's book. Winnicott reminded him that it was *Totem and Taboo* and commented:

It interests me that you refer to *Totem and Taboo* as unacceptable. . . . The brothers come together to kill the father. . . . The hostility between the brothers is suppressed for the purpose of the overthrow of the father. . . . I suggest that there is something you are leaving out. . . . You are not saying anything about the central theme, which is that all those who were antagonistic to each other loved their mother, and it was love of the mother that made them want to kill the father.[81]

Once again "love of the mother" ranked in Winnicott's mind as primary.

The Hands of the Living God

In 1969 Marion Milner published *The Hands of the Living God,* an account of the psychoanalytic treatment of a schizophrenic woman during the years 1943 to 1959. What is striking, and sometimes maddening, about Milner's account is its lack of closure: the myriad details of the material are not fitted into a tidy structure. Winnicott commented on this quality in his foreword to the book:

Any bit can be taken out and discussed, alternative theories can be applied, and the reader can make his or her own discoveries on the basis of the material presented. At no point does the author dogmatize, so that there is no barrier to disagreement about alternative interpretations or alternative methods of management.

Milner herself admitted forthrightly that she had not been able to "conceptualize" the "raw material . . . fully in terms of psycho-analytic theory":

I slowly came to accept the fact that the ideas that I was trying to clarify for myself might be still in the stage of private models for thinking, and that I would probably have to be content with leaving them in that condition.[82]

Milner's "private models for thinking" echoed those Winnicott was simultaneously working out, and the ideas each was trying to clarify resonated with the other's. Indeed, the material Milner presented gave the richest account of a "Winnicottian" case.

Throughout the years of "Susan's" therapy, her analyst had "kept some sort of notes for each day's session, even though often very scanty ones," concentrating on what her patient had said rather than on her own interpretations. Beyond that, she had Susan's drawings, roughly four thousand of them: her patient had sometimes brought as many as ninety in one day and "then another huge batch on the next" before Milner "had even had time to glance through those from the previous days." The analyst had simply filed most of them away; she discovered only later that no single drawing was the exact replica of another. Originally Milner had intended to meld together these diverse materials, to use her own diary notes along "with the drawings as the basis for a descriptive account of what had happened" between her and her patient. But the "problem of selection from verbal material" proved "too difficult." So she centered the account on the drawings, which in her view contained "in highly condensed form the essence" of what she and Susan "were trying to understand," and on the particularly rich phases of the treatment, 1950 and 1957–1958, during which they were produced.[83]

Susan's drawings, or rather the act of drawing itself, marked a crucial step—indeed suggested that after nearly seven years of treatment analysis might actually be possible. Throughout the early period when Susan had had "great difficulty in accepting the analytic process," one particular aspect of that difficulty had stood out: she had found intolerable the notion that "the conscious logical part of her ego might have at times to be abrogated temporarily during the sessions. . . . Any spontaneous happening in herself was felt as going crazy." Drawing broke this resistance: her productions "were practically all 'doodles', . . . that is, made without any conscious intention about what she was going to draw." And so she came to appreciate, as Milner put it, "the idea of dependence on the unconscious forces by which she is lived."[84]

At the same time the drawings paved the way for engaging in symbolic expression—again crucial for the analytic process. Susan had been trapped in literal-mindedness, in concrete thought: she would insist, "A thing is what it is and can't be anything else."[85] How did drawing help? (Here Milner's answer paralleled what Winncott would say.) The paper was a "pliable medium," external to Susan, but "not insisting" on its own "separate objective existence";[86] it functioned as a bridge to recognition of the " 'otherness' of the external world," and along with otherness, of duality. It thus became possible for Susan "to accept that a symbol" was "both itself and the thing" it stood for, "without being identical with it."[87]

In the case of Susan, the connection between Milner and Winnicott was not merely intellectual: Milner thanked him in her preface for carrying the medical responsibility—she was a lay analyst—and for always being "ready with an illuminating remark on the telephone in moments of crisis."[88] Confidentiality, however, kept her from publicly acknowledging in 1969 the most tangible and immediate links. It was with Winnicott and his first wife that Susan had lived throughout the intial period of the treatment, a period of almost seven years; it was Winnicott who had brought Susan to Milner and who, so long as she resided in his house, paid for the analysis itself; it was the collapse of Winnicott's marriage that precipitated the second of Susan's two breakdowns. By the mid-1980s Milner was prepared to disclose that the "Mr. and Mrs. X" of her account were in fact the Winnicotts.[89]

Alice Winnicott had found Susan "in great distress" at "N. I.," a hospital for functional and nervous diseases. Susan had been admitted in the summer of 1943 following a breakdown: the presenting symptoms were hypochondriacal heart pains, torturing obsessional doubts, guilt, and depression. When after a couple of months she showed no improvement, the hospital psychiatrist recommended electroconvulsive therapy (E.C.T.), otherwise known as shock. Susan resisted but finally gave way: "She was asked," Winnicott wrote, "to give her permission about 19 times and she refused, but after the 20th time when she said yes, the shock therapy was started." She "had two doses and following these she had a great disturbance of the right side' apart from a very severe degree of the usual amnesia and confusion."[90] (The longer-term effect of the E.C.T. remained unclear. The treatment itself and Susan's experience of it, however, figured prominently in the analysis.) When, according to Milner, "Mrs X saw 'the terrible state'" Susan was in, she persuaded the girl "to leave the hospital and come and stay with them."[91]

Winnicott recognized, whereas his wife did not, the full extent of what she was taking on. Susan herself recalled much later how "she would 'just sit'—her head down, knees up, for hours and hours, 'how awful for them'—and how Mr X would come in and put a hand out and maybe she would take no notice." By 1949 Milner had begun to observe an "inner movement that seemed to be bringing her alive as a person." At the same time she began to see "that there was another acute anxiety, a very realistic one, dominating her feelings: . . . there were increasing signs that the X's marriage was not going to last very long." When Winnicott's home broke up near the turn of the year, he found her a new one: "She was taken in by a seventy-year old friend . . . , Mrs Brown, who took total charge of her and expected nothing from her in the way of help in running the house."[92] Indeed by the time Susan moved in with Mrs. Brown, she had become unable to help. Her daily routine—so she reported to a psychiatric consultant in July 1950—consisted in going to bed at 10:30 P.M., sleeping with sedation, and sometimes remaining in bed until one o'clock the following afternoon, in sum, just sitting about and having her psychoanalytic sessions, and she usually went to them in a taxi.[93] Obviously the break-up of the marriage had produced a serious regression.[94]

Susan stayed with Mrs. Brown for roughly a year. Gradually she recovered from her "extreme dependence" and "became restless."

She first took a "daily house-cleaning job, though still sleeping at Mrs Brown's, and later an 'au pair' living-in job with a large family." In this position she remained for eight years, without being paid for her work. When she attempted to alter these arrangements and to receive a regular wage, there was a further crisis. The family refused, and Susan felt obliged to find a new situation and a new place to live. By then, that is, 1959, the five-days-a-week analysis had stopped, and Milner merely alluded to the vicissitudes of Susan's life thereafter.[95] There were ups and downs—she attempted briefly to live on her own, was hospitalized for a short time, and finally found a man. That man she held onto throughout the subsequent years, and with him around, she proved able to cope; she also found and held onto a good, though boring, job in a museum, from which she retired at the age of sixty. And throughout those years Milner continued to see her in therapy, ending it, however, before she might begin to fail; she feared that should she die with her patient still in treatment, Susan would blame herself for the death.[96]

So much for Susan's history during and after analysis. What had happened to her before treatment began? Winnicott made mention of the "extreme muddle of her home" and inferred that her environment had been "an extremely tantalising one." Beyond that he confessed himself not "very well informed, having deliberately left this to the analyst, who gradually comes at the details."[97] Milner was more skeptical about the analyst's ability to "come at" those details; only the general outlines of the historic past could be discerned, and in the analysis reconstruction played a minor role. One item, however, belonging to that past did get revised and reassessed: Susan had not realized until she was in analysis that her mother was "mad."[98]

Still, Milner's readers required that Susan be placed in a family context, and the author provided the necessary background information. It had not been an easy childhood. Susan had lived in chronic poverty with mother, older sister, and Jack, the lodger. "She remembered being always hungry but that her mother would tell her she was greedy." She remembered her house being "in a terrible mess: it always smelt, there was only newspaper on the meal table, and anyway . . . they hardly ever sat down to meals together."[99]

Susan also lived in chronic uncertainty. Who was her father? Her mother's husband, who had deserted the fold, or Jack, a victim of drink and unemployment? (In the second year of treatment she learned the truth from relatives: "Jack was her father.") Jack, Susan said, was hated by everyone, and "once when he had gone away temporarily and found work to do with an electric power station her mother had said that she hoped he would get electrocuted." (He did finally leave when Susan was still a child.)[100]

What about her "mad" mother?

> Susan could remember her mother having terrible black moods, and she would often walk out of the house and leave them in order to wander about the town. Also in the black moods she would often not speak for days, and sometimes they were all hating each other so much that none of them would speak. Susan also remembers how she would cling to her mother, not able to bear being separate from her; and once, when her mother asked, 'Do you love me?' she remembers saying, 'I love you the whole world.' . . . There were constant quarrels between Jack and her mother, mostly, she said, about her, and soon her mother took Susan into her bed altogether and made Jack sleep alone. . . .

> She always felt as a child that she was her mother's favourite and that her mother was very unkind to her sister. . . . When she was away staying with an aunt and uncle her mother would write to her beginning 'O moon of my delight'; but also, when in her bad moods, her mother would say that all their troubles were Susan's fault, meaning Susan supposed, that she ought not to have been born. Gradually, as Susan grew up, her mother lost all interest in her.[101]

From Susan's account of those growing-up years, analyst and reader alike could begin to glimpse the complexity of her personality: it certainly was not all of a piece, and what Milner referred to as neurotic and psychotic parts alternated and intermingled. The neurotic manifested itself in her obsessional rituals begun at the age of ten: "While doing them she became extremely good at school, and also . . . had friends 'because she was gay and didn't care', but the rituals became such hard work that she had to give them up just before puberty, and went back to being 'no good at school'."[102] She did not, however, give them up permanently. Winnicott later commented on what was a recurrent pattern: "While obsessional she felt all right, but the obsessions got in the way, but when she cured herself of them she became very much more ill." He himself always assumed that there was "a psychotic core to the illness."[103]

That psychotic core had few immediate manifestations. Writing about Susan as she was in the 1950s, Milner observed:

In part of her psyche she was able to discriminate between the various polarities, fantasy and reality, self and not-self, inner and outer, and hence was able to live what looked increasingly like a fairly normal life, [yet] there was another part of her which held grimly onto the fused state of no-difference, so that she could still go on saying that the world was not really outside herself.

Shortly before her initial hospitalization Susan had seen herself as

'breaking down into reality'. For the first time in her life, she felt she was 'in the world': she discovered that she was in her body, that space existed, that if she walked away from things they got farther away; and she discovered that she had not made herself—this was 'such a relief'. And her emotions were 'absolutely terrific' because she was getting into the world for the first time, her emotions were inside her and she felt terrific things were happening[104]

On January 8, 1959, Susan wrote, "I am in the world for the first time for sixteen years" (that is, as Milner noted, for the first time since the E.C.T.). A few weeks later she brought Milner a further written commentary:

The shock of the realization that one could have been unconscious for so long a time seems almost to send one into unconsciousness again. Maybe it will, I do not know, but it is something to have become conscious even for a few minutes.[105]

In early 1952 Susan, still at Mrs. Brown's, brought her analyst a drawing "which she said she had made nearly ten years before, on the first night at the X's, which was also the night before her first meeting" with Milner "and her first session. . . . She said . . . she had just found it amongst her belongings where it had presumably lain all those years, during seven of which" the analyst "had had no idea that she could draw at all."[106]

The drawing made a profound impression on Milner. It was a picture of someone holding her own head, of Susan, Milner conjectured, nursing her "sore head after the E.C.T." The head, without a neck, was positioned horizontally and encircled by arms; there were no breasts—"the curves that might suggest them" were "more the curves of an arm, . . . an arm that both holds the baby" and was "itself the baby." The fact that Susan had made the drawing just before her first analytic session suggested to Milner that "being safely held" had been the patient's "prime concern," and "that in this holding there would have to be no clear distinction for her between the holder and the held." At the same time the picture conveyed, so Milner further conjectured, a "faint glimmer of hope" on Susan's part that "she would somehow be able to find a psychic equivalent of the encircling arms":

> Whether or not all this was what the drawing meant to her, it certainly was by means of it that I came to see more clearly what I thought she needed from me. It became an intensely rich symbol, too, of what I felt I had to become able to achieve in myself, while with her in sessions. . . . I had to think once more about my own capacity to . . . hold in myself a blankness, an empty circle, emptiness of ideas, not always pushing myself to try and find an interpretation. And how difficult this still was![107]

Above all what Milner needed to accomplish in herself in order to "hold" Susan had "a deeply physical aspect." As time went on, she came to believe that the words she said were "often less important" than her "body-mind state of being," a state of " 'concentration of the body'. . . a kind of deliberate filling out of one's body with one's consciousness." And there was a link between Milner's capacity to avoid "premature formulations" and her ability to achieve "full 'body attention' ": both depended upon tolerating unclearness, "the unorganized, undifferentiated 'mess' " of the relationship.[108]

Milner's background awareness of her body figured prominently precisely because Susan had lost her own; she told her analyst that after the E.C.T.

> she felt cut off from all perceptions coming from inside herself, and was living in a narrow area at the very top of her head. . . . She had . . . apparently lost the capacity to become aware of the ever-present fluid inarticulate spatial background of her own body-mind feeling self.

And connected with this loss was "a loss of some essential part of her unconscious memories of her mother's hands and arms, holding her, sustaining her, protecting her, without which, however inadequate her mother had been, she would have died":

> Obviously the relation between these two aspects is very close, because the background awareness of one's own body, that which

one both holds and is held by, after infancy, must have been largely indistinguishable from the awareness of one's mother's body doing the holding; so it was not surprising, surely, that the loss of the one could feel like the loss of the other. So Susan was left feeling herself as a disembodied spirit.[109]

A passage of poetry from D. H. Lawrence's *Pansies,* which recurred again and again to Milner, prompted her speculation on these themes:

It is a fearful thing to fall into the hands of the living God.
But it is a much more fearful thing to fall out of them.

The hands out of which Susan had fallen stood in Milner's mind for both mother and Susan's own body. And when in early 1952 her patient finally brought the post-E.C.T. drawing to her session, Milner wondered—prematurely as it turned out—whether Susan "was showing that she herself could now take responsibility for what she knew she needed to find again, in some token way, the encircling arms, the re-discovered sense of the hands of the living god."[110]

In the more than four thousand drawings Susan brought her analyst one visual phenomenon stood out: her use of alternating perspective. The first time Susan employed this technique was in a representation of an insect. Initially the whole insect looked like an X figure; then it became two faces tightly pressed against each other, so tightly that they seemed to merge. In other such drawings human faces and body parts were more immediately apparent; two interlocking circles depicting faces in profile or one full face in the center were not uncommon. A particularly striking drawing showed "either two oval faces . . . with their noses pressed close together, or a full face with a mouth and drops of saliva," although it could "also be read as buttocks emitting faeces. Alternatively, the eyes in the middle of the two ovals" could "be seen as the nipples of two breasts." The final version of the alternating profiles "showed a swing between looking like one full face, with a lock of hair down the middle, and two profiles facing each other."[111]

These pictures taken together captured in Milner's view the central dilemma of the analysis:

They did all seem to suggest a feeling of bodily fusion with parts of me-mother. She [Susan] would agree, intellectually, with the idea that part of her was feeling totally fused with me, or part of me, so that interpretations in terms of any relationship to me as a whole separate person made no sense to her; but, at the same time, we could not proceed from that assumption because at once it seemed to rouse in her the terror of being fused with a mad mother, and this in turn then made her swing back to a sense of two-ness again.[112]

The theme of separation or differentiation went right along with the question of Susan's body image. "Living in a narrow area at the very top of her head," "cut off from conscious awareness of 'messages coming from inside'," Susan was "left with having to construct a body image from an agglomeration of bits taken in from outside." The most prominent bit was a phallus. Phallic forms appeared in a series of drawings, and one day, early in the analysis, she came "in a great state of panic because she felt she was actually growing a penis." Brains, phallus, omnipotence were all linked in Susan's mind: she seemed to conceive of her brain in terms of a penis and testicles, and brains and phallus were central to a fantasy of magical self-creation. In December 1950, Susan brought a drawing that suggested to Milner that she appreciated, at some level, what she needed to do: "climb down from the heights of her pride in a delusory possession of the urinating penis, and therefore once more fully inhabit her own body, once more become fully subject to time and space and the force of gravity."[113]

Nearly eight years passed. On March 4, 1958, Milner made a note that suddenly she saw Susan "as a woman, as if for the first time." After an extended interruption Susan had recently resumed drawing, but now only in the sessions themselves. In December 1957 she had produced what Milner regarded as a comically vivid representation of her "battle in coming down from the . . . heights":

Here is her infant self, . . . on the ground and looking like an unowned abandoned urchin, while far up above is the self that disowns, haughtily oblivious, even its hat taking part in the effort at levitation. As for the duck on the left, turning up its beak, as at a bad smell, but also looking rather weak at the knees, here was almost a hint of a dawning compassion, shown in the way it contemplates the disowned urchin. I suspected that I was the duck

with the turned-up beak, for I felt that part of her did expect me
to reject her smelly baby self and even thought of me as weak-
kneed if I did not.

Early the next year Susan drew, over and over again, water and waves,
and then ducks and more ducks. In February she put a duck in some
water: she drew a duck that was "actually supported by water and
actively swimming." Shortly thereafter Susan made a picture of "a little
duck inside a big one, the little duck wearing a hat." In so doing she
commented, "It's got a hat on; that means it's ready to come out."[114]

Although the little duck may have been ready to emerge, Susan
"herself did not 'come out' into the world for another ten months."
Toward the end of that period she "developed a new symbol, one that
was directly concerned with the problem of dividing a primary wholeness into two": many of her drawings now began with a diagonal line.
This symbol appeared "in the context of her struggle to get a firmer
hold on the concept of duality and hence on the related problem of
the boundary, including the boundary that is the skin." Susan, Milner
remarked, "seemed to know just how she wanted to use it, [and] so it
was best to let it develop in its own way."[115]

In October 1958 Susan drew her first diagonal, "a faint intermit-
tent line . . . right across the page from the top left corner," where it
emerged "from a small eight-pointed star." Two months later her
diagonal showed a change: "[T]he bisecting line" was "rhythmically
broken all the way along, being made of three bracket lines arranged
in alternating series so that the diagonal itself" was "permeable." Various familiar iconographic items appeared on either side of the line,
and in the bottom left were "four circles with an upright stroke in each
and labelled 'me's'." Milner reflected:

Somehow this new form of the diagonal made me think of laughter
and how, when Susan laughed, it broke up the rigid set of her face
and jaw, a quite startling transformation, especially when laughing
at herself. . . . This association of mine seemed to suggest that she is
saying . . . that when the idea of duality is accepted as one half of
living, it need not be only a matter of pain and hard endurance; it
can also be a source of delight, since the line which is the boundary
between two becomes also the meeting place. . . .
    I had to think also of what she might mean by the tiny circles
with an upright stroke in the middle of each and labelled 'me's'. In
fact, I came to think of them as representing the dawning idea of

the subjectivity of herself and other people, of people being 'me's' to themselves. I think of the straight vertical line in the middle of each circle, and how it could stand either for the pronoun, the first person singular, or for the digit 'one', both indicating surely the same thing, the dawning concept of the unified consciousness of oneself as a person, and therefore also of other people as persons.[116]

The last diagonal drawing accompanied Susan's reentry into the world. It was done the day after Milner had noticed feeling "in contact" with Susan "in a way that had never happened before." What stood out in the analyst's mind was Susan's placement of items "right across the dividing line," and she read the drawing as a commentary on the contact of the previous day. She did not verbalize these thoughts to her patient and was glad of it. Susan herself was able to report that she "felt herself to be once more in the world and the world once more outside her, and yet herself part of it."[117]

Susan's "capacity for excursion into the real world" proved precarious. The very next week she dreamed a dream that suggested to Milner the task still lying ahead: "There was a mad white horse on a bridge, blocking her way, but she felt she might get by, via the parapet." Susan associated: "The mad white horse made her think of her mother."[118]

■■■■ ■■■■ ■■■■ ■■■■ ■■■■

Not until *The Piggle,* Winnicott's posthumously published case history of a little girl, did he provide clinical material bearing on the issues with which Milner's Susan had been grappling for close to two decades. The task of sorting out self and objects and along with it those of inhabiting one's own body and perceiving it accurately may have reached psychotic proportions with Susan, but they plagued less seriously disturbed patients as well. And precisely because the analyst became implicated in the patient's confusion, the consulting room became the environment in which differentiation might be facilitated—and chronicled.

Transitions

As early as 1955 Harry Guntrip had "made a private note" that "Fairbairn could not do much more" for him, and he "wondered about going to Winnicott."[119] By the time he ended his analysis with Fairbairn, that wondering had hardened into a firm resolve. He, and

Fairbairn as well, had been reading Winnicott's papers as they appeared in print, and Guntrip underlined his analyst's description of Winnicott as "clinically brilliant." By 1962 Guntrip "had no doubt" that Winnicott was the man to "turn to for further help." And so he went to London, "once a month for a couple of sessions," and during the six-year period from 1962 to 1968 he managed to have just over 150 of them. Again, as in his analysis with Fairbairn, Guntrip kept detailed notes of every session; in this second case, however, the only record extant is the brief published assessment in his article "My Experience of Analysis with Fairbairn and Winnicott."[120]

According to this account Guntrip was far happier with Winnicott: from the outset he was "astonished at the rapidity" with which his new analyst went to the "heart of the matter," to the mother who Guntrip claimed had not called him to life, or as Fairbairn might have put it, to the mother who had not recognized him as a "person in his own right." At the end of the very first session, after forty or so minutes of very hard talking by Guntrip, Winnicott remarked—and his patient quoted him approvingly—"I've nothing particular to say yet, but if I don't say something, you may begin to feel I'm not here."[121] (Guntrip missed his analyst's irony: Winnicott was asking whether there was going to be a relationship or simply a monologue.)[122] He subsequently linked his patient's conviction of maternal failure with hard talking and note taking:

You can't take your ongoing being for granted. You have to work hard to keep yourself in existence. You're afraid to stop acting, talking or keeping awake. You feel you might die in a gap like . . . [your brother], because if you stop acting mother can't do anything. . . . You're bound to fear I can't keep you alive, so you link up monthly sessions for me by your records. No gaps. . . . You know about 'being active' but not about 'just growing, just breathing' while you sleep, without your having to do anything about it.

At the end of the analysis Guntrip was once again talking hard; his analyst interpreted: "You gave me half an hour of concentrated talk, rich in content. It felt strained listening and holding the situation for you. You had to know that I could stand your talking hard at me."[123]

In this setting the analysand's longing for his mother was powerfully revived—and satisfied as well, so Guntrip claimed. Winnicott became, he wrote, "a good breast mother" to his "infant self" in his "deep unconscious." And even death did not deprive the analyst of his maternal role: "Winnicott was not, and could not be, dead" for Guntrip; he had "come into living relation with precisely that earlier lost part" of himself "that fell ill" because of his mother's inadequacy. And when, near the end of Guntrip's own life, he had dreamed the dream of his mother as a "woman who had no face, arms or breasts," he drew the conclusion that because Winnicott had taken that mother's place, it had become "*safe*" for him "*to remember her in an actual dream-reliving of her paralysing schizoid aloofness.*"[124]

A curious conclusion: it betokened an attempt to disown his real mother while clinging to his two analysts, Winnicott, the good mother, and Fairbairn, the bad. Winnicott's title Guntrip openly bestowed; Fairbairn's he merely implied. (Guntrip remained deeply involved with his first analyst; at the very time he was writing his assessment of his two analyses, he had begun working on a manuscript entitled "Fairbairn Re-Examined in Historical Perspective.")[125] Indeed one suspects that Guntrip's description of Winnicott as a "good breast mother" was intended to serve as an object lesson to Fairbairn—albeit after the fact.

What would Winnicott have made of Guntrip's encomium? In giving his reading of the Kleinian good breast, he provided an answer:

I wish to add the reminder that a good breast introjection is sometimes highly pathological, a defence organization. The breast is then an idealized breast (mother) and this idealization indicates a hopelessness about inner chaos. . . . Such an introjected idealized breast dominates the scene; and all seems well for the patient. Not so for the patient's friends, however, since such an introjected good breast has to be advertised, and the patient becomes a 'good breast' advocate.

Analysts are faced with this difficult problem, shall we ourselves be recognizable in our patients? We always are. But we deplore it. We hate . . . to hear ourselves being advertised by those whose own inner chaos is being precariously held by the introjection of an idealized analyst.[126]

Elsewhere Winnicott drew a distinction between subjective objects and objects objectively perceived. The subjective object derived from Melanie Klein: it was a bundle of projections; it worked by magic; in short, it belonged to the inner world. In contrast, the object objectively perceived belonged to external reality and hence lay outside the sphere of subjective (or "omnipotent," as Winnicott put it) control.[127]

With this distinction, Winnicott landed once again "right in the territory of Fairbairn"—or perhaps it would be more accurate to say that here the interests of the two analysts converged. Fairbairn's summary comment about therapy written when Guntrip's analysis had reached an impasse underlined the convergence:

Psychoanalytical treatment resolves itself into a struggle on the part of the patient to press-gang his relationship with the analyst into the closed system of the inner world . . . , and a determination on the part of the analyst to effect a breach in this closed system and to provide conditions under which . . . the patient may be induced to accept the open system of outer reality.[128]

Having conceptualized the struggle, Fairbairn appeared at a loss how to do the same for its solution. Along with most psychoanalytic theorists, he fastened on stalemate rather than improvement—and in accounting for the former he had a measure of success. For his part Winnicott seemed intent on examining change rather than stasis, on investigating the transitions between inner and outer, and on exploring the moments when the patient moved in the direction of external reality.

In delineating transitions, Winnicott once again couched his observations in terms of development and once again made little attempt to sort out what derived from pediatric practice and what from analytic. At the same time he was assessing both infant and analytic experience from a different perspective. The focus now shifted: from analyst as environment to patient as creative, or, to put it another way, from analytic provision to patient cognition. Above all, this shift in focus facilitated a more consistently cognitive understanding of the analytic process.

Winnicott's initial observations and reports on "transitional phenomena" derived from his work with infants at the Paddington Green Children's Hospital. He had devised a "set situation" as an "instrument of research" without being altogether clear what the point of the research actually was—other than finding out more about mothers and babies. When a mother and her infant of six to fourteen months arrived for a consultation, Winnicott would ask her to take a seat opposite him with the corner of the table coming between them:

She sits down with the baby on her knee. As a routine, I place a right-angled shining tongue depressor at the edge of the table and I invite the mother to place the child in such a way that, if the child should wish to handle the spatula, it is possible. Ordinarily a mother will understand what I am about, and it is easy for me gradually to describe to her that there is to be a period of time in which she and I will contribute as little as possible to the situation, so that what happens can fairly be put down to the child's account.

The normal sequence of events—and Winnicott considered significant any deviation—fell into three stages:

Stage 1. The baby puts his hand to the spatula, but at this moment discovers unexpectedly that the situation must be given thought. He is in a fix. Either with his hand resting on the spatula and his body quite still he looks at me and his mother with big eyes, and watches and waits, or, in certain cases, he withdraws interest completely and buries his face in the front of his mother's blouse. . . .

Stage 2. All the time, in 'the period of hesitation' (as I call it), the baby holds his body still (but not rigid). Gradually he becomes brave enough to let his feelings develop, and then the picture changes quite quickly. The moment at which this first phase changes into the second is evident, for the child's acceptance of the reality of desire is heralded by a change in the inside of the mouth, which becomes flabby, while the tongue looks thick and soft, and saliva flows copiously. Before long he puts the spatula into his mouth and is chewing it with his gums. . . . Instead of expectancy and stillness there now develops self-confidence, and there is free bodily movement, the latter related to manipulation of the spatula.

Stage 3. In the third stage the baby first of all drops the spatula as if by mistake. If it is restored he is pleased, plays with it again, and drops it once more, but this time less by mistake. On its being restored again, he drops it on purpose, and thoroughly enjoys aggressively getting rid of it, and is especially pleased when it makes a ringing sound on contact with the floor.

The theoretical discussion that followed sounded like a pastiche of Freud and Klein. Winnicott sounded like himself when he observed more closely and reflected further on what the infant did with the spatula:

The baby . . . seems to feel that the spatula is in his possession, perhaps in his power, certainly available for the purposes of self-expression. He bangs with it on the table or on a metal bowl which is nearby on the table, making as much noise as he can; or else he holds it to my mouth and to his mother's mouth, very pleased if we *pretend* to be fed by it. He definitely wishes us to *play* at being fed, and is upset if we should be so stupid as to take the thing into our mouths and spoil the game as a game.

At this point I might mention that I have never seen any evidence of a baby being disappointed that the spatula is, in fact, neither food nor a container of food.[129]

The spatula did not rank as a "transitional object," but the way it was appropriated and treated bore a family resemblance to that Winnicottian object—or concept—par excellence. His paper "Transitional Objects and Transitional Phenomena" was first presented in 1951 and attracted more attention than any of his others. Mention "transitional object" and a teddy bear springs to mind; in fact, the concept was more complex. "After a few months," Winnicott wrote, "infants of either sex become fond of playing with dolls, and . . . most mothers allow their infants some special object and expect them to become, as it were, addicted to such objects." Again:

Perhaps some soft object or other type of object has been found and used by the infant, and this then becomes what I am calling a *transitional object*. This object goes on being important. The parents get to know its value and carry it around when travelling. The mother lets it get dirty and even smelly, knowing that by washing it she introduces a break in continuity in the infant's experience, a break that may destroy the meaning and value of the object for the infant.[130]

Although transitional objects were apparently material things, Winnicott did not define them by shared physical characteristics. He defined them instead by their similar use. In his words, "What I am referring to . . . is not the cloth or the teddy bear that the baby uses—not so much the object used as the use of the object." Herewith the summary he provided:

1. The infant assumes rights over the object, and we agree to this assumption. Nevertheless some abrogation of omnipotence is a feature from the start.

2. The object is affectionately cuddled as well as excitedly loved and mutilated.

3. It must never change, unless changed by the infant.

4. It must survive instinctual loving, and also hating. . . .

5. Yet it must seem to the infant to give warmth, or to move, or to have texture, or to do something that seems to show it has vitality or reality of its own.

6. It comes from without from our point of view, but not so from the point of view of the baby. Neither does it come from within; it it not a hallucination.

7. . . . In the course of years it becomes not so much forgotten as relegated to limbo. . . . It is not forgotten and it is not mourned. It loses meaning.[131]

Of these seven items the sixth stood out as providing the key to why the object warranted the name "transitional." This item also required further elaboration, and that elaboration introduced another crucial Winnicottian term: "illusion," the cognitive outcome of the environment-mother's adaptation to her infant:

At some theoretical point early in the development of every human individual an infant in a certain setting provided by the mother is capable of conceiving the idea of something which would meet the growing need which arises out of instinctual tension. The infant cannot be said to know at first what is to be created. At this point in time the mother presents herself. In the ordinary way she gives her breast and her potential feeding urge. The mother's adaptation to the infant's needs, when good enough, gives the *illusion* that there is an external reality that corresponds to the infant's own capacity to create. In other words, there is an overlap between what the mother supplies and what the child might conceive of. To the observer the child perceives what the mother actually presents, but this is not the whole truth. The infant perceives the breast only in so far as a breast could be created just there and then.

It followed from the above that

of the transitional object it can be said that it is a matter of agreement between us and the baby that we will never ask the question 'Did you conceive of this or was it presented to you from without?' The important point is that no decision on this point is expected. The question is not to be formulated.[132]

Nor was it to be posed when play was involved. Like the area of transitional objects and their cousins, transitional phenomena (which were to be recognized by their transitional, not their phenomenal, character), that of play was neither inner psychic reality nor the external world:

Into this play area the child gathers objects or phenomena from external reality and uses them in the service of some sample derived from inner . . . reality. Without hallucinating the child puts out a sample of dream potential and lives with this sample in a chosen setting of fragments from external reality.

In Winnicott's view, to enter the realm of transitional phenomena, to become able to play, ranked as a crucial step in a patient's freeing himself from bondage to his inner world.[133]

When a patient becomes able to play (which Guntrip never did), a bit of the external world has proved malleable—with the suggestion that it is different from a coercive inner world. Its malleability has made the external inviting, and hence conducive to taking a first step from inner to outer. In this context, an analyst is not a transitional object, but it may be a good sign when he is treated as such.

━━ ━━ ━━ ━━ ━━

Gabrielle, affectionately nicknamed "Piggle," was two years and four months old when in January 1964 her parents brought her for a consultation. She was five years and two months at the last such session. There were in all only sixteen consultations. (Winnicott refused to define analysis in terms of the frequency and regularity of the sessions. Whether this kind of treatment "on demand"—he saw Gabrielle at her request—warranted the label "analysis" should be decided, he argued, on the basis of how the work was done.)[134] His case history consists of the record, not verbatim but reasonably complete, of those sixteen sessions, along with his annotations, and, in addition, letters from Gabrielle's parents. Taken together, the materials provide a picture of the child and how child and analyst worked together. Perhaps "played"—and with gusto—would be more apt. In Winnicott's judgment, "[I]t is not possible for a child this age to get meaning out of a game unless first of all the game is *played and enjoyed*."[135] And the analyst's own enjoyment is palpable.

What was the matter with Gabrielle? Her difficulties had begun after the birth of her sister, at a time when there was tension in the parents' marriage. By day, Gabrielle seemed not herself: listless and bored, unable to play, she insisted she was either mother or sister and talked in an artificial voice. Nights were worse: she scratched her face and couldn't sleep for fear of the "black mummy." According to the mother's account:

She [Gabrielle] has a black mummy and daddy. The black mummy comes after her at night and says: "Where are my yams?" (To yam = to eat. She pointed out her breasts, calling them yams. . . .) Sometimes she is put into the toilet by the black mummy. The black mummy, who lives in her tummy, and who can be talked to there on the telephone, is often ill, and difficult to make better.

The second strand of fantasy, which started earlier, is about the 'babacar.' Every night she calls, again and again, 'Tell me about the babacar, *all* about the babacar.' The black mummy and daddy are often in the babacar together, or some man alone. There is very occasionally a black Piggle in evidence.[136]

Before Gabrielle saw Winnicott for the first time, her mother told her that he knew "about babacars and black mummys." Winnicott was less sure, and at the end of the third consultation he penned the following comment:

Importance of my not *understanding* what she had not yet been able to give me clues for. Only she knew the answers, and when she could encompass the meaning of the fears she would make it possible for me to understand too.

In the third session Gabrielle had begun to act out those anxieties— and to allow Winnicott to participate. But when he played the Piggle frightened of the black mummy and the babacar, she started putting everything away and then proclaimed, "The babacar is all tidied up." "The dark," Winnicott noted, "was packed away, i.e., forgotten."[137] It had not been understood.

It was during the ninth session—the most dramatic of all—that Gabrielle unpacked the dark, though in earlier sessions there were hints that she would be able to do so. Shortly into the session she started telling him about the black mummy:

"She comes every night. I can't do anything. She's very difficult. She gets on my bed. She is not allowed to touch. 'No, this is my bed. I'm going to have it. I've got to sleep in it.' Daddy and mummy are in bed in another room. 'No, that's *my* bed. No! No! No! That's *my* bed.' "

Gabrielle continued:

"I don't know what's happening to me. Goodness I am being forced out of bed by the black mummy and I've got such a nice bed. 'No, Piggle you have't got a nice bed' " (here she was "in" an experience). " 'No, Piggle you haven't got a nice bed.' "

After an interval in the doldrums, Gabrielle went on:

"This is my bed so I can't go by train to Mr. Winnicott. No you don't want to go to Mr. Winnicott. He really does know about bad dreams. No he doesn't" (this was a conversation between herself and another part of herself). "He doesn't want me to get rid of her."

Winnicott interpreted and commented:

I talked about the black mummy as a dream, trying to make it quite clear to Gabrielle that the black mummy belongs to dreaming, and that upon waking there are the contrasting ideas of the black mummy and real people. The time had come when we could talk about dreams instead of an inner reality, delusionally "actual" inside.

Winnicott noted Gabrielle's intense anxiety. Still he pushed on, asking her about her dreams. She replied: "I dreamed she was dead. She wasn't there."

At this point she [Gabrielle] did something which I am sure had great significance, whatever it symbolized. I could tell this from the fact that the whole quality of the session altered. It was as if everything had been held back for this to happen. She took . . . [a] blue eyebath and put it in and out of her mouth, making sucking noises, and it could be said that she experienced something very near to a generalized orgasm.

Finally Gabrielle blurted out, "I loved her very much." With that, Winnicott said it was time to go. In his view, "anxiety had been overcome in some way during the hour."[138]

In what way? A striking shift was apparent: from being "in" an experience to being able to talk about it in dream terms. And in playing with that dream material—in actually sucking it—Gabrielle found the black mummy appetizing. Indeed she was a black mummy no longer; she had become a facet of her own mother. (As Winnicott put it, "black phenomena" had "become aspects of objects in the actual world external to herself, and separate from her.") Gabrielle could now say to her mother, as the latter reported, "You become a black mummy when you are cross."[139]

Dominated by the black mummy, Gabrielle had felt herself helpless—or not existing at all. The establishment of her sense of self, its emergence and consolidation, ran as a theme throughout the treatment. In the second consultation Gabrielle together with Winnicott— her father was conscripted into the game as well—acted out a variety of birth fantasies. (Early in the session Winnicott interpreted the babacar: "It was the mother's inside where the baby is born from." "The black inside," Gabrielle added.) When Gabrielle appeared on the doorstep for the sixth consultation, Winnicott, acting on clues from the previous session, said for the first time, "Hullo Gabrielle," rather than "Piggle." (She subsequently commented to her mother, "I wanted to tell Dr. Winnicott that my name is Gabrielle, but he knew it already.") In the seventh session she made a very careful toy arrangement:

There was a central S-shaped line of houses with a church at each end, and on her side there was herself and many objects representing herself. On the other side, i.e., on my side of the S-shaped line, was the tractor she had thrown at me and also myself and other objects. This was a not-me representation. It was an absolutely deliberate communication showing she had achieved this separation from me as part of the establishment of herself. It was also a defense against being reinvaded.[140]

And so it went, not in a straight line; there were swings, a forward movement, and then a loss of ground. In the fourteenth session Gabrielle invented a game that brought together ideas of birth and separation, and the fear and sorrow they provoked. Winnicott reported:

We kneel close together opposite each other. . . . She rolls it [a cylindrical ruler] to me and that kills me. I die and she hides. Then I come alive and I can't find her. . . .

By the time we had done it many times, and sometimes I was the one killing her, it became very clear that it had to do with sadness. For instance, if she killed me, then when I recovered I couldn't remember her. This was represented by her hiding, but I did eventually find her and then I said: "Oh I remember what it was I had forgotten." . . . Whoever was hiding had to leave a leg or something showing so that the agony of not being able to remember the lost person would not be prolonged or absolute. . . . Gradually the game altered by specializing in its hiding aspect. . . . Eventually it was fairly clear she was playing a game belonging to the idea of being born. . . .

I had to repeat a bursting out from under the curtains which seemed to be a kind of birth. Then I had to become a house, and she crept inside the house, rapidly becoming bigger until I could not contain her any longer and pushed her out. As the game developed, I said: "I hate you," as I pushed her out.

Gabrielle had put out a "sample of dream potential" and had played with it. In that play, Winnicott commented, she had gotten "in touch with the mother's need to be rid of the baby when it was too big." And she was quite ready to emerge; she was now aware of being herself and fully alive. "The session ended with a period in which she took the two curtains . . . and rushed backwards and forwards with them." "I am the wind," she said, "look out!"[141]

In the course of the treatment, how had Gabrielle used Winnicott? As "mender"; that was a notion she entertained in the thirteenth session just at the point when she was ready to take over that task from him. Then, in play, she reviewed the various roles she had assigned him. Winnicott interpreted: "Now the mending Winnicott and the cooking Winnicott have gone away, and there is another Winnicott, the teaching Winnicott. And then there is the play Winnicott." Gabrielle subsequently reminded herself, and him, of the "Dustbin Winnicott"— "a Winnicott that helps her get rid of what she has finished with."[142]

In the fifteenth session she made it clear that she had finished with him:

She took the father figure (about three inches long, very realistic, made on a basis of pipe-cleaner) and started to ill-treat it.

GABRIELLE: I'm twisting his legs (etc.).

ME: Ow! Ow! (as an interpretation of acceptance of the role assigned me).

GABRIELLE: I'm twisting him more—yes—his arm now.

ME: Ow!

GABRIELLE: Now his neck!

ME: Ow!

GABRIELLE: Now there's nothing left—he's all twisted up. I am going to twist you some more. You cry more.

ME: Ow! Ow! Ooooooo!

She was very pleased.

GABRIELLE: Now there's nothing left. It's all twisted up and his leg came off, and now his head has come off, so you can't cry. I'm throwing you right away. Nobody loves you. . . . Everyone hates you. . . .

In the middle of all this I said "So the Winnicott you invented was all yours and he's now finished with, and no one else can ever have him.". . .

GABRIELLE: Nobody will ever see you again. Are you a doctor?

ME: Yes, I am a doctor . . . , but the Winnicott that you invented is finished forever.

GABRIELLE: I made you.[143]

She made him; she destroyed him; he survived. "The subject," Winnicott wrote elsewhere, "says to the object, 'I destroyed you,' and the object is there to receive the communication. From now on the subject says: 'Hullo object!' 'I destroyed you.' 'I love you.' 'You have value for me because of your survival of my destruction of you.' "[144] The "subject" might have added: "You survived. You are not controlled by my thoughts. Hence you must exist in external reality." And that was how Gabrielle had come to perceive Winnicott:

There was a period at the end in which she got the feeling that she was staying a little longer than usual *simply because she liked being with me when she was not feeling frightened,* and when she was able to get pleasure and to express in a positive way her relationship to me as a person.[145]

Conclusion: Paradigms Transformed

CHAPTER 6

During the controversial discussions the British Psycho-Analytical Society grappled with theoretical disputes and failed to resolve the points at issue. Intransigence ruled when it came to theory; permissiveness, however, reigned when it came to patients. In the 1920s the British had been eager to include children in their patient population, and it was this eagerness that had made them so receptive to Melanie Klein. In the 1940s a number of analysts influenced by Klein insisted on extending the boundaries further to include psychotics; Winnicott, for one, considered that "there was no class of illness . . . impossible to analyse."[1] (To be sure there were individuals impossible to analyze.) Such catholicity did not so much betoken therapeutic optimism as point to a conviction that the consulting room was the heart of the psychoanalytic domain. What riveted the attention of the British in general, and of the protagonists of this study in particular, were clinical phenomena. What they felt compelled to account for was material produced in the consulting room, the more varied the better.

Along the way they transformed Freud's overarching paradigms. Of the two, developmental and structural, the developmental was initially and more consistently exploited. Here the work of Karl Abraham, whose premature death cut short any reckoning with Freud's structural hypothesis, had a telling effect. Here also Klein and Winnicott's focus on children made developmental language seem especially appropriate. Fairbairn alone dealt little, if at all, with children, and he alone consistently struggled with structural concepts.

At this point it may be useful to review the trio's transformations of Freudian paradigms as a series of steps, and to recall them in words that figured earlier in the text.

172

Melanie Klein made the first move in transforming libido theory:

As I see it, the boy's and girl's sexual and emotional development *from early infancy onwards* includes genital trends, which constitute the first stages of the inverted and positive Oedipus complex; they are experienced under the primacy of oral libido and mingle with urethral and anal desires and phantasies.[2]

Klein's long-standing contention that libidinal trends—and she considered them overlapping trends rather than neatly demarcated stages—interacted with oedipal tendencies from the earliest months of life meant reuniting aim and object. What Freud had sundered, Klein joined together again. And with that she arrived at one of her cardinal postulates, one that Anna Freud refused to accept: object relations existed from birth onward.[3]

Though aim and object were reunited, conceptually they remained distinct—and Klein continued her pursuit of the object. (As for "aim," she stuck with libido and aggression while emphasizing the latter.) In antedating superego formation, she took a second step. If that formation went hand in hand with oedipal experiences, it followed that object relations were not simply to external objects; they were to internal ones as well. (And because internal objects so obviously descended from the Freudian superego, this concept little by little lapsed as a focus of contention.)

In contrast, Fairbairn took off in pursuit of aim. He made a radical move when he transformed libido into "*the object-seeking principle*."[4] "The real libidinal aim," he claimed, was "the establishment of satisfactory relationships with objects."[5] Clearly "libido" had been shorn of its grossly sexual meaning, and it might have been better if Fairbairn had devised a different term. What he intended, after all, was to reconceptualize development: to replace sexuality with dependency. In his view what needed mapping was not infantile sexuality broken down into component instincts and erotogenic zones but infantile dependence and its transitions to mature dependence.

Fairbairn next took a comparatively short step: he linked his libido to Klein's internal objects and then maintained that persistent infantile dependency amounted to dependence on internal objects. Here he discerned Freud's primary identification and Klein's oral incorporation at work. Not until he elaborated his structural model of paired egos and objects did it become clear why Fairbairn expected to find evidence of both processes, why he assumed that an internal object might be confused with part of the ego and also be experienced as a foreign body.

What about external objects, more particularly mother, who, for all three protagonists of this study, in contrast to Freud, ranked as the external object par excellence? Though Freud, in replacing sexual seduction by sexual fantasy, had made early external object ties problematic (and they remained so ever after), no one was prepared to dismiss them out of hand. Not even Melanie Klein. Her views were merely asymmetrical: bad objects derived from a child's aggression, good objects from the external world: wicked mammas of whom "everything evil . . . was anticipated . . . differed fundamentally from the real objects";[6] fairy mammas—and good breasts—more closely approximated actual mothers who had been on hand in early infancy. Fairbairn did not waver: he regarded the real mother, not a mere fantasy, as central to development and psychopathology. Yet in the work of both Klein and Fairbairn, mother remained an elusive figure; as a concept, she was still, by and large, an empty box.

It was Winnicott who did most to fill in that box and, along the way, tried to convince Klein that the effort was worthwhile. As he wrote to Joan Riviere:

My trouble when I start to speak to Melanie about her statement of early infancy is that I feel as if I were talking about colour to the colour-blind. She simply says that she has not forgotten the mother and the part the mother plays, but in fact I find that she has shown no evidence of understanding the part the mother plays at the very beginning. I must say this quite boldly in spite of the fact that I have never been a mother and she, of course, has. . . .

The "good breast" is not a thing, it is a name given to a technique. It is the name given to the presentation of breast (or bottle) to the infant, a most delicate affair and one which can only be done well enough at the beginning, if the mother is in a most curious state of sensitivity. . . . Unless she can identify very closely with her infant at the beginning, she cannot "have a good breast," because just having the thing means nothing whatever to the infant.[7]

This theme, Winnicott thought, should be developed, and he attempted to do so with his notion of the environment mother and her adaptation. In his usage "adaptation" was not something demanded of the infant; it was the mother who, if "good-enough," did the adapting.

Had psychoanalytic theory come full circle? Had paternal seduction simply been replaced by maternal failure? The answer is no. Like Freud, Winnicott considered both sterile and uninformed the either-or fashion in which the nature-nurture debate was frequently framed—a debate in which Freud's seduction theory was commonly construed as a major argument for nurture and against nature. Indeed it was not to that debate that Winnicott hoped to contribute. What he intended, and accomplished, was to insist that the mother, whom Fairbairn epitomized in terms of treating, or failing to treat, her child as a person in his own right, should herself be regarded as a person in *her* own right. In short, the psychoanalytic domain now included two highly variable systems, and, as a consequence, a once simple and determinist account of etiology had become increasingly complex and approximate.

How did development leave an imprint or get encoded and hence continue to have influence? Such questions structural theory was supposed to address. Of this study's three protagonists, only Fairbairn systematically scrutinized structure, and only he directly challenged Freudian theory.

The first step he took was to replace what he referred to as impulse psychology with a psychology of dynamic structure. Fairbairn's proposal was simplicity itself: impulse, he maintained, should be thought of "as inseparable from structure and as representing" its dynamic character.[8] This notion of dynamic structure was liberating: it enabled Fairbairn to take for granted energy at work behind acceptance or rejection, avowal or disavowal; it enabled him tacitly to acknowledge that purposes, programs, and plans required for their actualization real physical energy driving specific causal mechanisms—but that purposes and mechanisms remained on two distinct conceptual levels.[9] In this fashion he freed object relations theory from the ghost of "energy," which nonetheless continued to haunt psychoanalytic ego psychology.

The next step Fairbairn took was to draw his own picture of endopsychic structure. Again it was a simple step: he moved to structure from the Kleinian notion of unconscious fantasy. In his written contribution to the controversial discussions he commented:

The concept of 'phantasy' is purely functional and can only be applied to activity on the part of the Ego. It is quite inadequate to describe inner situations involving the relationships of the Ego to internal objects possessing an endopsychic structure and dynamic qualities.[10]

In Fairbairn's view the ego and its internal objects, in contrast to fantasy, were entitled to structural status. Splits in the ego with such a status allowed him to depict mental states as encoded and thereby to assume their durability. At the same time, that status allowed him to represent intrapsychic conflict in hierarchical fashion. What emerged was mind with plans and subplans operating unbeknownst to one another and potentially in conflict.

In revising Freud's structural hypothesis, Fairbairn unwittingly resumed an enterprise with which Freud had grappled in the "Project" and subsequently abandoned: sorting out in systematic fashion the relations between psychoanalysis and neighboring scientific disciplines. Freud had looked to neurophysiology, and he had hoped that by modeling clinical phenomena, he might more easily specify assumptions that neurophysiology could one day confirm or at least make reasonable. Fairbairn was less explicit about signaling the relevance of neighboring psychological disciplines. His model, however, invited spelling out assumptions about mind that such disciplines—cognitive psychology being the closest neighbor—might justify or render plausible. What his work made clear was not only the desirability of this kind of enterprise but its feasibility as well.

A similar reorientation was implied in the metamorphosis of developmental theory. By different routes, all three protagonists of this study bumped up against the connection between psychoanalysis and biology of the evolutionary variety—and, *mutatis mutandis*, the connection between psychoanalysis and developmental psychology. From Fairbairn's writings, but not from Klein's and Winnicott's, a clear view emerged: although psychoanalysis might derive support from biology, the two constituted separate scientific domains. The obvious next imperative was to specify the nature of such support.

In sum the cumulative transformation of Freudian paradigms brought to the fore the possibility of replacing outmoded metatheory with background knowledge from related fields.

━━━ ━━━ ━━━ ━━━ ━━━

What about clinical practice? After all, the consulting room was the center of the psychoanalytic domain. In the 1940s, in the heat of controversy, the question of the relation between theory and practice or theory and technique had been sharply posed—and left in suspense. In that context James Strachey's position, his game attempt to sever "views on aetiology or theory" from "valid technique," made political sense—despite his failure to preserve a single teaching program.[11] Yet even someone as theoretically disinclined as Strachey would have acknowledged that psychoanalytic paradigms informed the analyst's understanding of what changes were occurring in his patient, or indeed, his belief that change was possible at all. It was the understanding of how analysis might bring about change, or how evolution might take place in the consulting room, that Winnicott and Fairbairn did so much to articulate and refine.

Of the trio, Winnicott made the greatest effort to describe the analytic environment, and in the process he compared that setting to mothering. Freud, he pointed out, had long ago grasped the family resemblance between the two: he had taken "for granted the early mothering situation . . . and . . . *it [had] turned up in his provision of a setting for his work*, almost without his being aware" of it. The analyst, like mother, "would be reliably there, on time, alive, breathing"; he "would keep awake and become preoccupied with the patient"; he would remain "free from temper tantrums, free from compulsive falling in love."[12] Beyond reliability and being reliably present, protection from impingement, provision of ego support, and, more generally, "holding" found a place in Winnicott's discussion of both mother and analyst. Once again, it was the analyst, in Winnicott's view, who should do the adapting; yet he insisted that such adaptation, such "corrective provision," was "never enough" for his "patients to get well."[13]

What, then, was necessary? Here the interests of Fairbairn and Winnicott converged. The latter would have endorsed Fairbairn's pithy comment about therapy:

Psychoanalytical treatment resolves itself into a struggle on the part of the patient to press-gang his relationship with the analyst into the closed system of the inner world . . . , and a determination on the part of the analyst to effect a breach in this closed system and to provide conditions under which . . . the patient may be induced to accept the open system of outer reality.[14]

Marion Milner's description of her patient Susan's inching toward autonomy captured the same drama in slightly different terms:

For Susan to achieve . . . this separating herself off from mother-me, claiming the right to be 'behind her eyes' . . . , claiming her own point of view which could not be identical with anyone else's, for her such an act of affirming and claiming her own privacy within her skin could be felt as an ultimate selfishness. . . . What she would not see, or only intellectually, was that in fact such an affirming . . . , far from cutting her off from people, would in fact become the only basis for a true relationship to them.[15]

What needed further elucidation—and Winnicott took up that task when he turned to transitions—was the moment when the patient moved in the direction of external reality, when confusion with a subjective object gave way to acceptance of the object's independent existence.

In the psychoanalytic universe, as opposed to the Darwinian, that change, that evolution, could be brought to consciousness—and by the same token, the analytic setting has proved a privileged locale for its investigation.

Notes

Preface

1. Phyllis Grosskurth, *Melanie Klein: Her World and Her Work* (New York: Knopf, 1986).
2. Jay R. Greenberg and Stephen A. Mitchell, *Object Relations in Psychoanalytic Theory* (Cambridge, Mass.: Harvard University Press, 1983).

Chapter 1. Reshaping the Psychoanalytic Domain

1. Ernest Jones, *The Life and Work of Sigmund Freud*, vol. 2, *Years of Maturity 1901–1919* (New York: Basic Books, 1955), pp. 152–153, and Ernest Jones, *Free Associations: Memories of a Psycho-Analyst* (New York: Basic Books, 1959), p. 227.
2. Freud to Jones, August 1, 1912, quoted in Jones, *Years of Maturity*, p. 153.
3. Freud to Eitingon, November 23, 1919, quoted ibid., p. 154.
4. Jones to Freud, June 25, 1913, quoted in Vincent Brome, *Ernest Jones: Freud's Alter Ego* (New York and London: Norton, 1983), p. 89.
5. Jones, *Free Associations*, pp. 229–231; see also Edward Glover, "Psychoanalysis in England," in Franz Alexander, Samuel Eisenstein, and Martin Grotjahn, eds., *Psychoanalytic Pioneers* (New York: Basic Books, 1966), pp. 535–536.
6. Jones, *Free Associations*, p. 230.
7. Pearl H. M. King, "The Contributions of Ernest Jones to the British Psycho-Analytical Society," *The International Journal of Psycho-Analysis* 60 (1979): 280–281.
8. Jones, *Free Associations*, pp. 41, 57, 58, 61.
9. On James Glover, see Ernest Jones, "James Glover: Obituary," *The International Journal of Psycho-Analysis* 8 (1927): 1–9; on Edward Glover, see Charles William Wahl, "Edward Glover: Theory of Technique," in Alexander, Eisenstein, and Grotjahn, *Psychoanalytic Pioneers*, pp. 501–507.
10. Sylvia Payne, in Training Committee Documents, British Psycho-Analytical Society, October 25, 1943. Institute of Psycho-Analysis, London.
11. James to Alix Strachey, December 29, 1924, *Bloomsbury/Freud: The Letters of James and Alix Strachey 1924–1925*, ed. Perry Meisel and Walter Kendrick (New York: Basic Books, 1985), p. 164.
12. James Strachey, "Joan Riviere: Obituary," *The International Journal of Psycho-Analysis* 44 (1963): 228.
13. Jones to Freud, January 21, 1921, quoted in Brome, *Ernest Jones*, p. 132.

14. Meisel and Kendrick, editors' introduction to *Bloomsbury/Freud,* p. 27.
15. James Strachey, "Jubilee dinner Speech. The British Psycho-Analytical Society: Fiftieth Anniversary," The British Psycho-Analytical Society, London, 1963 (unpublished), quoted in Gregorio Kohon, ed., *The British School of Psychoanalysis: The Independent Tradition* (London: Free Association Books, 1986), p. 47. See also D. W. Winnicott, "James Strachey: Obituary," *The International Journal of Psycho-Analysis* 50 (1969): 129–131, and M. Masud R. Khan, "Mrs Alix Strachey," *The International Journal of Psycho-Analysis* 54 (1973): 370.
16. Alix to James Strachey, February 9, 1925, *Bloomsbury/Freud,* p. 198.
17. On Ella Sharpe, see Sylvia M. Payne, "Ella Freeman Sharpe: Obituary," *The International Journal of Psycho-Analysis* 28 (1947): 54–56; Charles William Wahl, "Ella Freeman Sharpe: The Search for Empathy," in Alexander, Eisenstein, and Grotjahn, *Psychoanalytic Pioneers,* pp. 265–271; and Carol Netzer, "Annals of Psychoanalysis: Ella Freeman Sharpe," *Psychoanalytic Review* 69 (1982): 207–219. On Susan Isaacs, see John Rickman, "Susan Sutherland Isaacs: Obituary," *The International Journal of Psycho-Analysis* 31 (1950): 279–285; D. E. M. Gardner, *Susan Isaacs* (London: Methuen, 1969); and Elyse Levy, *Susan Isaacs: An Intellectual Biography* (Ann Arbor, Mich.: University Microfilms, 1977). On John Rickman, see Sylvia M. Payne, "Dr. John Rickman: Obituary," *The International Journal of Psycho-Analysis* 33 (1952): 54–60.
18. James Strachey, editor's note on Sigmund Freud, *The Question of Lay Analysis: Conversations with an Impartial Person* (1926), in *The Standard Edition of the Complete Psychological Works of Sigmund Freud,* translated under the general editorship of James Strachey (London: Hogarth, 1953–1974), 20:180.
19. Freud to Eitingon, September 27, 1926, quoted in Ernest Jones, *The Life and Work of Sigmund Freud,* vol. 3, *The Last Phase 1919–1939* (New York: Basic Books, 1957), p. 292.
20. Strachey, editor's note on Freud, *Question of Lay Analysis,* p. 180.
21. Freud, *Question of Lay Analysis,* pp. 248, 252.
22. Resolutions of the New York Psycho-Analytical Society, in International Psycho-Analytical Association, "Discussion on Lay Analysis," *The International Journal of Psycho-Analysis* 8 (1927): 283.
23. Freud, postscript (1927) to *Question of Lay Analysis,* p. 258.
24. A. A. Brill, in International Psycho-Analytical Association, "Discussion on Lay Analysis," p. 221.
25. C. P. Oberndorf, in International Psycho-Analytical Association, "Discussion on Lay Analysis," p. 206.
26. James to Alix Strachey, October 5, 1924, *Bloomsbury/Freud,* p. 79.
27. Ernest Jones, in International Psycho-Analytical Association, "Discussion on Lay Analysis," p. 188.
28. Ernest Jones, "The Future of Psycho-Analysis," *The International Journal of Psycho-Analysis* 17 (1936): 272.
29. Freud, *Question of Lay Analysis,* p. 240.
30. For Jones's reference to Klein, see Jones, in International Psycho-Analytical Association, "Discussion on Lay Analysis," p. 185. For his appreciative comments on his children's analyses, see Jones to Freud, May

16, 1927, quoted in Riccardo Steiner, "Some Thoughts about Tradition and Change Arising from an Examination of the British Psychoanalytical Society's Controversial Discussions (1943–1944)," *The International Review of Psycho-Analysis* 12 (1985): 30.

31. James to Alix Strachey, January 24, 1925, *Bloomsbury/Freud*, p. 187.
32. Freud, *Question of Lay Analysis*, pp. 228, 233 (emphasis in the original).
33. Ella Sharpe, in Training Committee Documents, October 25, 1943, Institute of Psycho-Analysis, London.
34. Susan Isaacs, in Extraordinary Business Meetings, British Psycho-Analytical Society, February 25, 1942, Institute of Psycho-Analysis, London.
35. Edward Glover, in Training Committee Documents, October 25, 1943, Institute of Psycho-Analysis, London.
36. Melanie Klein, "Autobiography," quoted in Grosskurth, *Melanie Klein*, p. 16.
37. Klein, "Autobiography," quoted ibid., p. 72. See also Ilse Grubich-Simitis, "Six Letters of Sigmund Freud and Sándor Ferenczi on the Interrelationship of Psychoanalytic Theory and Technique," *The International Review of Psycho-Analysis* 13 (1986): 259–277.
38. Klein, "Autobiography," quoted in Grosskurth, *Melanie Klein*, p. 74.
39. Jean-Michel Petot, *Melanie Klein, premières découvertes, premier système, 1919–1932* (Paris: Dunod, 1979), pp. 25–30, 35–66.
40. Sigmund Freud, "Analysis of a Phobia in a Five-Year-Old Boy" (1909), in *Standard Edition* 10:6.
41. Alix to James Strachey, February 11, 1925, *Bloomsbury/Freud*, p. 201.
42. Grosskurth, *Melanie Klein*, p. 95.
43. Alix to James Strachey, December 14, 1924, *Bloomsbury/Freud*, p. 145 (emphasis in the original); compare Alix to James Strachey, January 12, 1925, ibid., p. 182, and Alix to James Strachey, January 25, 1925, ibid., p. 188. For Abraham's appraisal of Klein, see Abraham to Freud, October 7, 1923, *A Psycho-Analytic Dialogue: The Letters of Sigmund Freud and Karl Abraham 1907–1926*, ed. Hilda C. Abraham and Ernest L. Freud, trans. Bernard Marsh and Hilda C. Abraham (New York: Basic Books, 1965), p. 339.
44. James to Alix Strachey, December 16, 1924, *Bloomsbury/Freud*, p. 147; James to Alix Strachey, January 8, 1925, ibid., p. 175; James to Alix Strachey, May 7, 1925, ibid., pp. 258–259.
45. Alix to James Strachey, January 12, 1924, ibid., p. 182.
46. Ferenczi to Freud, n.d., quoted in Grosskurth, *Melanie Klein*, p. 162.
47. Pearl H. M. King, "The Life and Work of Melanie Klein in the British Psycho-Analytical Society," *The International Journal of Psycho-Analysis* 64 (1983): 252.
48. Edward Glover, review of *The Psychoanalysis of Children*, by Melanie Klein, *The International Journal of Psycho-Analysis* 14 (1933): 119. For his views after his change of mind, see Edward Glover, "Examination of the Klein System of Child Psychology," *The Psychoanalytic Study of the Child* 1 (1945): 75–118.
49. Grosskurth, *Melanie Klein*, pp. 215, 219.
50. Melanie Klein, "Mourning and Its Relation to Manic-Depressive States" (1940), in *The Writings of Melanie Klein*, under the general editorship of

Roger Money-Kyrle, in collaboration with Betty Joseph, Edna O'Shaughnessy, and Hanna Segal (London: Hogarth, 1975), vol. 1, *Love, Guilt and Reparation and Other Works 1921–1945*, pp. 355, 361.

51. Eva Rosenfeld, interview with Pearl King, 1974, and Dr. William Gillespie, interview with Grosskurth, September 24, 1981, both quoted in Grosskurth, *Melanie Klein*, pp. 214, 242 (emphasis in the original). For Melitta's account, see Melitta Schmideberg, "A Contribution to the History of the Psycho-Analytic Movement in Britain," *British Journal of Psychiatry* 118 (1971): 61–68.

52. Pearl H. M. King, "Paula Heimann and the British Psychoanalytical Society," Scientific Bulletin, The British Psycho-Analytical Society, June 1983 (mimeo); see also Grosskurth, *Melanie Klein*, pp. 420–422.

53. D. W. Winnicott to Harry Guntrip, July 20, 1954, *The Spontaneous Gesture: Selected Letters of D. W. Winnicott*, ed. F. Robert Rodman (Cambridge, Mass.: Harvard University Press, 1987), p. 75. See also Harry Guntrip, "My Experience of Analysis with Fairbairn and Winnicott (How Complete a Result Does Psycho-Analytic Therapy Achieve?)," *The International Review of Psycho-Analysis* 2 (1975): 151, and D. W. Winnicott and M. Masud R. Khan, review of *Psychoanalytic Studies of the Personality*, by W. R. D. Fairbairn, *The International Journal of Psycho-Analysis* 34 (1953): 329–333.

54. W. Ronald D. Fairbairn, "Object-Relationships and Dynamic Structure," *The International Journal of Psycho-Analysis* 27 (1946): 36.

55. Dr. John D. Sutherland, interviews with Michael Dawson, March 31, 1981, and October 22, 1985, quoted in Michael Dawson, "W. R. D. Fairbairn: Relating His Work to His Life" (M.A. thesis, Harvard University, 1985), pp. 5–7.

56. W. Ronald D. Fairbairn, "Autobiographical Note," *The British Journal of Medical Psychology* 36 (1963): 107.

57. Dawson, "Fairbairn," p. 10.

58. Fairbairn, "Autobiographical Note," p. 107; see also John D. Sutherland, "W. R. D. Fairbairn: Obituary," *The International Journal of Psycho-Analysis* 46 (1965): 245.

59. Fairbairn, "Autobiographical Note," p. 107.

60. W. Ronald D. Fairbairn, *Psychoanalytic Studies of the Personality* (London: Tavistock and Routledge and Kegan Paul, 1952), p. 260.

61. Dr. John D. Sutherland, interview with the author, March 31, 1981.

62. Dr. John Bowlby, interview with Michael Dawson, November 12, 1984 (typescript generously provided to the author by Michael Dawson).

63. Sutherland, interview with the author, March 31, 1981; see also Sutherland, "Fairbairn: Obituary," pp. 245–246.

64. Bowlby, interview with Dawson, November 12, 1984.

65. Sutherland, interview with the author, October 22, 1985.

66. Controversial Series of Discussions, 1943–1944," British Psycho-Analytical Society, February 17, 1943, Institute of Psycho-Analysis, London.

67. Dr. Charles Rycroft, interview with Michael Dawson, November 1984, quoted in Dawson, "Fairbairn," p. 23.

68. Bowlby, interview with Dawson, November 12, 1984.

69. Susan Isaacs, in "Controversial Discussions," May 19, 1943, Institute of Psycho-Analysis, London.

70. Fairbairn, *Psychoanalytic Studies of the Personality*, p. 154.
71. Sutherland, interview with the author, March 31, 1981.
72. D. W. Winnicott to Michael Fordham, September 26, 1955, *Spontaneous Gesture*, p. 87.
73. D. W. Winnicott to Michael Balint, February 5, 1960, *Spontaneous Gesture*, pp. 127–128.
74. Dr. Martin James to D. W. Winnicott, December 6, 1961, Box 2 of D. W. Winnicott, Correspondence, Boxes 1–4, Archives of Psychiatry, New York Hospital–Cornell Medical Center; see also Charles Rycroft, *Psychoanalysis and Beyond* (London: Chatto and Windus and Hogarth, 1985), p. 141.
75. Rodman, editor's introduction to Winnicott, *Spontaneous Gesture*, p. xiii.
76. D. W. Winnicott, "Not Less Than Everything" (unpublished autobiographical notebook), quoted in Clare Winnicott, "D. W. W.: A Reflection," in Simon A. Grolnick and Leonard Barkin, eds., *Between Reality and Fantasy: Transitional Objects and Phenomena* (New York: Jason Aronson, 1978), pp. 23–24.
77. D. W. Winnicott to Katherine Whitehorn, September 23, 1966, Winnicott, Correspondence, Box 3.
78. D. W. Winnicott to a Confidant, April 15, 1966, *Spontaneous Gesture*, p. 155.
79. Clare Winnicott, "D. W. W.: A Reflection," pp. 24–28.
80. D. W. Winnicott, "Introduction on the Occasion of the 8th Ernest Jones Lecture" (undated), Winnicott, Correspondence, Box 1.
81. Alix to James Strachey, December 29, 1924, *Bloomsbury/Freud*, pp. 165–166.
82. Dr. John Padel, interview with the author, October 10, 1985; see also Grosskurth, *Melanie Klein*, p. 233.
83. Grosskurth, *Melanie Klein*, p. 396.
84. D. W. Winnicott, "A Personal View of the Kleinian Contribution" (1962), in his *The Maturational Processes and the Facilitating Environment: Studies in the Theory of Emotional Development* (London: Hogarth, 1965), pp. 172–173.
85. D. W. Winnicott to Donald Meltzer, October 25, 1966, *Spontaneous Gesture*, p. 160.
86. Winnicott, "Kleinian Contribution," p. 173.
87. Grosskurth, *Melanie Klein*, p. 400.
88. Dr. John Padel, interview with Grosskurth, December 8, 1981, quoted ibid., p. 399.
89. D. W. Winnicott to Adam Limentani, September 27, 1968, *Spontaneous Gesture*, p. 179.
90. William H. Gillespie, "Donald W. Winnicott: Obituary," *The International Journal of Psycho-Analysis* 52 (1971): 228.
91. Clare Winnicott, interview with the author, June 4, 1982; see also Grosskurth, *Melanie Klein*, pp. 451–453.
92. D. W. Winnicott, *The Piggle: An Account of the Psychoanalytic Treatment of a Little Girl* (New York: International Universities Press, 1977), p. 124.
93. D. W. Winnicott, "Not Less Than Everything," quoted in Clare Winnicott, "D. W. W.: A Reflection," p. 19.

184

94. Anna Freud, "Personal Memories of Ernest Jones," *The International Journal of Psycho-Analysis* 60 (1979): 286.
95. Grosskurth, *Melanie Klein,* p. 241. For slightly higher figures, see Kohon, *British School,* p. 40.
96. John Rickman, "Reflections on the Function and Organization of a Psychoanalytic Society," *The International Journal of Psycho-Analysis* 32 (1951): 236.
97. Klein, quoted by Clare Winnicott, interview with Grosskurth, September 18, 1981, quoted in Grosskurth, *Melanie Klein,* p. 241; see also Sylvia Payne to D. W. Winnicott, May 24, 1966, Winnicott, Correspondence, Box 4.
98. Anna Freud, "Personal Memories of Ernest Jones," p. 286.
99. Katherine Jones, Diary, September 19, 20, and 21, 1939, and Ernest Jones, interview with Lancelot Whyte, both quoted in Brome, *Ernest Jones,* p. 200.
100. Ernest Jones to Melanie Klein (1940), quoted in Grosskurth, *Melanie Klein,* p. 256.
101. On Anna Freud's career, see Raymond Dyer, *Her Father's Daughter: The Work of Anna Freud* (New York: Jason Aronson, 1983), and Uwe Henrik Peters, *Anna Freud: A Life Dedicated to Children* (New York: Schocken Books, 1985).
102. Jones to Freud, May 16, 1927; Freud to Jones, September 23, 1927; and Freud to Jones, October 9, 1927, quoted in Steiner, "Some Thoughts," pp. 30, 32, 35.
103. James Strachey to Edward Glover, April 1940, and Anna Freud, quoted in memorandum by Sylvia Payne, April 1940, both quoted in Grosskurth, *Melanie Klein,* pp. 256–257.
104. Susan Isaacs, in "Controversial Discussions," May 19, 1943, Institute of Psycho-Analysis; London; also quoted in Steiner, "Some Thoughts," p. 49.
105. Melanie Klein to Marjorie Brierley, June 1942, and memorandum by Melanie Klein, June 1942, both quoted in Grosskurth, *Melanie Klein,* pp. 313–314.
106. Grosskurth, *Melanie Klein,* p. 315; see also William Gillespie, review of *Klein,* by Hanna Segal, *The International Journal of Psycho-Analysis* 61 (1980): 85–88.
107. Edward Glover, in Scientific Meeting, British Psycho-Analytical Society, October 21, 1942, Institute of Psycho-Analysis, London.
108. Joan Riviere, general introduction to Melanie Klein, Paula Heimann, Susan Isaacs, and Joan Riviere, *Developments in Psycho-Analysis* (London: Hogarth, 1952), pp. 10–11.
109. On Marjorie Brierley, see Anne Hayman, "On Marjorie Brierley," *The International Review of Psycho-Analysis* 13 (1986): 383–392.
110. Anna Freud, in Scientific Meeting, October 21, 1942, Institute of Psycho-Analysis, London.
111. The exchange lectures were arranged by Ernest Jones and Paul Federn, and the following lectures were eventually published: Ernest Jones, "Early Female Sexuality," *The International Journal of Psycho-Analysis* 16 (1935): 263–273; Joan Riviere, "On the Genesis of Psychi-

cal Conflict in Earliest Infancy," *The International Journal of Psycho-Analysis* 17 (1936): 398–422; and Robert Waelder, "The Problem of the Genesis of Psychical Conflict in Earliest Infancy: Remarks on a Paper by Joan Riviere," *The International Journal of Psycho-Analysis* 18 (1937): 406–473.

112. Memorandum by James Strachey, February 24, 1943, Training Committee Documents, Institute of Psycho-Analysis, London (emphasis in the original).

113. Steiner, "Some Thoughts," p. 43.

114. Memorandum by Anna Freud, September 29, 1943, Training Committee Documents, Institute of Psycho-Analysis, London; also quoted in Steiner, "Some Thoughts," pp. 45–46.

115. Anna Freud, in Extraordinary Business Meetings, May 13, 1942, Institute of Psycho-Analysis, London; also quoted in Grosskurth, *Melanie Klein,* p. 303.

116. Pearl H. M. King, "The Education of a Psycho-Analyst," Scientific Bulletin, The British Psycho-Analytical Society, February 1981, pp. 1–20 (mimeo).

117. Extraordinary Business Meetings, February 2, 1944, and March 8, 1944, Institute of Psycho-Analysis, London.

118. Barbara Low, quoted in Grosskurth, *Melanie Klein,* p. 346.

119. Extraordinary Business Meetings, February 2, 1944, Institute of Psycho-Analysis, London.

120. King, "Melanie Klein," pp. 255–256, and Kohon, *British School,* pp. 44–45.

Chapter 2. Freudian Paradigms

1. Ilza Veith, *Hysteria: The History of a Disease* (Chicago: University of Chicago Press, 1965), p. 171.

2. Kenneth Levin, *Freud's Early Psychology of the Neuroses: A Historical Perspective* (Pittsburgh, Pa.: University of Pittsburgh Press, 1978), p. 21.

3. Ibid., p. 25. The most thorough and wide-ranging treatment of nineteenth-century psychiatry is Henri Ellenberger, *The Discovery of the Unconscious: The History and Evolution of Dynamic Psychiatry* (New York: Basic Books, 1970). See also Gregory Zilboorg, in collaboration with George W. Henry, *A History of Medical Psychology* (New York: Norton, 1941); Walter Riese, "The Neuropsychologic Phase in the History of Psychiatric Thought," in Iago Gladston, ed., *Historic Derivations of Modern Psychiatry* (New York: McGraw-Hill, 1967), pp. 75–137; Hannah S. Decker, *Freud in Germany: Revolution and Reaction in Science, 1893–1907,* Psychological Issues Monographs, no. 41 (New York: International Universities Press, 1977); and Francis Schiller, *A Möbius Strip: Fin-de-Siècle Neuropsychiatry and Paul Möbius* (Berkeley, Los Angeles, and London: University of California Press, 1982).

4. Levin, *Freud's Early Psychology,* p. 44. See also A. R. G. Owen, *Hysteria, Hypnosis and Healing: The Work of J.-M. Charcot* (London: Dennis Dobson, 1971).

5. American Psychiatric Association, *Diagnostic and Statistical Manual of Men-*

tal Disorders, 3d ed. (Washington, D.C.: American Psychiatric Association, 1980), p. 241.

6. Sigmund Freud, "Preface and Footnotes to the Translation of Charcot's *Tuesday Lectures*" (1892–1894), in *Standard Edition* 1:134.

7. Sigmund Freud, "Report on My Studies in Paris and Berlin" (1886), in *Standard Edition* 1:10–12.

8. Josef Breuer and Sigmund Freud, *Studies on Hysteria* (1895), in Freud, *Standard Edition* 2:258–259.

9. Among secondary works dealing with Freud's early writings, see Ola Andersson, *Studies in the Prehistory of Psychoanalysis: The Etiology of Psycho-neuroses and Some Related Themes in Sigmund Freud's Scientific Writings and Letters 1886–1896* (Norstedts, Sweden: Svenska Bokförlaget, 1962), and Walter A. Stewart, *Psychoanalysis: The First Ten Years 1888–1898* (New York: Macmillan, 1967).

10. Sigmund Freud, "The Neuro-Psychoses of Defence" (1894), in *Standard Edition* 3:47 (emphasis in the original).

11. Ibid., pp. 49, 51–52 (emphasis in the original).

12. Breuer and Freud, *Studies on Hysteria,* pp. 214, 216, 250.

13. Ibid., p. 286.

14. Freud, "Neuro-Psychoses of Defence," p. 53.

15. Freud to Fliess, November 29, 1895, *The Complete Letters of Sigmund Freud to Wilhelm Fliess 1887–1904,* trans. and ed. Jeffrey Moussaieff Masson (Cambridge, Mass.: Harvard University Press, 1985), p. 152.

16. James Strachey, editor's introduction to Sigmund Freud, "Project for a Scientific Psychology" (1895), in *Standard Edition* 1:290. See also Peter Amacher, *Freud's Neurological Education and Its Influence on Psychoanalytic Theory,* Psychological Issues Monographs, no. 16 (New York: International Universities Press, 1965), and Robert R. Holt, "A Review of Some of Freud's Biological Assumptions and Their Influence on His Theories," in Norman S. Greenfield and William C. Lewis, eds., *Psychoanalysis and Current Biological Thought* (Madison and Milwaukee: University of Wisconsin Press, 1965), pp. 93–124. For more recent work, see John Friedman and James Alexander, "Psychoanalysis and Natural Science: Freud's 1895 Project Revisited," *The International Review of Psycho-Analysis* 10 (1893): 303–318; Isabel F. Knight, "Freud's 'Project': A Theory for *Studies on Hysteria,*" *Journal of the History of the Behavioral Sciences* 20 (1984): 340–358; and Mark Solms and Michael Saling, "On Psychoanalysis and Neuroscience: Freud's Attitude to the Localizationist Tradition," *The International Journal of Psycho-Analysis* 67 (1986): 397–416.

17. In the past decade the "Project" has received scientific attention in its own right. Many of its concepts, it has been argued, anticipate those currently in circulation, and with the proper transmutations they could serve to forge a link—as Freud hoped long ago—between the phenomena of psychology and the mechanisms of neurophysiology. See Karl H. Pribram and Merton M. Gill, *Freud's 'Project' Reassessed: Preface to Contemporary Cognitive Theory and Neuropsychology* (New York: Basic Books, 1976). Among articles by Karl H. Pribram, see "The Neuropsychology of Sigmund Freud," in Arthur J. Bachrach, ed., *Experimental Foundations of Clinical Psychology* (New York: Basic Books, 1962), pp. 442–468; "Freud's

Project: An Open Biologically Based Model for Psychoanalysis," in Greenfield and Lewis, *Psychoanalysis and Current Biological Thought*, pp. 81–92; and "The Foundation of Psychoanalytic Theory: Freud's Neuropsychological Model," in Karl H. Pribram, ed., *Brain and Behavior*, vol. 4, *Adaptation* (Harmondsworth, England: Penguin Books, 1969), pp. 395–432.

18. See James Strachey, "Appendix C: The Nature of Q," in Freud, "Project," p. 393.
19. Pribram and Gill, *Freud's 'Project' Reassessed*, p. 32.
20. Freud, "Project," p. 298 (emphasis in the original).
21. Ibid., pp. 298, 299–300, 302.
22. Ibid., p. 323.
23. Pribram and Gill, *Freud's 'Project' Reassessed*, p. 80.
24. Freud, "Project," pp. 309–310, 311–312.
25. Ibid., p. 299.
26. Ibid., pp. 299–300 (emphasis in the original).
27. See Freud, "Project," pp. 351–353, 357–358.
28. Sigmund Freud, "Draft K—The Neuroses of Defense (A Christmas Fairy Tale)" (enclosed in Freud's letter to Fliess, January 1, 1896), in Freud, "Extracts from the Fliess Papers" (1892–1899), *Standard Edition* 1:222; also in *Complete Letters of Freud to Fliess*, p. 164.
29. Sigmund Freud, "Further Remarks on the Neuro-Psychoses of Defence" (1896), in *Standard Edition* 3:169 (emphasis in the original).
30. See Freud, "Project," p. 353.
31. Freud, "Draft K," p. 221; also in *Complete Letters of Freud to Fliess*, p. 163.
32. Freud to Fliess, Letter 69, September 21, 1897, "Extracts from the Fliess Papers," pp. 259–260; also in *Complete Letters of Freud to Fliess*, pp. 264–265. For a notorious, but unconvincing, account of Freud's abandonment of the seduction hypothesis, see Jeffrey Moussaieff Masson, *The Assault on Truth: Freud's Suppression of the Seduction Theory* (New York: Farrar, Straus, and Giroux, 1984).
33. James Strachey, "Notes on Some Technical Terms Whose Translation Calls for Comment," in Freud, *Standard Edition* 1:xxiv–xxv.
34. Sigmund Freud, "An Autobiographical Study" (1925), in *Standard Edition* 20:56–57.
35. Sigmund Freud, "Instincts and Their Vicissitudes" (1915), in *Standard Edition* 14:124.
36. Freud to Fliess, Letter 61, May 2, 1897, "Extracts from the Fliess Papers," p. 247 (emphasis in the original); also in *Complete Letters of Freud to Fliess*, p. 239.
37. For comments on erotogenic zones, see the following letters from Freud to Fliess: Letter 52, December 6, 1896, "Extracts from the Fliess Papers," p. 239; Letter 55, January 11, 1897, ibid., p. 241; and Letter 75, November 14, 1897, ibid., pp. 268–271; also in *Complete Letters of Freud to Fliess*, pp. 212, 223, 279–281.
38. Sigmund Freud, *Three Essays on the Theory of Sexuality* (1905), in *Standard Edition* 7:218–219.
39. For a useful discussion of late nineteenth-century research into sexuality, see Frank J. Sulloway, *Freud, Biologist of the Mind: Beyond the Psychoanalytic*

Legend (New York: Basic Books, 1979), pp. 134–319. See also Stephen Kern, "Freud and the Discovery of Child Sexuality," *History of Childhood Quarterly: The Journal of Psychohistory* 1 (1973): 117–141.

40. Albert Moll, *Untersuchungen über die Libido sexualis* (Berlin: Fischer's Medizinsche Buchhandlung, 1897); trans. and abridged by David Berger as *Libido Sexualis: Studies in the Psychosexual Laws of Love Verified by Clinical Sexual Case Histories* (New York: American Ethnological Press, 1933). For Freud's references to Moll, see Freud to Fliess, Letter 75, November 14, 1897, "Extracts from the Fliess Papers," p. 268 (also in *Complete Letters of Freud to Fliess*, p. 279), and *Three Essays*, pp. 169n, 180n.

41. Freud, *Three Essays*, p. 148.

42. Richard von Krafft-Ebing, *Psychopathia sexualis, mit besonderer Berücksichtigung der conträren Sexualempfindung. Eine medizinisch-gerichtliche Studie für Ärtze und Juristen,* 12th ed. (Stuttgart: F. Enke, 1903); trans. by Franklin S. Klaf as *Psychopathia Sexualis, With Especial Reference to the Antipathic Sexual Instinct: A Medico-Forensic Study* (New York: Bell, 1965).

43. Freud, *Three Essays*, p. 150.

44. Freud to Fliess, Letter 52, December 6, 1896, "Extracts from the Fliess Papers," p. 239; also in *Complete Letters of Freud to Fliess*, p. 212.

45. Freud, *Three Essays*, pp. 153, 183.

46. Ibid., pp. 155–156, 157, 158, 162 (emphasis in the original).

47. Ibid., pp. 179–180.

48. Ibid., pp. 181–182.

49. Sigmund Freud, *Introductory Lectures on Psycho-Analysis* (1916–1917), in *Standard Edition* 16:323–325.

50. For Fliess's influence on this conceptualization, see Sulloway, *Freud, Biologist of the Mind*, pp. 171–173.

51. See Sigmund Freud, "The Infantile Genital Organization: An Interpolation into the Theory of Sexuality" (1923), in *Standard Edition* 19:141–145.

52. Sigmund Freud, *New Introductory Lectures on Psycho-Analysis* (1933), in *Standard Edition* 22:98–99 (emphasis in the original).

53. Karl Abraham, "A Short Study of the Development of the Libido, Viewed in the Light of Mental Disorders" (1924), in his *Selected Papers of Karl Abraham,* trans. Douglas Bryan and Alix Strachey (London: Hogarth, 1927; reprint, London: Karnac, Maresfield Reprints, 1979), pp. 432, 450.

54. Freud to Fliess, Letter 46, May 30, 1896, "Extracts from the Fliess Papers," pp. 229–230; see also Letter 52, December 6, 1896, p. 237. Both of these are also in *Complete Letters of Freud to Fliess*, pp. 187–188, 210.

55. Karl Abraham, "Contribution to a Discussion on Tic" (1921), in *Selected Papers,* p. 325.

56. Sigmund Freud, "On the History of the Psycho-Analytic Movement" (1914), in *Standard Edition* 14:29.

57. Freud, *Introductory Lectures*, p. 341.

58. Ibid., pp. 340–341.

59. Ibid., p. 337.

60. Freud, *Three Essays*, p. 226n.

61. Ibid., p. 222.

62. Freud to Fliess, Letter 71, October 15, 1897, "Extracts from the Fliess Papers," p. 265; also published with a translation differing in phraseology but not in substance in *Complete Letters of Freud to Fliess*, p. 272.

Chapter 3. Melanie Klein

1. The best brief treatments of Melanie Klein's works are both by Hanna Segal: *Introduction to the Work of Melanie Klein,* enl. ed. (London: Hogarth, 1978), and *Melanie Klein* (New York: Viking, 1980).
2. *The Writings of Melanie Klein,* vol. 2, *The Psycho-Analysis of Children,* trans. Alix Strachey (London: Hogarth, 1975), p. 124.
3. Sigmund Freud, *Inhibitions, Symptoms and Anxiety* (1926), in *Standard Edition* 20:109.
4. Sigmund Freud, "Draft E—How Anxiety Originates" (undated), in "Extracts from the Fliess Papers, p. 191 (emphasis in the original); also in *Complete Letters of Freud to Fliess,* p. 79.
5. Freud, "Project," pp. 322, 358.
6. Freud, *Inhibitions, Symptoms and Anxiety,* p. 93.
7. Freud, *New Introductory Lectures,* p. 85.
8. Freud, *Inhibitions, Symptoms and Anxiety,* pp. 130, 135.
9. Freud, *New Introductory Lectures,* pp. 85–87.
10. Melanie Klein, "Criminal Tendencies in Normal Children" (1927), in *Love, Guilt and Reparation,* pp. 170–185.
11. Melanie Klein, "The Early Development of Conscience in the Child" (1933), in *Love, Guilt and Reparation,* p. 250. See also Melanie Klein, "On the Theory of Anxiety and Guilt" (1948), in *The Writings of Melanie Klein,* vol. 3, *Envy and Gratitude and Other works 1946–1963* (London: Hogarth, 1975), pp. 28–30. In the course of the British Society's controversial discussions Klein declared that "her conclusions did not stand or fall on the concept of the death instinct. Many colleagues had come to conclusions similar to hers without believing in the death instinct. She did not think the difference of opinion need affect later conclusions. It is known that aggression is stirred by frustration, and that the first frustration occurs at birth" ("Controversial Discussions," February 16, 1944, Institute of Psycho-Analysis, London).
12. Fantasy will be spelled with an *f,* despite the fact that in psychoanalytic literature it has been the practice—although it is now gradually eroding—to spell it with a *ph.*
13. Sigmund Freud, "Formulations on the Two Principles of Mental Functioning" (1911), in *Standard Edition* 12:218–219, 222 (emphasis in the original).
14. For a helpful discussion of Freud's writings on fantasy, see Joseph Sandler and Humberto Nagera, "Aspects of the Metapsychology of Fantasy," *The Psychoanalytic Study of the Child* 18 (1963): 159–194.
15. Freud, quoted in James Strachey, editor's note on Freud, "Instincts and Their Vicissitudes," in *Standard Edition* 14:112–113.
16. Susan Isaacs, "The Nature and Function of Phantasy," in Klein et al., *Developments in Psycho-Analysis,* p. 83.
17. Ibid., p. 93.

18. To the extent that Susan Isaacs retained the Freudian concept, she stripped it of its energetic referents: "The 'primary process' is . . . not to be regarded as governing the *whole* mental life of the child during any measurable period of development. It might conceivably occupy the main field for the first few days, but we must not overlook the first adaptations of the infant to his external environment, and the fact that both gratification and frustration are experienced from birth onwards" (Isaacs, "The Nature and Function of Phantasy," p. 97, emphasis in the original).

19. Ibid., p. 78.

20. Sándor Ferenczi, "Introjection and Transference" (1909), in his *First Contributions to Psycho-Analysis*, 2d. ed., trans. Ernest Jones (London: Hogarth, 1950), pp. 35–93.

21. Paula Heimann, "Certain Functions of Introjection and Projection in Early Infancy," in Klein et al., *Developments in Psycho-Analysis*, p. 125.

22. Sigmund Freud, "A Special Type of Choice of Object Made by Men" (1910), in *Standard Edition* 11:171.

23. Sigmund Freud, *The Ego and the Id* (1923), in *Standard Edition* 19:33.

24. Sigmund Freud, "From the History of an Infantile Neurosis" (1918), in *Standard Edition* 17:47.

25. Sigmund Freud, *Leonardo da Vinci and a Memory of His Childhood* (1910), in *Standard Edition* 11:96. See also Sigmund Freud, "Some Neurotic Mechanisms in Jealousy, Paranoia and Homosexuality" (1922), in *Standard Edition* 18:231.

26. Freud, *Leonardo da Vinci*, p. 99.

27. Freud, *New Introductory Lectures*, p. 113.

28. Sigmund Freud, "Female Sexuality" (1931), in *Standard Edition* 21:226, 228.

29. Freud, *New Introductory Lectures*, p. 121.

30. Ibid., pp. 124, 125.

31. Sigmund Freud, "Some Psychical Consequences of the Anatomical Distinction between the Sexes" (1925), in *Standard Edition* 19:256–257 (emphasis in the original).

32. Freud, *New Introductory Lectures*, p. 129.

33. Freud, "Female Sexuality," pp. 226, 236.

34. Melanie Klein, "The Oedipus Complex in the Light of Early Anxieties" (1945), in *Love, Guilt and Reparation*, p. 416 (emphasis in the original).

35. Klein, "Early Stages of the Oedipus Conflict" (1928), in *Love, Guilt and Reparation*, p. 186 (emphasis in the original).

36. Klein, *Psycho-Analysis of Children*, p. 239.

37. See Klein, "Oedipus Complex in the Light of Early Anxieties," pp. 416–417.

38. Klein, *Psycho-Analysis of Children*, p. 195.

39. Ibid., p. 196.

40. Klein, "Early Stages of the Oedipus Conflict," p. 192; see also Klein, *Psycho-Analysis of Children*, p. 217.

41. Klein, *Psycho-Analysis of Children*, pp. 196, 199.

42. Klein, "Oedipus Complex in the Light of Early Anxieties," p. 419.

43. Ibid., p. 411.

44. Klein, *Psycho-Analysis of Children*, p. 251.
45. Klein, "Oedipus Complex in the Light of Early Anxieties," p. 412.
46 Klein, *Psycho-Analysis of Children*, p. 250.
47. Freud, *The Ego and the Id*, p. 33.
48. Sigmund Freud, *Group Psychology and the Analysis of the Ego* (1921), in *Standard Edition* 18:106–109; see also Sigmund Freud, "Mourning and Melancholia" (1917), in *Standard Edition* 14:249.
49. Freud, *The Ego and the Id*, p. 34 (emphasis in the original).
50. Klein, "Early Development of Conscience in the Child," p. 251.
51. Klein, *Psycho-Analysis of Children*, p. 138.
52. Sigmund Freud, *Civilization and Its Discontents* (1930), in *Standard Edition* 21:130n.
53. Freud, *New Introductory Lectures*, p. 67.
54. Melanie Klein, contribution to "Symposium on Child Analysis" (1927), in *Love, Guilt and Reparation*, pp. 157–158. The complete "Symposium," by Klein, Joan Riviere, M. N. Searl, Ella F. Sharpe, Edward Glover, and Ernest Jones, was published in *The International Journal of Psycho-Analysis* 8 (1927): 331–391. All citations of Klein's contribution are to its republication in her *Love, Guilt and Reparation*.
55. Melanie Klein, "Personification in the Play of Children" (1929), in *Love, Guilt and Reparation*, pp. 203–205, and Klein, "Early Development of Conscience in the Child," p. 252; see also Klein, *Psycho-Analysis of Children*, pp. 151–152.
56. Melanie Klein, "The Origins of Transference" (1952), in *Envy and Gratitude*, p. 49.
57. Melanie Klein, "Mourning and Its Relation to Manic-Depressive States," p. 362.
58. See, for example, Roy Schafer, *Aspects of Internalization* (New York: International Universities Press, 1968).
59. Alix Strachey, "A Note on the Use of the Word 'Internal,' " *The International Journal of Psycho-Analysis* 22 (1941): 37.
60. *The Writings of Melanie Klein*, vol. 4, *Narrative of a Child Analysis* (London: Hogarth, 1975), p. 31; see also Klein, "Mourning and Its Relation to Manic-Depressive States," p. 365n.
61. Richard Wollheim, "The Mind and the Mind's Image of Itself," in his *On Art and the Mind: Essays and Lectures* (London: Allen Lane, 1973), p. 43.
62. Ella Sharpe and Susan Isaacs, in "Controversial Discussions," March 17, 1943, and May 19, 1943, Institute of Psycho-Analysis, London.
63. Marjorie Brierley, *Trends in Psycho-Analysis* (London: Hogarth, 1951) p. 72.
64. Schafer, *Aspects of Internalization*, pp. 138–139.
65. Melanie Klein, "A Contribution to the Psychogenesis of Manic-Depressive States" (1935), in *Love, Guilt and Reparation*, p. 275n; Klein *Psycho-Analysis of Children*, p. xiii; "Controversial Discussions," May 3, 1944, Institute of Psycho-Analysis, London.
66. Klein, "A Contribution to the Psychogenesis of Manic-Depressive States," pp. 262, 285.
67. Melanie Klein, "On Observing the Behaviour of Young Infants" (1952), in *Envy and Gratitude*, p. 117 n. 1.

68. See, for example, Klein, *Psycho-Analysis of Children,* p. xiii.
69. Klein, "A Contribution to the Psychogenesis of Manic-Depressive States," p. 264. Subsequently she made less sharp a distinction between relations to part objects and to whole objects; see Klein, "On the Theory of Anxiety and Guilt," pp. 35–36, and Melanie Klein, "Some Theoretical Conclusions Regarding the Emotional Life of the Infant" (1952), in *Envy and Gratitude,* p. 66n.
70. D. W. Winnicott, "The Depressive Position in Normal Emotional Development" (1954), in his *Collected Papers: Through Paediatrics to Psycho-Analysis* (London: Tavistock, 1958), p. 265.
71. Klein, "A Contribution to the Psychogenesis of Manic-Depressive States," p. 266.
72. Klein, "Mourning and Its Relation to Manic-Depressive States," pp. 350–351 (emphasis in the original).
73. Ibid., p. 349n.
74. Ibid., p. 368.
75. Ibid., p. 353.
76. Klein, *Psycho-Analysis of Children,* p. xiii.
77. Klein, "Mourning and Its Relation to Manic-Depressive States," p. 345.
78. Marjorie Brierley, in "Controversial Discussions," March 1, 1944, Institute of Psycho-Analysis, London.
79. Ibid., March 1, 1944.
80. Freud, "Analysis of a Phobia in a Five-Year-Old Boy," p. 5.
81. Freud, "History of an Infantile Neurosis," pp. 8–9.
82. H. von Hug-Hellmuth, "On the Technique of Child-Analysis," trans. R. Gabler and Barbara Low, *The International Journal of Psycho-Analysis* 2 (1921): 287–305.
83. Klein et al., "Symposium on Child-Analysis."
84. *The Writings of Anna Freud,* vol. 1, *Introduction to Psychoanalysis: Lectures for Child Analysts and Teachers 1922–1935* (New York: International Universities Press, 1965), p. 23.
85. Ibid., pp. 35–39.
86. Melanie Klein, "The Psychological Principles of Early Analysis" (1926), in *Love, Guilt and Reparation,* pp. 134–135.
87. Segal, *Melanie Klein,* p. 34.
88. Melanie Klein, "The Psycho-Analytic Play Technique: Its History and Significance" (1955), in *Envy and Gratitude,* pp. 126–127 (emphasis in the original).
89. A. Freud, *Introduction to Psychoanalysis,* pp. 37–38.
90. Klein, contribution to "Symposium on Child Analysis," p. 147.
91. Klein, *Psycho-Analysis of Children,* p. 8.
92. Sigmund Freud, "Fragment of an Analysis of a Case of Hysteria" (1905), in *Standard Edition* 7:116–118. See also Breuer and Freud, *Studies on Hysteria,* p. 303.
93. A. Freud, *Introduction to Psychoanalysis,* pp. 44–45.
94. Riviere, in Klein et al., "Symposium on Child-Analysis," p. 373.
95. Klein, contribution to "Symposium on Child-Analysis," p. 151.
96. On this point, Freud echoed his daughter; see S. Freud, *Question of Lay Analysis,* p. 215.

97. A. Freud, *Introduction to Psychoanalysis,* pp. 40–41, 50.

98. Klein, contribution to "Symposium on Child-Analysis," p. 167.

99. Klein, "Psycho-Analytic Play Technique," pp. 127–128, 132 (emphasis in the original).

100. Melanie Klein, "The Development of a Child" (1921), in *Love, Guilt and Reparation,* pp. 31, 32–33, 35.

101. Melanie Klein, "Early Analysis" (1923), in *Love, Guilt and Reparation,* pp. 96–97.

102. Melanie Klein, "The Importance of Symbol-Formation in the Development of the Ego" (1930), in *Love, Guilt and Reparation,* pp. 222, 224, 225, 228–229.

103. For Freud's best-known discussion of the primal scene, see "History of an Infantile Neurosis," p. 97.

104. Klein, "Importance of Symbol-Formation in the Development of the Ego," p. 219.

105. Sigmund Freud, "On Beginning the Treatment (Further Recommendations on the Technique of Psycho-Analysis I)" (1913), in *Standard Edition* 12:139–140.

106. For a discussion of the technical differences between Freudians and Kleinians, see Ralph R. Greenson, "Transference: Freud or Klein," and Herbert Rosenfeld, "A Discussion of the Paper by Ralph R. Greenson on 'Transference: Freud or Klein'," *The International Journal of Psycho-Analysis* 55 (1974): 37–48 and 49–51. For a review of changes in Kleinian technique, see Elizabeth Bott Spillius, "Some Developments from the Work of Melanie Klein," *The International Journal of Psycho-Analysis* 64 (1983): 324–327.

107. Klein, "Psycho-Analytic Play Technique," p. 123.

108. For an explicit statement of this principle, see Klein, *Narrative of a Child Analysis,* p. 193.

109. Klein, contribution to "Symposium on Child-Analysis," p. 148 (emphasis in the original).

110. Klein, *Psycho-Analysis of Children,* p. 16 and 16n.

111. Klein "Psycho-Analytic Play Technique," p. 130.

112. Klein, *Psycho-Analysis of Children,* p. 17. Klein stressed the technical point: "I always find out beforehand from the child's mother what special words the child uses for the genitals, excremental processes, etc., and adopt them in speaking of it" (*Psycho-Analysis of Children,* p. 17n).

113. Ibid., pp. 17–18.

114. Freud, "On Beginning the Treatment," p. 140.

115. Elliott Jaques, foreword to Klein, *Narrative of a Child Analysis.*

116. Sigmund Freud, "Recommendations to Physicians Practising Psycho-Analysis" (1912), in *Standard Edition* 12:113.

117. Klein, *Narrative of a Child Analysis,* p. 11.

118. Ibid., p. 18.

119. Donald Meltzer, *The Kleinian Development: Part II, Richard Week-by-Week* (Perthshire, Scotland: Clunie, 1978), p. 93.

120. Klein, *Narrative of a Child Analysis,* p. 13.

121. Ibid., pp. 13, 16–17.

122. Ibid., p. 15.

123. Ibid., p. 15.
124. Klein, *The Psycho-Analysis of Children*, p. 58.
125. Elisabeth R. Geleerd, evaluation of *Narrative of a Child Analysis*, by Melanie Klein, *The International Journal of Psycho-Analysis* 44 (1963): 500. See also Hanna Segal and Donald Meltzer, evaluation of *Narrative of a Child Analysis*, by Melanie Klein, *The International Journal of Psycho-Analysis* 44 (1963): 507–513.
126. Klein, *Narrative of a Child Analysis*, pp. 19–20.
127. Ibid., pp. 21–22 (emphasis in the original).
128. Klein, "Oedipus Complex in the Light of Early Anxieties," p. 373.
129. Klein, *Narrative of a Child Analysis*, pp. 196–197 (emphasis in the original).
130. Klein, "Oedipus Complex in the Light of Early Anxieties," p. 380.
131. Ibid., pp. 378, 380, 381 (emphasis in the original).
132. Klein, *Narrative of a Child Analysis*, pp. 127–129 (emphasis in the original).
133. Ibid., p. 130.
134. D. W. Winnicott, "On the Contribution of Direct Child Observation to Psycho-Analysis" (1957), in *Maturational Processes*, p. 112.
135. Freud, *Introductory Lectures on Psycho-Analysis*, p. 421; see also Sigmund Freud, "Psycho-Analytic Notes on an Autobiographical Account of a Case of Paranoia (Dementia Paranoides)" (1911), in *Standard Edition* 12:62.
136. Melanie Klein, "Notes on Some Schizoid Mechanisms" (1946), in *Envy and Gratitude*, p. 2.
137. Freud, *Introductory Lectures on Psycho-Analysis*, p. 447.
138. Klein, "Origins of Transference," pp. 53–54.
139. Freud, *Introductory Lectures on Psycho-Analysis*, p. 424; see also Sigmund Freud, "On Narcissism: An Introduction" (1914), in *Standard Edition* 14:74.
140. American Psychiatric Association, *Diagnostic and Statistical Manual*, pp. 315–317.
141. Klein, "Notes on Some Schizoid Mechanisms," p. 2n.
142. Ibid., p. 1.
143. Freud, "Notes on a Case of Paranoia," p. 75.
144. Ibid., p. 68.
145. Ibid., p. 70; Klein, "Notes on Some Schizoid Mechanisms," p. 23.
146. Klein, "Notes on Some Schizoid Mechanisms," p. 6.
147. Wollheim, "Mind and the Mind's Image of Itself," pp. 49–50.
148. See Klein, "Notes on Some Schizoid Mechanisms," p. 11.
149. Ibid., p. 21.
150. See Meltzer, *Richard Week-by-Week*, pp. 37–41.
151. Klein, "Notes on Some Schizoid Mechanisms," p. 6.
152. Sigmund Freud, *An Outline of Psycho-Analysis* (1940), in *Standard Edition* 23:203.
153. Sigmund Freud, "Splitting of the Ego in the Process of Defence" (1940), in *Standard Edition* 23:276.
154. Klein, "Notes on Some Schizoid Mechanisms," p. 10.

155. Melanie Klein, "Envy and Gratitude" (1957), in *Envy and Gratitude*, p. 183.
156. Ibid., p. 180.

Chapter 4. W. R. D. Fairbairn

1. Ernest Jones, preface to W. Ronald D. Fairbairn, *Psychoanalytic Studies of the Personality*, p. v.
2. Arnold H. Modell, "The Ego and the Id: Fifty Years Later," *The International Journal of Psycho-Analysis* 56 (1975): 57.
3. See Edward Bibring, "The Development and Problems of the Theory of the Instincts," *The International Journal of Psycho-Analysis* 22 (1941): 102–131.
4. See Abram Kardiner, *My Analysis with Freud: Reminiscences* (New York: Norton, 1977).
5. Bernard Apfelbaum, "On Ego Psychology: A Critique of the Structural Approach to Psycho-Analytic Theory," *The International Journal of Psycho-Analysis* 47 (1966): 451–475. See also Arnold Rothstein, *The Structural Hypothesis: An Evolutionary Perspective* (New York: International Universities Press, 1983).
6. James Strachey, editor's introduction to Freud, *The Ego and the Id*, in *Standard Edition* 19:7.
7. Freud, *The Ego and the Id*, p. 23.
8. Freud, *New Introductory Lectures*, p. 73.
9. Ibid., p. 72.
10. See above, "Mind: Psychological Speculation," the second section of chapter 2.
11. Freud, *New Introductory Lectures*, p. 77.
12. Freud, *Outline of Psycho-Analysis*, pp. 145–146 (emphasis in the original).
13. Freud, *The Ego and the Id*, p. 44.
14. Heinz Hartmann, "Comments on the Psychoanalytic Theory of the Ego" (1950), in his *Essays on Ego Psychology: Selected Problems in Psychoanalytic Theory* (New York: International Universities Press, 1964), p. 128.
15. Heinz Hartmann, "Notes on the Theory of Sublimation" (1955), in *Essays on Ego Psychology*, p. 228.
16. Hartmann, "Psychoanalytic Theory of the Ego," p. 130.
17. Heinz Hartmann, *Ego Psychology and the Problem of Adaptation* (1939), trans. David Rapaport (New York: International Universities Press, 1958).
18. Hartmann, "Psychoanalytic Theory of the Ego," p. 130.
19. Heinz Hartmann, "The Mutual Influences in the Development of the Ego and Id" (1952), in *Essays on Ego Psychology*, p. 177.
20. Freud, *New Introductory Lectures*, p. 80.
21. Hartmann, *Ego Psychology and the Problem of Adaptation*, p. 5.
22. See Allan D. Rosenblatt and James T. Thickstun, "A Study of the Concept of Psychic Energy," *The International Journal of Psycho-Analysis* 51 (1970): 265–278. See also Judith M. Hughes, "Psychoanalysis as a General Psychology, Revisited," paper presented at the 75th Anniversary

Meeting of the American Psychoanalytic Association, Washington D.C., May 9, 1986.

23. H. Stuart Hughes, *The Sea Change: The Migration of Social Thought 1930–1965* (New York: Harper and Row, 1975), pp. 201–217.

24. Freud, *New Introductory Lectures,* p. 64.

25. Freud, *The Ego and the Id,* p. 48.

26. Ibid., p. 34.

27. Ibid., p. 53.

28. On psychoanalysis and single-subject research, see Marshall Edelson, *Hypothesis and Evidence in Psychoanalysis* (Chicago and London: University of Chicago Press, 1984).

29. W. R. D. Fairbairn, "Fundamental Principles of Psychoanalysis," *Edinburgh Medical Journal* 36 (1929): 329–345.

30. Sutherland, interview with the author, March 31, 1981.

31. Fairbairn, *Psychoanalytic Studies of the Personality,* p. 154.

32. Ibid., pp. 31, 137, 138 (emphasis in the original).

33. Michael Balint, "Pleasure, Object and Libido: Some Reflexions on Fairbairn's Modification of Psychoanalytic Theory," *The British Journal of Medical Psychology* 29 (1956): 163.

34. W. Ronald D. Fairbairn, "Observations in Defence of the Object-Relations Theory of the Personality," *The British Journal of Medical Psychology* 28 (1955): 145 (emphasis in the original).

35. Fairbairn, *Psychoanalytic Studies of the Personality,* pp. 140, 157.

36. Freud, *Three Essays,* p. 182.

37. Fairbairn, *Psychoanalytic Studies of the Personality,* p. 33.

38. Ibid., pp. 80n, 260–261, 266.

39. Ibid., pp. 261–262, 264.

40. Ibid., p. 33.

41. Ibid., p. 35.

42. Ibid., pp. 32, 34 (emphasis in the original).

43. See Freud, *The Ego and the Id,* p. 29.

44. Fairbairn, *Psychoanalytic Studies of the Personality,* p. 42 (emphasis in the original).

45. Ibid., p. 35 (emphasis in the original).

46. Ibid., p. 120.

47. Ibid., p. 121.

48. Ibid., p. 124 (emphasis in the original).

49. Ibid., p. 122.

50. Ibid., p. 122.

51. Ibid., p. 37.

52. Ibid., p. 124.

53. Klein, "Notes on Some Schizoid Mechanisms," p. 3.

54. Stephen A. Mitchell, "The Origin and Nature of the 'Object' in the Theories of Klein and Fairbairn," *Contemporary Psychoanalysis* 17 (1981): 379, 381, 384.

55. Fairbairn, *Psychoanalytic Studies of the Personality,* pp. 55–56.

56. Ibid., pp. 55, 56.

57. Ibid., pp. 17–18, 23.

58. Ibid., p. 56.

59. Morris N. Eagle, *Recent Developments in Psychoanalysis: A Critical Evaluation* (New York: McGraw Hill, 1984), p. 86.
60. W. Ronald D. Fairbairn, "A Critical Evaluation of Certain Basic Psycho-Analytical Conceptions," *The British Journal for the Philosophy of Science* 7 (1956): 53. For evidence of Fairbairn's interest in ethology, see Fairbairn, "Object-Relationships and Dynamic Structure," p. 32, and Fairbairn, *Psychoanalytic Studies of the Personality*, pp. 140–141; compare John Bowlby, *Attachment and Loss*, vol. 1, *Attachment* (New York: Basic Books, 1969), part 2.
61. Guntrip, "Analysis with Fairbairn and Winnicott," p. 146.
62. Harry Guntrip, "First Training Analysis, with W. R. D. Fairbairn" n.d., p. 4, The Menninger Foundation, Topeka, Kansas.
63. Harry Guntrip, "Psychoanalytical Autobiography (A Study of the 'Dream Process' over Thirty-Six Years, Showing the Effects of an Amnesia for an Infancy Trauma)," n.d., p. 1, The Menninger Foundation, Topeka, Kansas.
64. Guntrip, "Analysis with Fairbairn and Winnicott," p. 154.
65. Ibid., p. 149.
66. Guntrip, "Psychoanalytical Autobiography," p. 47.
67. Ibid., p. 38.
68. Guntrip, "Analysis with Fairbairn and Winnicott," p. 148 (emphasis in the original).
69. Guntrip, "Psychoanalytical Autobiography," pp. 39, 294, 342–343.
70. Ibid., pp. 340–341.
71. Guntrip, "Analysis with Fairbairn and Winnicott," pp. 148, 151.
72. Guntrip, "Training Analysis," p. 284, with, as an attachment, letter from Fairbairn to Guntrip, June 27, 1956.
73. Guntrip, "Analysis with Fairbairn and Winnicott," p. 147.
74. Guntrip, "Training Analysis," pp. 138, 234 (emphasis in the original).
75. W. Ronald D. Fairbairn, "Observations on the Nature of Hysterical States," *The British Journal of Medical Psychology* 27 (1954): 114.
76. Guntrip, "Training Analysis," pp. 263–264.
77. W. Ronald D. Fairbairn, "Considerations Arising Out of the Schreber Case," *The British Journal of Medical Psychology* 29 (1956): 113–127.
78. Guntrip, "Training Analysis," pp. 364, 366.
79. Guntrip, "Analysis with Fairbairn and Winnicott," pp. 146–147. See also Henriette T. Glatzer and William N. Evans, "On Guntrip's Analysis with Fairbairn and Winnicott," *International Journal of Psychoanalytic Psychotherapy* 6 (1977): 95, and Otto F. Kernberg, *Internal World and External Reality: Object Relations Theory Applied* (New York and London: Jason Aronson, 1980), p. 59.
80. Fairbairn, quoted in Guntrip, "Analysis with Fairbairn and Winnicott," p. 147.
81. Ibid., p. 148.
82. Guntrip, "Training Analysis," p. 16.
83. Fairbairn, quoted ibid., pp. 38, 43, 101.
84. Fairbairn, quoted ibid., p. 79 (emphasis in the original).
85. Ibid., p. 80.
86. Ibid., p. 245 (emphasis in the original).

87. Ibid., p. 322.
88. Ibid., p. 337.
89. Ibid., pp. 337, 338.
90. Ibid., p. 349.
91. See ibid., pp. 334–335, 344.
92. In Guntrip's view, losing Fairbairn would represent the death of his brother, and he "would be left with a full scale eruption of that traumatic event, and no one to help" him with it. (Guntrip, "Analysis with Fairbairn and Winnicott," p. 151; see also Guntrip, "Training Analysis," p. 402).
93. W. Ronald D. Fairbairn, "On the Nature and Aims of Psycho-Analytical Treatment," *The International Journal of Psycho-Analysis* 39 (1958): 381, 385.
94. See Harry Guntrip, *Personality Structure and Human Interaction: The Developing Synthesis of Psychodynamic Theory* (London: Hogarth, 1961).
95. See Hartmann, "Psychoanalytic Theory of the Ego," p. 127.
96. Fairbairn, *Psychoanalytic Studies of the Personality,* pp. 88, 119, 150.
97. Ibid., p. 88.
98. Ibid., p. 106.
99. Eagle, *Recent Developments in Psychoanalysis,* p. 83.
100. Fairbairn, *Psychoanalytic Studies of the Personality,* pp. 89–90.
101. Ibid., pp. 95, 99.
102. Ibid., pp. 100–101, 133; see also Fairbairn, "Nature of Hysterical States," p. 108n.
103. Fairbairn, *Psychoanalytic Studies of the Personality,* pp. 115–116.
104. Ibid., pp. 116–117.
105. Ibid., pp. 109, 169.
106. Ibid., p. 109.
107. Ibid., pp. 110–111; compare p. 93n.
108. Ibid., pp. 134–135 (emphasis in the original).
109. See Richard L. Rubens, "The Meaning of Structure in Fairbairn," *The International Review of Psycho-Analysis* 11 (1984): 438.
110. Fairbairn, *Psychoanalytic Studies of the Personality,* p. 130.
111. Ibid., p. 107.
112. Ibid., pp. 66, 178–179 (emphasis in the original).
113. Ibid., pp. 106–107.
114. Ibid., p. 129.

Chapter 5. D. W. Winnicott

1. For reports on his wartime work, see D. W. Winnicott, *The Child and the Outside World: Studies in Developing Relationships* (London: Tavistock, 1957), and D. W. Winnicott, *Deprivation and Delinquency* (London: Tavistock, 1984).
2. D. W. Winnicott, preface to *Collected Papers,* p. ix.
3. D. W. Winnicott, "Ego Integration in Child Development" (1962), in *Maturational Processes,* p. 54.
4. D. W. Winnicott, "Ego Distortion in Terms of True and False Self" (1960), in *Maturational Processes,* p. 141.
5. D. W. Winnicott, *Playing and Reality* (London: Tavistock, 1971), p. 101.

6. D. W. Winnicott, *Therapeutic Consultations in Child Psychiatry* (London: Hogarth, 1971).

7. Ibid., pp. 4–5.

8. Ibid., p. 3.

9. Ibid., pp. 85, 86.

10. Ibid., pp. 68–69, 70, 72.

11. Ibid., pp. 77, 78–79, 81, 82.

12. Ibid., pp. 82, 86.

13. Ibid., p. 83.

14. Ibid., p. 86.

15. D. W. Winnicott, *The Child and the Family: First Relationships* (London: Tavistock, 1957), p. 141.

16. D. W. Winnicott. *Clinical Notes on Disorders of Childhood* (London: William Heinemann, 1931), p. 126.

17. D. W. Winnicott to Donald Meltzer, October 25, 1966, *Spontaneous Gesture*, p. 159.

18. D. W. Winnicott, "Envy and Jealousy," Scientific Bulletin, The British Psycho-Analytic Society 29 (1969): 1 (mimeo).

19. D. W. Winnicott, "Primary Maternal Preoccupation" (1956), in *Collected Papers*, p. 302.

20. Ibid., pp. 302, 304.

21. D. W. Winnicott, "The Theory of the Parent-Infant Relationship" (1960), in *Maturational Processes*, p. 54.

22. Ibid., pp. 50–51, 53–54.

23. D. W. Winnicott, *The Child, the Family, and the Outside World* (Harmondsworth; England: Penguin, 1964), p. 88.

24. Sigmund Freud, "Formulations on the Two Principles of Mental Functioning," p. 220n.

25. D. W. Winnicott, "The Development of the Capacity for Concern" (1963), in *Maturational Processes*, p. 75.

26. Winnicott, "Ego Integration in Child Development," p. 47.

27. D. W. Winnicott, "The Capacity to Be Alone" (1958), in *Maturational Processes*, pp. 30, 32.

28. Winnicott, "Depressive Position in Normal Emotional Development," pp. 267–268.

29. D. W. Winnicott, "Mind and Its Relation to the Psyche-Soma" (1949), in *Collected Papers*, p. 246; see also Winnicott, "Ego Integration in Child Development," p. 50.

30. See, for example, D. W. Winnicott, "Primitive Emotional Development" (1945), in *Collected Papers*, p. 145; Winnicott, "Mind and Its Relation to the Psyche-Soma," p. 245; and Winnicott, "Ego Distortion in Terms of True and False Self," p. 141.

31. Freud, *New Introductory Lectures*, p. 77.

32. Winnicott, "Ego Integration in Child Development," pp. 56, 60; Winnicott, "Mind and Its Relation to the Psyche-Soma," p. 244.

33. Winnicott, "Mind and Its Relation to the Psyche-Soma," p. 246.

34. Ibid., pp. 245–247.

35. D. W. Winnicott, "Psychoses and Child Care" (1952), in *Collected Papers*, p. 226.

36. Winnicott, "Ego Distortion in Terms of True and False Self," p. 148.
37. D. W. Winnicott, "Communicating and Not Communicating Leading to a Study of Certain Opposites" (1963), in *Maturational Processes,* p. 187.
38. Guntrip, *Personality Structure and Human Interaction,* pp. 412–413; see also Stephen J. Morse, "Structure and Reconstruction: A Critical Comparison of Michael Balint and D. W. Winnicott," *The International Journal of Psycho-Analysis* 53 (1972): 487–500; John D. Sutherland, "The British Object Relations Theorists: Balint, Winnicott, Fairbairn, Guntrip," *Journal of the American Psychoanalytic Association* 28 (1980): 829–860; and John Padel, "Ego in Current Thinking," *The International Review of Psycho-Analysis* 12 (1985): 273–282.
39. In an initial attempt to join his work to that of Freud and Klein, Winnicott divided cases of mental disorder into three rough categories: neurotic, depressive, and borderline-psychotic. This division suggests, as Greenberg and Mitchell have observed, that for Winnicott, "Freud was right with respect to neurosis, Klein was right with respect to depressives," but that he reserved for himself "the relatively unexplored area of psychotic and borderline-psychotic phenomena" (Greenberg and Mitchell, *Object Relations,* p. 208). By the mid-1950s Winnicott had reduced the number of categories to two: neurotics, who scarcely figured as ill, and the rest, now conceptualized in terms of a false self. He had "come to use the false self concept as a single diagnostic principle, representing a continuum of psychopathology from psychotic states, in which the false self has collapsed, to nearly healthy states, in which the false self mediates selectively and sparingly between the true self and the outside world" (ibid.).
40. Winnicott, "Ego Distortion in Terms of True and False Self," p. 151.
41. Winnicott, *Therapeutic Consultations in Child Psychiatry,* p. 239.
42. Ibid., pp. 240–241.
43. Ibid., pp. 265, 268.
44. Ibid., p. 243.
45. Ibid., pp. 244, 249, 250.
46. Ibid., p. 251.
47. Ibid., pp. 252–253, 263.
48. Ibid., pp. 260, 262.
49. Ibid., pp. 262–263; D. W. Winnicott, "Withdrawal and Regression" (1954), in *Collected Papers,* p. 261.
50. Winnicott, *Therapeutic Consultations in Child Psychiatry,* p. 265.
51. Winnicott, "Primary Maternal Preoccupation," pp. 302–303.
52. Winnicott, "Ego Distortion in Terms of True and False Self," p. 141.
53. D. W. Winnicott, "Metapsychological and Clinical Aspects of Regression within the Psycho-Analytical Set-Up" (1954), in *Collected Papers,* p. 285.
54. Freud, "On Beginning the Treatment," p. 134.
55. Fairbairn, "On the Nature and Aims of Psycho-Analytical Treatment," pp. 378, 379.
56. Guntrip, "Analysis with Fairbairn and Winnicott," p. 149.
57. Winnicott, "Metapsychological and Clinical Aspects of Regression," pp. 284, 285–286 (emphasis in the original).

58. D. W. Winnicott, "Birth Memories, Birth Trauma, and Anxiety" (1949), in *Collected Papers*, p. 192.

59. D. W. Winnicott, "The Aims of Psycho-Analytical Treatment" (1962), in *Maturational Processes*, p. 167.

60. D. W. Winnicott, "Dependence in Infant-Care, in Child-Care, and in the Psycho-Analytic Setting" (1963), in *Maturational Processes*, pp. 249–250 (emphasis in the original).

61. Winnicott, "Withdrawal and Regression," p. 261.

62. See Sigmund Freud, "Observations on Transference-Love (Further Recommendations on the Technique of Psycho-Analysis III)" (1915), in *Standard Edition* 12:170, and Sigmund Freud, "On the History of the Psycho-Analytic Movement" (1914), in *Standard Edition* 14:10.

63. Winnicott, "Birth Memories, Birth Trauma, and Anxiety," p. 181, and Winnicott, "Metapsychological and Clinical Aspects of Regression," p. 293.

64. Winnicott, "Metapsychological and Clinical Aspects of Regression," p. 281.

65. Ibid., pp. 281–282 (emphasis in the original).

66. Ibid., p. 281.

67. Ibid., pp. 290–291, 293; see also D. W. Winnicott, Clinical Papers, file 1869, Archives of Psychiatry, New York Hospital–Cornell Medical Center.

68. D. W. Winnicott, *Holding and Interpretation: Fragment of an Analysis* (London: Hogarth, 1986), p. 19.

69. Winnicott, "Withdrawal and Regression," pp. 255–257 (emphasis in the original).

70. Winnicott, Clinical Papers, file 1869.

71. Winnicott, "Withdrawal and Regression," p. 257.

72. Winnicott, Clinical Papers, file 1869.

73. Winnicott, "Withdrawal and Regression," p. 257.

74. Winnicott, "Dependence in Infant-Care," p. 258 (emphasis in the original).

75. Winnicott, Clinical Papers, file 1869.

76. Winnicott, *Holding and Interpretation*, pp. 69–70.

77. Winnicott, *The Child, the Family, and the Outside World*, p. 114.

78. Ibid., p. 115.

79. Winnicott, *Holding and Interpretation*, pp. 98, 165.

80. Ibid., p. 75–76.

81. Ibid., pp. 184–185.

82. D. W. Winnicott, foreword to Marion Milner, *The Hands of the Living God: An Account of a Psycho-Analytic Treatment* (London: Hogarth, 1969), pp. ix–x; Milner, *Hands of the Living God*, pp. xxi–xxii.

83. Milner, *Hands of the Living God*, pp. xxix, xx–xxi, 240.

84. Ibid., pp. 30, 81.

85. Ibid., p. 40.

86. Marion Milner, "The Role of Illusion in Symbol Formation," in Melanie Klein, Paula Heimann, and R. E. Money-Kyrle, eds., *New Directions in Psycho-Analysis: The Significance of Infant Conflict in the Pattern of Adult Behaviour* (London: Tavistock, 1955), p. 91.

87. Milner, *Hands of the Living God,* pp. 40, 242.
88. Ibid., pp. xxx–xxxi.
89. Marion Milner, letter to the author, April 8, 1986.
90. Winnicott, Clinical Papers, file 470.
91. Milner, *Hands of the Living God,* p. 3.
92. Ibid., pp. 58–60, 367.
93. Winnicott, Clinical Papers, file 470.
94. Marion Milner, interview with the author, May 27, 1982.
95. Milner, *Hands of the Living God,* pp. 235, 386–387.
96. Milner, interview with the author, May 27, 1982.
97. Winnicott, Clinical Papers, file 470.
98. Milner, interview with the author, May 27, 1982.
99. Milner, *Hands of the Living God,* p. 5.
100. Ibid., p. 4.
101. Ibid., pp. 5, 8.
102. Ibid., pp. xxix, 7.
103. Winnicott, Clinical Papers, file 470.
104. Milner, *Hands of the Living God,* pp. 9, 258.
105. Ibid., p. xix.
106. Ibid., p. 239.
107. Ibid., pp. 250–252, 253.
108. Ibid., pp. 42, 49, 50.
109. Ibid., pp. 45–46, 52–53.
110. Ibid., p. 252.
111. Ibid., pp. 111, 200, 258.
112. Ibid., p. 257.
113. Ibid., pp. 208, 223, 291.
114. Ibid., pp. 284–285, 296, 299, 302.
115. Ibid., pp. 304, 324, 355, 356.
116. Ibid., pp. 328, 354–356.
117. Ibid., pp. 373, 404.
118. Ibid., pp. 376, 396.
119. Guntrip, "Training Analysis," p. 332.
120. Guntrip, "Analysis with Fairbairn and Winnicott," pp. 146, 151, 152.
121. Winnicott, quoted ibid., p. 152.
122. Dr. John Padel, interview with the author, October 10, 1985. See also Michael Eigen, "Guntrip's Analysis with Winnicott: A Critique of Glatzer and Evans," *Contemporary Psychoanalysis* 17 (1981): 103–117.
123. Winnicott, quoted in Guntrip, "Analysis with Fairbairn and Winnicott," pp. 152–153.
124. Ibid., pp. 153–154 (emphasis in the original).
125. Harry Guntrip, "Fairbairn Re-Examined in Historical Perspective (The Development of Personal 'Object Relations' Theory)" n.d., The Menninger Foundation, Topeka, Kansas.
126. Winnicott, "Depressive Position in Normal Emotional Development," p. 276.
127. Winnicott, *Playing and Reality,* pp. 88–89; see also Winnicott, "Communicating and Not Communicating," pp. 180–181.
128. Fairbairn, "On the Nature and Aims of Psycho-Analytical Treatment," p. 385.

129. D. W. Winnicott, "The Observation of Infants in a Set Situation" (1941), in *Collected Papers,* pp. 52–54 (emphasis in the original).
130. Winnicott, *Playing and Reality,* pp. 1, 4 (emphasis in the original).
131. Ibid., pp. xi–xii, 5.
132. Ibid., pp. 11–12 (emphasis in the original).
133. Ibid., pp. 51, 54.
134. Ishak Ramzy, editor's foreword to Winnicott, *The Piggle,* p. xv.
135. Winnicott, *The Piggle,* p. 175 (emphasis in the original).
136. Ibid., pp. 6–7 (emphasis in the original).
137. Ibid., pp. 7, 47–48 (emphasis in the original).
138. Ibid., pp. 113–114, 116–118 (emphasis in the original).
139. Ibid., pp. 96, 119.
140. Ibid., pp. 24, 77, 84, 91.
141. Ibid., pp. 182–184.
142. Ibid., pp. 174–175.
143. Ibid., pp. 188–190. See also Margaret I. Little, "Winnicott Working in Areas Where Psychotic Anxieties Predominate: A Personal Record," *Free Associations: Psychoanalysis, Groups, Politics, Culture* 3 (1985): 36.
144. Winnicott, *Playing and Reality,* p. 90.
145. Winnicott, *The Piggle,* p. 176 (emphasis in the original).

Chapter 6. Conclusion: Paradigms Transformed

1. Little, "Winnicott Working in Areas Where Psychotic Anxieties Predominate," p. 39.
2. Klein, "Oedipus Complex in the Light of Early Anxieties," p. 416 (emphasis in the original).
3. "Controversial Discussions," April 7, 1943, Institute of Psycho-Analysis, London. See also John Bowlby, "The Nature of the Child's Tie to His Mother," *The International Journal of Psycho-Analysis* 39 (1958): 350–373.
4. Fairbairn, "Observations in Defence of the Object-Relations Theory of the Personality," p. 145 (emphasis in the original).
5. Fairbairn, *Psychoanalytic Studies of the Personality,* p. 138.
6. Klein, contribution to "Symposium on Child Analysis," p. 157.
7. D. W. Winnicott to Joan Riviere, *Spontaneous Gesture,* February 3, 1956, pp. 95–96.
8. Fairbairn, *Psychoanalytic Studies of the Personality,* p. 119.
9. Compare Margaret A. Boden, *Purposive Explanation in Psychology* (Cambridge, Mass.: Harvard University Press, 1972), pp. 194–198, 281–290.
10. Fairbairn, in "Controversial Discussions," February 17, 1943, Institute of Psycho-Analysis, London; see also Fairbairn, *Psychoanalytic Studies of the Personality,* p. 154.
11. Memorandum by James Strachey, February 24, 1943, in Training Committee Documents, Institute of Psycho-Analysis, London.
12. Winnicott, "Metapsychological and Clinical Aspects of Regression," pp. 284–285 (emphasis in the original).
13. Winnicott, "Dependence in Infant-Care," p. 258.
14. Fairbairn, "On the Nature and Aims of Psycho-Analytical Treatment," p. 385.
15. Milner, *Hands of the Living God,* p. 272.

Bibliography

ABENHEIMER, KARL. "Critical Observations on Fairbairn's Theory of Object-Relations." *The British Journal of Medical Psychology* 28 (1955): 29–41.
ABRAHAM, HILDA C., and ERNEST L. FREUD, eds. *A Psycho-Analytic Dialogue: The Letters of Sigmund Freud and Karl Abraham 1907–1926.* Translated by Bernard Marsh and Hilda C. Abraham. New York: Basic Books, 1965.
ABRAHAM, KARL. The works listed below are in *Selected Papers of Karl Abraham*, translated by Douglas Bryan and Alix Strachey. London: Hogarth, 1927. (Reprint. London: Karnac, Maresfield Reprints, 1979.)
———. "The Psycho-Sexual Differences between Hysteria and Dementia Praecox" (1908).
———. "Hysterical Dream States" (1910).
———. "Notes on the Psycho-Analytical Investigation and Treatment of Manic-Depressive Insanity and Allied Conditions" (1911).
———. "The First Pregenital Stage of the Libido" (1916).
———. "Ejacultio Praecox" (1917).
———. "A Particular Form of Neurotic Resistance Against the Psycho-Analytic Method" (1919).
———. "Manifestations of the Female Castration Complex" (1920).
———. "The Narcissistic Evaluation of Excretory Processes in Dreams and Neurosis" (1920).
———. "Contribution to a Discussion on Tic" (1921).
———. "Contribution to the Theory of the Anal Character" (1921).
———. "An Infantile Theory of the Origin of the Female Sex" (1923).
———. "The Influence of Oral Erotism on Character Formation" (1924).
———. "A Short Study of the Development of the Libido, Viewed in the Light of Mental Disorders" (1924).
———. "Character-Formation on the Genital Level of the Libido" (1925).
———. "An Infantile Sexual Theory Not Hitherto Noted" (1925).
ACHINSTEIN, PETER, and STEPHEN F. BARKER, eds. *The Legacy of Logical Positivism: Studies in the Philosophy of Science.* Baltimore, Md.: Johns Hopkins University Press, 1969.
ACKERKNECHT, ERWIN H. *A Short History of Psychiatry.* 2d ed. Translated by Sula Wolff. New York and London: Hafner, 1968.

ALEXANDER, F. G., and S. T. SELESNICK. *The History of Psychiatry: An Evaluation of Psychiatric Thought and Practice from Prehistoric Times to the Present.* New York: Harper and Row, 1966.

AMACHER, PETER. *Freud's Neurological Education and Its Influence on Psychoanalytic Theory.* Psychological Issues Monographs, no. 16. New York: International Universities Press, 1965.

————. "The Concepts of the Pleasure Principle and Infantile Erogenous Zones Shaped by Freud's Neurological Education." *The Psychoanalytic Quarterly* 43 (1974): 341–362.

American Psychiatric Association. *Diagnostic and Statistical Manual of Mental Disorders.* 3d ed. Washington, D.C.: American Psychiatric Association, 1980.

ANDERSSON, OLA. *Studies in the Prehistory of Psychoanalysis: The Etiology of Psychoneuroses and Some Related Themes in Sigmund Freud's Scientific Writings and Letters 1886–1896.* Norstedts, Sweden: Svenska Bokförlaget, 1962.

ANZIEU, DIDIER. "Comment devient-on Melanie Klein?" *Nouvelle Revue de Psychanalyse* 26 (1982): 235–251.

ANZIEU, DIDIER; J.-B. PONTALIS; and GUY ROSOLATO. "A propos du texte de Guntrip." *Nouvelle Revue de Psychanalyse* 15 (1977): 29–37.

APFELBAUM, BERNARD. "On Ego Psychology: A Critique of the Structural Approach to Psycho-Analytic Theory." *The International Journal of Psycho-Analysis* 47 (1966): 451–475.

ARDEN, MARGARET. " 'A Concept of Femininity': Sylvia Payne's 1935 Paper Reassessed." *The International Review of Psycho-Analysis* 14 (1987): 237–244.

ARLOW, JACOB A., and CHARLES BRENNER. *Psychoanalytic Concepts and the Structural Theory.* New York: International Universities Press, 1964.

AYALA, FRANCISCO JOSÉ, and THEODOSIUS DOBZHANSKY, eds. *Studies in the Philosophy of Biology: Reduction and Related Problems.* Berkeley, Los Angeles, London: University of California Press, 1974.

BACAL, HOWARD A. "British Object-Relations Theorists and Self-Psychology: Some Critical Reflections." *The International Journal of Psycho-Analysis* 68 (1987): 87–98.

BALINT, MICHAEL. *Primary Love and Psycho-Analytic Technique.* London: Hogarth, 1952. (Reprint. London: Karnac, Maresfield Library, 1985.)

————. "Pleasure, Object and Libido: Some Reflexions on Fairbairn's Modification of Psychoanalytic Theory." *The British Journal of Medical Psychology* 29 (1956): 162–167.

————. "The Concepts of Subject and Object in Psychoanalysis." *The British Journal of Medical Psychology* 31 (1958): 83–91.

————. *Thrills and Regressions.* London: Hogarth; New York: International Universities Press, 1959.

————. *The Basic Fault: Therapeutic Aspects of Regression.* London: Tavistock, 1968.

BECKNER, MORTON. *The Biological Way of Thought.* Berkeley and Los Angeles: University of California Press, 1968.

BELLAK, L., ed. *Contemporary European Psychiatry.* New York: Grove, 1961.

BERES, DAVID. "Structure and Function in Psycho-Analysis." *The International Journal of Psycho-Analysis* 46 (1965): 53–63.

BERES, DAVID, and EDWARD D. JOSEPH. "The Concept of Mental Representation in Psychoanalysis." *The International Journal of Psycho-Analysis* 51 (1970): 1–9.

BETTELHEIM, BRUNO. *Freud and Man's Soul.* New York: Knopf, 1982.

BIBRING, EDWARD. "The Development and Problems of the Theory of the Instincts." *The International Journal of Psycho-Analysis* 22 (1941): 102–131.

―――. "The So-Called English School of Psychoanalysis." *The Psychoanalytic Quarterly* 16 (1947): 69–93.

BION, W. R. "Notes on the Theory of Schizophrenia." *The International Journal of Psycho-Analysis* 35 (1954): 113–118.

―――. "Differentiation of the Psychotic from the Non-Psychotic Personalities." *The International Journal of Psycho-Analysis* 38 (1957): 266–275.

―――. "A Theory of Thinking." *The International Journal of Psycho-Analysis* 43 (1962): 306–310.

BODEN, MARGARET A. *Purposive Explanation in Psychology.* Cambridge, Mass.: Harvard University Press, 1972.

BOWLBY, JOHN. "The Nature of the Child's Tie to His Mother." *The International Journal of Psycho-Analysis* 39 (1958): 350–373.

―――. "Psycho-Analysis and Child Care." In *Psychoanalysis and Contemporary Thought,* edited by John D. Sutherland. London: Hogarth, 1958.

―――. "Separation Anxiety." *The International Journal of Psycho-Analysis* 41 (1960): 89–113.

―――. "Symposium on Psycho-Analysis and Ethology. II. Ethology and the Development of Object Relations." *The International Journal of Psycho-Analysis* 41 (1960): 313–317.

―――. "Separation Anxiety: A Critical Review of the Literature." *Journal of Child Psychology and Psychiatry* 1 (1961): 251–265.

―――. *Attachment and Loss.* Vol. 1, *Attachment.* New York: Basic Books, 1969.

―――. *Attachment and Loss.* Vol. 2, *Separation: Anxiety and Anger.* New York: Basic Books, 1973.

―――. *Attachment and Loss.* Vol. 3, *Loss: Sadness and Depression.* New York: Basic Books, 1980.

―――. "Psychoanalysis as a Natural Science." *The International Review of Psycho-Analysis* 3 (1981): 243–256.

BREUER, JOSEF, and SIGMUND FREUD. "On the Psychical Mechanism of Hysterical Phenomena: Preliminary Communication" (1893). In *Standard Edition,* vol. 2. *See* Freud.

―――. *Studies on Hysteria* (1895). In *Standard Edition,* vol. 2. *See* Freud.

BRIERLEY, MARJORIE. "Some Problems of Integration in Women." *The International Journal of Psycho-Analysis* 13 (1932): 433–448.

―――. *Trends in Psycho-Analysis.* London: Hogarth, 1951.

BROME, VINCENT. *Freud and His Early Circle: The Struggles of Psycho-Analysis.* London: Heinemann, 1967.

―――. *Ernest Jones: Freud's Alter Ego.* New York and London: Norton, 1983.

BROWN, J. A. C. *Freud and the Post-Freudians.* Harmondsworth, England: Penguin Books, 1961.

BRY, ILSE, and ALFRED H. RIFKIN. "Freud and the History of Ideas: Primary Sources, 1886–1910." In *Psychoanalytic Education. Science and Psychoanalysis,* edited by J. Masserman, vol. 5. New York: Grune and Stratton, 1962.

CLANCIER, ANNE, and JEANNINE KALMANOVITCH, *Winnicott and Paradox: From Birth to Creation.* Translated by Alan Sheridan. London: Tavistock, 1987.

CLARK, RONALD W. *Freud: The Man and the Cause.* London: Jonathan Cape and Weidenfeld and Nicolson; New York: Random House, 1980.

CRANEFIELD, PAUL F. "Freud and the 'School of Helmholtz.'" *Gesnerus* 23 (1966): 35–39.

D'AMORE, ARCANGELO R. T. "Ernest Jones: Founder of the American Psychoanalytic Association." *The International Journal of Psycho-Analysis* 60 (1979): 287–290.

DAVIS, MADELEINE. "The Writing of D. W. Winnicott." *The International Review of Psycho-Analysis* 14 (1987): 491–502.

DAVIS, MADELEINE, and DAVID WALLBRIDGE. *Boundary and Space: An Introduction to the Work of D. W. Winnicott.* London: Karnac, 1981.

DAWSON, MICHAEL. "W. R. D. Fairbairn: Relating His Work to His Life." Master's thesis, Harvard University, 1985.

DECKER, HANNAH S. *Freud in Germany: Revolution and Reaction in Science, 1893– 1907.* Psychological Issues Monographs, no. 41. New York: International Universities Press, 1977.

DICKS, HENRY V. "Object Relations Theory and Marital Studies." *The British Journal of Medical Psychology* 36 (1963): 125–129.

DREVER, JAMES. *Instincts in Man: A Contribution to the Psychology of Education.* 2d ed. Cambridge: Cambridge University Press, 1921.

DYER, RAYMOND. *Her Father's Daughter: The Work of Anna Freud.* New York: Jason Aronson, 1983.

EAGLE, MORRIS N. "Interests as Object Relations." *Psychoanalysis and Contemporary Thought* 4 (1981): 527–565.

———. *Recent Developments in Psychoanalysis: A Critical Evaluation.* New York: McGraw Hill, 1984.

EDELSON, MARSHALL. *Hypothesis and Evidence in Psychoanalysis.* Chicago and London: University of Chicago Press, 1984.

EIGEN, MICHAEL. "Guntrip's Analysis with Winnicott: A Critique of Glatzer and Evans." *Contemporary Psychoanalysis* 17 (1981): 103–117.

EISSLER, KURT R. *Medical Orthodoxy and the Future of Psychoanalysis.* New York: International Universities Press, 1965.

ELLENBERGER, HENRI. *The Discovery of the Unconscious: The History and Evolution of Dynamic Psychiatry.* New York: Basic Books, 1970.

ERDELYI, M. H. *Psychoanalysis: Freud's Cognitive Science.* New York: Freeman, 1985.

EZRIEL, HENRY. "The Scientific Testing of Psycho-Analytic Findings and Theory." *The British Journal of Medical Psychology* 24 (1951): 30–34.

FAIRBAIRN, W. RONALD D. "Fundamental Principles of Psychoanalysis." *Edinburgh Medical Journal* 36 (1929): 329–345.

———. "Prolegomena to a Psychology of Art." *The British Journal of Psychology* 28 (1937–1938): 288–303.

———. "The Ultimate Basis of Aesthetic Experience." *The British Journal of Psychology* 29 (1938–1939): 167–181.

———. "Is Aggression an Irreducible Factor?" *The British Journal of Medical Psychology* 18 (1939): 163–170.

————. "Object-Relationships and Dynamic Structure." *The International Journal of Psycho-Analysis* 27 (1946): 30–37.

————. Review of *On Not Being Able to Paint*, by Joanna Field. *The British Journal of Medical Psychology* 24 (1951): 69–72.

————. *Psychoanalytic Studies of the Personality.* London: Tavistock and Routledge and Kegan Paul, 1952.

————. "Theoretical and Experimental Aspects of Psycho-Analysis." *The British Journal of Medical Psychology* 25 (1952): 122–127.

————. Review of *Psychoanalytic Explorations in Art*, by Ernst Kris. *The British Journal of Medical Psychology* 26 (1953): 164–169.

————. "Observations on the Nature of Hysterical States." *The British Journal of Medical Psychology* 27 (1954): 105–125.

————. "Observations in Defence of the Object-Relations Theory of the Personality." *The British Journal of Medical Psychology* 28 (1955): 144–156.

————. Considerations Arising Out of the Schreber Case." *The British Journal of Medical Psychology* 29 (1956): 113–127.

————. "A Critical Evaluation of Certain Basic Psycho-Analytical Conceptions." *The British Journal for the Philosophy of Science* 7 (1956): 49–60.

————. "Freud, the Psycho-Analytical Method and Mental Health." *The British Journal of Medical Psychology* 30 (1957): 53–62.

————. "On the Nature and Aims of Psycho-Analytical Treatment." *The International Journal of Psycho-Analysis* 39 (1958): 374–385.

————. "Autobiographical Note." *The British Journal of Medical Psychology* 36 (1963): 107.

————. "Synopsis of an Object-Relations Theory of the Personality." *The International Journal of Psycho-Analysis* 44 (1963): 224–225.

Farrell, B. A. *The Standing of Psychoanalysis.* Oxford: Oxford University Press, 1981.

Fenichel, Otto. *The Psychoanalytic Theory of Neurosis.* New York: Norton, 1945.

Ferenczi, Sándor. The works listed below are, as indicated, in one of these two volumes: *First Contributions to Psycho-Analysis*, 2d ed., by Sándor Ferenczi, translated by Ernest Jones. London: Hogarth, 1950. *Further Contributions to the Theory and Technique of Psycho-Analysis*, 2d ed., by Sándor Ferenczi, compiled by John Rickman and translated by Jane Isabel Suttie. London: Hogarth, 1950.

————. "Introjection and Transference" (1909). In *First Contributions*.

————. "Stages in the Development of the Sense of Reality" (1913). In *First Contributions*.

————. "Psycho-Analytic Observations on Tic" (1921). In *Further Contributions*.

————. "Psycho-Analysis of Sexual Habits" (1925). In *Further Contributions*.

————. "The Problem of Acceptance of Unpleasant Ideas" (1926). In *Further Contributions*.

First, Elsa. "The Good Doctor." Review of *The Piggle: An Account of the Psychoanalytic Treatment of a Little Girl*, by D. W. Winnicott. *The New York Review of Books*, August 17, 1978, pp. 32–36.

Flew, Antony. "Transitional Objects and Transitional Phenomena: Comments and Interpretations." In *Between Reality and Fantasy: Transitional Objects and Phenomena*, edited by Simon A. Grolnick and Leonard Barkin. New York: Jason Aronson, 1978.

FLÜGEL, J. C. "Clothes Symbolism and Clothes Ambivalence." *The International Journal of Psycho-Analysis* 10 (1929): 205–217.

FORDHAM, MICHAEL. Review of *On Not Being Able to Paint,* by Joanna Field. *The British Journal of Medical Psychology* 24 (1951): 72–75.

FORRESTER, JOHN. *Language and the Origins of Psychoanalysis.* London: Macmillan, 1980.

FREUD, ANNA. *The Writings of Anna Freud.* Vol. 1, *Introduction to Psychoanalysis: Lectures for Child Analysts and Teachers 1922–1935.* New York: International Universities Press, 1965.

———. *The Writings of Anna Freud.* Vol. 2, *The Ego and the Mechanisms of Defense.* Rev. ed. New York: International Universities Press, 1966.

———. "James Strachey: Obituary." *The International Journal of Psycho-Analysis* 50 (1969): 131–132.

———. "Personal Memories of Ernest Jones." *The International Journal of Psycho-Analysis* 60 (1979): 285–290.

FREUD, SIGMUND. Most of the works listed below are, as indicated, in *The Standard Edition of the Complete Psychological Works of Sigmund Freud,* translated from the German under the general editorship of James Strachey. 24 vols. London: Hogarth, 1953–1974.

———. "Report on my Studies in Paris and Berlin" (1886). In *Standard Edition,* vol. 1.

———. "Hysteria" (1888). In *Standard Edition,* vol. 1.

———. "Preface to the Translation of Bernheim's *Suggestion*" (1888). In *Standard Edition,* vol. 1.

———. *On Aphasia: A Critical Study* (1891). Translated by Erwin Stengel. New York: International Universities Press, 1953.

———. "Sketches for the 'Preliminary Communication' of 1893" (1892). In *Standard Edition,* vol. 1.

———. "A Case of Successful Hypnotic Treatment: With Some Remarks on the Origin of Hysterical Symptoms through 'Counter-Will' " (1892–1893). In *Standard Edition,* vol. 1.

———. "Preface and Footnotes to the Translation of Charcot's *Tuesday Lectures*" (1892–1894). In *Standard Edition,* vol. 1.

———. "Extracts from the Fliess Papers" (1892–1899). In *Standard Edition,* vol. 1.

———. "Charcot" (1893). In *Standard Edition,* vol. 3.

———. "On the Mechanism of Hysterical Phenomena: A Lecture" (1893). In *Standard Edition,* vol. 3.

———. "Some Points for a Comparative Study of Organic and Hysterical Motor Paralyses" (1893). In *Standard Edition,* vol. 1.

———. "The Neuro-Psychoses of Defence" (1894). In *Standard Edition,* vol. 3.

———. "Obsessions and Phobias: Their Psychical Mechanism and Their Aetiology" (1895). In *Standard Edition,* vol. 3.

———. "On the Grounds for Detaching a Particular Syndrome from Neurasthenia under the Description of 'Anxiety Neurosis' " (1895). In *Standard Edition,* vol. 3.

———. "Project for a Scientific Psychology" (1895). In *Standard Edition,* vol. 1.

———. "A Reply to Criticisms of My Paper on Anxiety Neurosis" (1895). In *Standard Edition,* vol. 3.

————. "Further Remarks on the Neuro-Psychoses of Defence" (1896). In *Standard Edition*, vol. 3.

————. "Heredity and the Aetiology of the Neuroses" (1896). In *Standard Edition*, vol. 3.

————. "Sexuality in the Aetiology of the Neuroses" (1898). In *Standard Edition*, vol. 3.

————. *The Interpretation of Dreams* (1900). In *Standard Edition*, vols. 4–5.

————. "On Dreams" (1901). In *Standard Edition*, vol. 5.

————. *The Psychopathology of Everyday Life* (1901). In *Standard Edition*, vol. 6.

————. "Fragment of an Analysis of a Case of Hysteria" (1905). In *Standard Edition*, vol. 7.

————. *Jokes and Their Relation to the Unconscious* (1905). In *Standard Edition*, vol. 8.

————. "Psychical (or Mental) Treatment" (1905). In *Standard Edition*, vol. 7.

————. *Three Essays on the Theory of Sexuality* (1905). In *Standard Edition*, vol. 7.

————. "My Views on the Part Played by Sexuality in the Aetiology of the Neuroses" (1906). In *Standard Edition*, vol. 7.

————. "Character and Anal Erotism" (1908). In *Standard Edition*, vol. 9.

————. "On the Sexual Theories of Children" (1908). In *Standard Edition*, vol. 9.

————. "Analysis of a Phobia in a Five-Year-Old Boy" (1909). In *Standard Edition*, vol. 10.

————. "Family Romances" (1909). In *Standard Edition*, vol. 9.

————. "Notes upon a Case of Obsessional Neurosis" (1909). In *Standard Edition*, vol. 10.

————. "Five Lectures on Psycho-Analysis" (1910). In *Standard Edition*, vol. 11.

————. *Leonardo da Vinci and a Memory of His Childhood* (1910). In *Standard Edition*, vol. 11.

————. "The Psycho-Analytic View of Psychogenic Disturbance of Vision" (1910). In *Standard Edition*, vol. 11.

————. "A Special Type of Choice of Object Made by Men" (1910). In *Standard Edition*, vol. 11.

————. "Formulations on the Two Principles of Mental Functioning" (1911). In *Standard Edition*, vol. 12.

————. "Psycho-Analytic Notes on an Autobiographical Account of a Case of Paranoia (Dementia Paranoides)" (1911). In *Standard Edition*, vol. 12.

————. "The Dynamics of Transference" (1912). In *Standard Edition*, vol. 12.

————. "A Note on the Unconscious in Psycho-Analysis" (1912). In *Standard Edition*, vol. 12.

————. "On the Universal Tendency to Debasement in the Sphere of Love" (1912). In *Standard Edition*, vol. 11.

————. "Recommendations to Physicians Practising Psycho-Analysis" (1912). In *Standard Edition*, vol. 12.

————. "Types of Onset of Neurosis" (1912). In *Standard Edition*, vol. 12.

————. "The Disposition to Obsessional Neurosis: A Contribution to the Problem of Choice of Neurosis" (1913). In *Standard Edition*, vol. 12.

————. "On Beginning the Treatment (Further Recommendations on The Technique of Psycho-Analysis I)" (1913). In *Standard Edition*, vol. 12.

————. *Totem and Taboo* (1913). In *Standard Edition*, vol. 13.

―――. "On Narcissism: An Introduction" (1914). In *Standard Edition*, vol. 14.

―――. "On the History of the Psycho-Analytic Movement" (1914). In *Standard Edition*, vol. 14.

―――. "Remembering, Repeating and Working-Through (Further Recommendations on the Technique of Psycho-Analysis II)" (1914). In *Standard Edition*, vol. 12.

―――. "A Case of Paranoia Running Counter to the Psycho-Analytical Theory of the Disease" (1915). In *Standard Edition*, vol. 14.

―――. "Instincts and Their Vicissitudes" (1915). In *Standard Edition*, vol. 14.

―――. "Observations on Transference-Love (Further Recommendations on the Technique of Psycho-Analysis III)" (1915). In *Standard Edition* vol. 12.

―――. "Repression" (1915). In *Standard Edition*, vol. 14.

―――. "The Unconscious" (1915). In *Standard Edition*, vol. 14.

―――. "Some Character-Types Met with in Psycho-Analytic Work" (1916). In *Standard Edition*, vol. 14.

―――. *Introductory Lectures on Psycho-Analysis* (1916–1917). In *Standard Edition*, vols. 15–16.

―――. "A Metapsychological Supplement to the Theory of Dreams" (1917). In *Standard Edition*, vol. 14.

―――. "Mourning and Melancholia" (1917). In *Standard Edition*, vol. 14.

―――. "On Transformations of Instinct as Exemplified in Anal Erotism" (1917). In *Standard Edition*, vol. 17.

―――. "From the History of an Infantile Neurosis" (1918). In *Standard Edition*, vol. 17.

―――. "The Taboo of Virginity (Contributions to the Psychology of Love III)" (1918). In *Standard Edition*, vol. 11.

―――. " 'A Child Is Being Beaten': A Contribution to the Study of the Origin of Sexual Perversions" (1919). In *Standard Edition*, vol. 17.

―――. "Lines of Advance in Psycho-Analytic Therapy" (1919). In *Standard Edition*, vol. 17.

―――. *Beyond the Pleasure Principle* (1920). In *Standard Edition*, vol. 18.

―――. "The Psychogenesis of a Case of Homosexuality in a Woman" (1920). In *Standard Edition*, vol. 18.

―――. *Group Psychology and the Analysis of the Ego* (1921). In *Standard Edition*, vol. 18.

―――. "Some Neurotic Mechanisms in Jealousy, Paranoia and Homosexuality" (1922). In *Standard Edition*, vol. 18.

―――. *The Ego and the Id* (1923). In *Standard Edition*, vol. 19.

―――. "The Infantile Genital Organization: An Interpolation into the Theory of Sexuality" (1923). In *Standard Edition*, vol. 19.

―――. "A Seventeenth-Century Demonological Neurosis" (1923). In *Standard Edition*, vol. 19.

―――. "The Dissolution of the Oedipus Complex" (1924). In *Standard Edition*, vol. 19.

―――. "The Economic Problem of Masochism" (1924). In *Standard Edition*, vol. 19.

―――. "The Loss of Reality in Neurosis and Psychosis" (1924). In *Standard Edition*, vol. 19.

―――. "Neurosis and Psychosis" (1924). In *Standard Edition*, vol. 19.

———. "An Autobiographical Study" (1925). In *Standard Edition*, vol. 20.

———. "Negation" (1925). In *Standard Edition*, vol. 19.

———. "A Note upon the 'Mystic Writing Pad' " (1925). In *Standard Edition*, vol. 19.

———. "Some Psychical Consequences of the Anatomical Distinction between the Sexes" (1925). In *Standard Edition*, vol. 19.

———. *Inhibitions, Symptoms and Anxiety* (1926). In *Standard Edition*, vol. 20.

———. "Psycho-Analysis" (1926). In *Standard Edition*, vol. 20.

———. *The Question of Lay Analysis: Conversations with an Impartial Person* (1926). In *Standard Edition*, vol. 20.

———. "Fetishism" (1927). In *Standard Edition*, vol. 21.

———. *Civilization and Its Discontents* (1930). In *Standard Edition*, vol. 21.

———. "Female Sexuality" (1931). In *Standard Edition*, vol. 21.

———. *New Introductory Lectures on Psycho-Analysis* (1933). In *Standard Edition*, vol. 22.

———. "Analysis Terminable and Interminable" (1937). In *Standard Edition*, vol. 23.

———. "Constructions in Analysis" (1937). In *Standard Edition*, vol. 23.

———. *An Outline of Psycho-Analysis* (1940). In *Standard Edition*, vol. 23.

———. "Splitting of the Ego in the Process of Defence" (1940). In *Standard Edition*, vol. 23.

———. *Letters of Sigmund Freud 1873–1939*. Edited by Ernst L. Freud. Translated by Tania Stern and James Stern. London: Hogarth, 1970.

———. *The Complete Letters of Sigmund Freud to Wilhelm Fliess 1887–1904*. Translated and edited by Jeffrey Moussaieff Masson. Cambridge, Mass.: Harvard University Press, 1985.

FRIEDMAN, JOHN, and JAMES ALEXANDER. "Psychoanalysis and Natural Science: Freud's 1895 Project Revisited." *The International Review of Psycho-Analysis* 10 (1983): 303–318.

FRIEDMAN, LAWRENCE. "Trends in the Psychoanalytic Theory of Treatment." *The Psychoanalytic Quarterly* 47 (1978): 524–567.

FRIEDMAN, LEONARD J. "Current Psychoanalytic Object Relations Theory and Its Clinical Implications." *The International Journal of Psycho-Analysis* 56 (1975): 137–146.

GADDINI, E., and A. KUCHENBUCH. "Dialogue on Different Types of Anxiety and Their Handling in the Psychoanalytic Situation." *The International Journal of Psycho-Analysis* 59 (1978): 237–243.

GARDNER, D. E. M. *Susan Isaacs*. London: Methuen, 1969.

GEDO, JOHN E. *Beyond Interpretation: Toward a Revised Theory for Psychoanalysis*. New York: International Universities Press, 1979.

GEDO, JOHN E., and ARNOLD GOLDBERG. *Models of the Mind: A Psychoanalytic Theory*. Chicago: University of Chicago Press, 1973.

GELEERD, ELISABETH R. Evaluation of *Narrative of a Child Analysis*, by Melanie Klein. *The International Journal of Psycho-Analysis* 44 (1963): 493–506.

GILL, MERTON M. *Topography and Systems in Psychoanalytic Theory*. Psychological Issues Monographs, no. 10. New York: International Universities Press, 1963.

———. "Psychoanalysis and Psychotherapy: A Revision." *The International Review of Psycho-Analysis* 11 (1984): 161–179.

GILL, MERTON M., and PHILIP S. HOLZMAN, eds. *Psychology versus Metapsychology: Psychoanalytic Essays in Memory of George S. Klein.* Psychological Issues Monographs, no. 36. New York: International Universities Press, 1975.

GILLESPIE, WILLIAM H. "Donald W. Winnicott: Obituary." *The International Journal of Psycho-Analysis* 52 (1971): 227–228.

———. "Ernest Jones: The Bonny Fighter." *The International Journal of Psycho-Analysis* 60 (1979): 273–279.

———. Review of *Klein,* by Hanna Segal. *The International Journal of Psycho-Analysis* 61 (1980): 85–88.

GLATZER, HENRIETTE T., and WILLIAM N. EVANS. "On Guntrip's Analysis with Fairbairn and Winnicott." *International Journal of Psychoanalytic Psychotherapy* 6 (1977): 81–98.

GLOVER, EDWARD. "Notes on Oral Character Formation." *The International Journal of Psycho-Analysis* 6 (1925): 131–154.

———. "The Therapeutic Effect of Inexact Interpretation: A Contribution to the Theory of Suggestion." *The International Journal of Psycho-Analysis* 12 (1931): 397–411.

———. Review of *The Psychoanalysis of Children,* by Melanie Klein. *The International Journal of Psycho-Analysis* 14 (1933): 119–129.

———. "Examination of the Klein System of Child Psychology." *The Psychoanalytic Study of the Child* 1 (1945): 75–118.

———. "The Position of Psycho-Analysis in Britain." *British Medical Bulletin* 6 (1949): 27–31. (Also published in *On the Early Development of Mind,* by Edward Glover. London: Imago, 1956.)

———. *The Technique of Psycho-Analysis.* London: Baillière, Tindall and Cox; New York: International Universities Press, 1955.

———. "Psychoanalysis in England." In *Psychoanalytic Pioneers,* edited by Franz Alexander, Samuel Eisenstein, and Martin Grotjahn. New York: Basic Books, 1966.

GLYMOUR, CLARK. "The Theory of Your Dreams." In *Physics, Philosophy and Psychoanalysis: Essays in Honor of Adolf Grünbaum.* Boston Studies in the Philosophy of Science, edited by R. S. Cohen and L. Laudan, no. 76. Dordrecht, Holland: Reidel, 1983.

GOULD, STEPHEN JAY. *Ever Since Darwin.* New York: Norton, 1977.

———. *Ontogeny and Phylogeny.* Cambridge, Mass.: Harvard University Press, 1977.

GREENACRE, PHYLLIS. "The Fetish and the Transitional Object." *The Psychoanalytic Study of the Child* 24 (1969): 144–164.

GREENBERG, JAY R., and STEPHEN A. MITCHELL. *Object Relations in Psychoanalytic Theory.* Cambridge, Mass.: Harvard University Press, 1983.

GREENSON, RALPH R. "Transference: Freud or Klein." *The International Journal of Psycho-Analysis* 55 (1974): 37–48.

GRENE, MARJORIE, and EVERETT MENDELSOHN, eds. *Topics in the Philosophy of Biology.* Boston Studies in the Philosophy of Science, no. 27. Dordrecht, Holland: Reidel, 1976.

GROSSKURTH, PHYLLIS. *Melanie Klein: Her World and Her Work.* New York: Knopf, 1986.

GROTSTEIN, JAMES. "The Significance of Kleinian Contributions to Psycho-analysis I. Kleinian Instinct Theory." *International Journal of Psychoanalytic Psychotherapy* 8 (1980–1981): 375–392.

———. "The Significance of Kleinian Contributions to Psychoanalysis II. Freudian and Kleinian Conceptions of Early Mental Development." *International Journal of Psychoanalytic Psychotherapy* 8 (1980–1981): 393–428.

———. *Splitting and Projective Identification.* New York: Jason Aronson, 1981.

———. "The Significance of Kleinian Contributions to Psychoanalysis III. The Kleinian Theory of Ego Psychology and Object Relations." *International Journal of Psychoanalytic Psychotherapy* 9 (1982–1983): 487–510.

———. "The Significance of Kleinian Contributions to Psychoanalysis IV. Critiques of Klein." *International Journal of Psychoanalytic Psychotherapy* 9 (1982–1983): 511–535.

GRUBICH-SIMITIS, ILSE. "Six Letters of Sigmund Freud and Sándor Ferenczi on the Interrelationship of Psychoanalytic Theory and Technique." *The International Review of Psycho-Analysis* 13 (1986): 259–277.

GRÜNBAUM, ADOLF. *The Foundations of Psychoanalysis: A Philosophical Critique.* Berkeley, Los Angeles, and London: University of California Press, 1984.

GUNTRIP, HARRY. *Personality Structure and Human Interaction: The Developing Synthesis of Psychodynamic Theory.* London: Hogarth, 1961.

———. "Psychodynamic Theory and the Problem of Psychotherapy." *The British Journal of Medical Psychology* 36 (1963): 161–172.

———. *Schizoid Phenomena, Object-Relations and the Self.* London: Hogarth; New York: International Universities Press, 1968.

———. *Psychoanalytic Theory, Therapy, and the Self.* New York: Basic Books, 1971. (Reprint. London: Karnac, Maresfield Reprints, 1977.)

———. "My Experience of Analysis with Fairbairn and Winnicott (How Complete a Result Does Psycho-Analytic Therapy Achieve?)." *The International Review of Psycho-Analysis* 2 (1975): 145–156.

———. "Fairbairn Re-Examined in Historical Perspective (The Development of Personal 'Object-Relations' Theory)." N.d. The Menninger Foundation, Topeka, Kansas.

———. "First Training Analysis, with W. R. D. Fairbairn." N.d. The Menninger Foundation, Topeka, Kansas.

———. "Psychoanalytical Autobiography (A Study of the 'Dream Process' over Thirty-Six Years, Showing the Effects of an Amnesia for an Infancy Trauma)." N.d. The Menninger Foundation, Topeka, Kansas.

HALE, NATHAN, ed. *James Jackson Putnam and Psychoanalysis: Letters between Putnam and Sigmund Freud, Ernest Jones, William James, Sándor Ferenczi, and Morton Prince, 1877–1917.* Cambridge, Mass.: Harvard University Press, 1971.

HAMILTON, VICTORIA. *Narcissus and Oedipus: The Children of Psychoanalysis.* London: Routledge and Kegan Paul, 1982.

HARTMANN, HEINZ. Unless otherwise noted, the works listed below are in *Essays on Ego Psychology: Selected Problems in Psychoanalytic Theory,* by Heinz Hartmann. New York: International Universities Press, 1964.

———. *Ego Psychology and the Problem of Adaptation* (1939). Translated by David Rapaport. New York: International Universities, Press, 1958.

———. "Comments on the Psychoanalytic Theory of Instinctual Drives" (1948).

———. "Comments on the Psychoanalytic Theory of the Ego" (1950).

———. "The Mutual Influences in the Development of the Ego and Id" (1952).

———. "Notes on the Theory of Sublimation" (1955).

———. "The Ego Concept in Freud's Work" (1956).

HAYMAN, ANNE. "On Marjorie Brierley." *The International Review of Psycho-Analysis* 13 (1986): 383–392.

HEIMANN, PAULA. "A Contribution to the Problem of Sublimation and Its Relation to the Processes of Internalization." *The International Journal of Psycho-Analysis* 23 (1942): 8–17.

———. "On Counter-Transference." *The International Journal of Psycho-Analysis* 31 (1950): 81–84.

———. "Certain Functions of Introjection and Projection in Early Infancy." In *Developments in Psycho-Analysis,* Melanie Klein, Paula Heimann, Susan Isaacs, and Joan Riviere. London: Hogarth, 1952.

———. "A Contribution to the Re-Evaluation of the Oedipus Complex—The Early Stages." *The International Journal of Psycho-Analysis* 33 (1952): 84–92. (Also published in *New Directions in Psycho-Analysis. See* Heimann 1955.)

———. "Notes on the Theory of the Life and Death Instincts." In *Developments in Psycho-Analysis. See* Heimann 1952, "Certain Functions."

———. "Preliminary Notes on Some Defence Mechanisms in Paranoid States." *The International Journal of Psycho-Analysis* 33 (1952): 208–213.

———. "Problems of the Training Analysis." *The International Journal of Psycho-Analysis* 35 (1954): 163–168.

———. "A Combination of Defence Mechanisms in Paranoid States." In *New Directions in Psycho-Analysis: The Significance of Infant Conflict in the Pattern of Adult Behaviour,* edited by Melanie Klein, Paula Heimann, and R. E. Money-Kyrle. London: Tavistock, 1955.

———. "Dynamics of Transference Interpretations." *The International Journal of Psycho-Analysis* 37 (1956): 303–310.

———. "Joan Riviere: Obituary." *The International Journal of Psycho-Analysis* 44 (1963): 230–233.

———. "Comment on Dr Kernberg's Paper, 'Structural Derivatives of Object Relationships.' " *The International Journal of Psycho-Analysis* 47 (1966): 254–260.

HEIMANN, PAULA, and SUSAN ISAACS. "Regression." In *Developments in Psycho-Analysis. See* Heimann 1952, "Certain Functions."

HILGARD, ERNEST R. "Dissociation Revisited." In *Historical Concepts of Psychology,* edited by Mary Henle, Julian Jaynes, and John J. Sullivan. New York: Springer, 1973.

———. "A Neodissociation Interpretation of Pain Reduction in Hypnosis." *Psychological Review* 80 (1973): 396–411.

———. "Toward a Neodissociation Theory: Multiple Cognitive Controls in Human Functioning." *Perspectives in Biology and Medicine* 17 (1974): 301–316.

HINDE, ROBERT A. *Animal Behavior: A Synthesis of Ethology and Comparative Psychology.* 2d ed. New York: McGraw-Hill, 1970.

HOLT, ROBERT R. "A Critical Examination of Freud's Concept of Bound vs.

Free Cathexis." *Journal of the American Psychoanalytic Association* 10 (1962): 475–525.

————. "A Review of Some of Freud's Biological Assumptions and Their Influence on His Theories." In *Psychoanalysis and Current Biological Thought*, edited by Norman S. Greenfield and William S. Lewis. Madison and Milwaukee: University of Wisconsin Press, 1965.

————. "The Development of the Primary Process: A Structural View." In *Motives and Thought: Psychoanalytic Essays in Honor of David Rapaport*, edited by Robert R. Holt. New York: International Universities Press, 1967.

————. "Beyond Vitalism and Mechanism: Freud's Concept of Psychic Energy." In *The Historical Roots of Contemporary Psychology*, edited by E. Wolman. New York: Harper and Row, 1968.

————. "Freud's Theory of the Primary Process—Present Status." In *Psychoanalysis and Contemporary Science: An Annual of Integrative and Interdisciplinary Studies,* edited by Theodore Shapiro. New York: International Universities Press, 1977.

————. "The Death and Transformation of Metapsychology." *The International Review of Psycho-Analysis* 8 (1981): 129–143.

HOOK, SIDNEY, ed. *Psychoanalysis, Scientific Method, and Philosophy.* New York: New York University Press, 1959.

HUG-HELLMUTH, H. VON. "On the Technique of Child-Analysis." Translated by R. Gabler and Barbara Low. *The International Journal of Psycho-Analysis* 2 (1921): 287–305.

HUGHES, H. STUART. *The Sea Change: The Migration of Social Thought 1930–1965.* New York: Harper and Row, 1975.

HUGHES, JUDITH M. "Psychoanalysis as a General Psychology, Revisited." Paper presented at the 75th Anniversary Meeting of the American Psychoanalytic Association, Washington, D.C., May 9, 1986.

HULL, DAVID L. *Philosophy of Biological Science.* Englewood Cliffs, N.J.: Prentice-Hall, 1974.

Institute of Psycho-Analysis, London. Business Meetings, British Psycho-Analytical Society. 1942.

————. Scientific Meeting, British Psycho-Analytical Society. October 21, 1942.

————. Extraordinary Business Meetings, British Psycho-Analytical Society. 1942, 1944.

————. Training Committee Documents, British Psycho-Analytical Society. 1943.

————. "Controversial Series of Discussions, 1943–1944," British Psycho-Analytical Society.

International Psychoanalytical Association. "Discussion on Lay Analysis." *The International Journal of Psycho-Analysis* 8 (1927): 174–283.

ISAACS, SUSAN. "Privation and Guilt." *The International Journal of Psycho-Analysis* 10 (1929): 335–347.

————. *Intellectual Growth in Young Children.* London: Routledge and Kegan Paul, 1930.

————. *Social Development of Young Children.* London: Routledge and Kegan Paul, 1933.

————. *The Psychological Aspects of Child Development.* London: Evans Brothers, 1935.

————. "Criteria for Interpretation." *The International Journal of Psycho-Analysis* 20 (1939): 148–160.

————. "Temper Tantrums in Early Childhood in Their Relation to Internal Objects." *The International Journal of Psycho-Analysis* 21 (1940): 280–293.

————. "The Nature and Function of Phantasy." In *Developments in Psycho-Analysis. See* Heimann 1952, "Certain Functions."

JACKSON, STANLEY W. "The History of Freud's Concept of Regression." *Journal of the American Psychoanalytic Association* 17 (1969): 743–784.

JACOBSON, EDITH. *The Self and the Object World.* New York: International Universities Press, 1964.

JAMES, MARTIN. "Premature Ego Development. Some Observations on Disturbances in the First Three Months of Life." *The International Journal of Psycho-Analysis* 41 (1960): 288–294.

————. "Infantile Narcissistic Trauma: Observations on Winnicott's Work in Infant Care and Child Development." *The International Journal of Psycho-Analysis* 43 (1962): 69–78.

————. "Preverbal Communications." In *Tactics and Techniques in Psychoanalytic Therapy,* edited by Peter L. Giovacchini. London: Hogarth; New York: Science House, 1972.

————. "The Non-Symbolic Nature of Psychosomatic Disorder: A Test Case of both Klein and Classical Theory." *The International Review of Psycho-Analysis* 6 (1979): 413–422.

JOFFE, WALTER. "A Critical Review of the Status of the Envy Concept." *The International Journal of Psycho-Analysis* 50 (1969): 533–545.

JONES, ERNEST. Unless otherwise noted, the works listed below are in *Papers on Psycho-Analysis,* 5th ed., by Ernest Jones. London: Baillière, Tindall and Cox, 1948. (Reprint. London: Karnac, Maresfield Reprints, 1977.)

————. "The Theory of Symbolism" (1916).

————. "Anal-Erotic Character Traits" (1918).

————. "The Origin and Structure of the Super-Ego." *The International Journal of Psycho-Analysis* 7 (1926): 303–311.

————. "The Early Development of Female Sexuality" (1927).

————. Introductory Memoir for *Selected Papers of Karl Abraham.* Translated by Douglas Bryan and Alix Strachey. London: Hogarth, 1927. (Reprint. London: Karnac, Maresfield Reprints, 1979.)

————. "James Glover: Obituary." *The International Journal of Psycho-Analysis* 8 (1927): 1–9.

————. "Fear, Guilt and Hate" (1929).

————. "The Psychopathology of Anxiety" (1929).

————. "The Phallic Phase" (1933).

————. "Early Female Sexuality." *The International Journal of Psycho-Analysis* 16 (1935): 263–273. (Also published in *Papers on Psycho-Analysis.*)

————. "The Future of Psycho-Analysis." *The International Journal of Psycho-Analysis* 17 (1936): 269–277.

————. "Psycho-Analysis and the Instincts" (1936).

————. "A Valedictory Address." *The International Journal of Psycho-Analysis* 27 (1946): 7–12.

———. "The Genesis of the Super-Ego" (1947).

———. *The Life and Work of Sigmund Freud.* Vol. 1, *The Formative Years and the Great Discoveries 1856–1900.* New York: Basic Books, 1953.

———. *The Life and Work of Sigmund Freud.* Vol. 2, *Years of Maturity 1901–1919.* New York: Basic Books, 1955.

———. *The Life and Work of Sigmund Freud.* Vol. 3, *The Last Phase 1919–1939.* New York: Basic Books, 1957.

———. *Free Associations: Memories of a Psycho-Analyst.* New York: Basic Books 1959.

JONES, KATHERINE. "A Sketch of E. J.'s Personality." *The International Journal of Psycho-Analysis* 60 (1979): 271–273.

JOSEPH, BETTY. "The Patient Who Is Difficult to Reach." In *Tactics and Techniques in Psychoanalytic Therapy,* vol. 2, *Countertransference,* edited by Peter L. Giovacchini. New York: Jason Aronson, 1975.

———. "Different Types of Anxiety and Their Handling in the Analytic Situation." *The International Journal of Psycho-Analysis* 59 (1978): 223–228.

KANZER, MARK. Review of *On Not Being Able to Paint,* by Marion Milner. *The International Journal of Psycho-Analysis* 43 (1962): 357–358.

———. "Two Prevalent Misconceptions about Freud's Project (1895)." *Annual of Psychoanalysis* 1 (1973): 88–103.

KARDINER, ABRAM. *My Analysis with Freud: Reminiscences.* New York: Norton, 1977.

KARDINER, ABRAM; AARON KARUSH; and LIONEL OVERSEY. "A Methodological Study of Freudian Theory: I. Basic Concepts." *Journal of Nervous and Mental Disease* 129 (1959): 11–19.

———. "A Methodological Study of Freudian Theory: II. The Libido Theory." *Journal of Nervous and Mental Disease* 129 (1959): 133–143.

———. "A Methodological Study of Freudian Theory: III. Narcissism, Bisexuality and the Dual Instinct Theory." *Journal of Nervous and Mental Disease* 129 (1959): 207–221.

———. "A Methodological Study of Freudian Theory: IV. The Structural Hypothesis, the Problem of Anxiety, and Post-Freudian Ego Psychology." *Journal of Nervous and Mental Disease* 129 (1959): 341–356.

KAYE, KENNETH. *The Mental and Social Life of Babies: How Parents Create Persons.* Chicago: University of Chicago Press, 1982.

KERN, STEPHEN. "Freud and the Discovery of Child Sexuality." *History of Childhood Quarterly: The Journal of Psychohistory* 1 (1973): 117–141.

KERNBERG, OTTO F. "A Contribution to the Ego-Psychological Critique of the Kleinian School." *The International Journal of Psycho-Analysis* 50 (1969): 317–333.

———. *Borderline Conditions and Pathological Narcissism.* New York: Jason Aronson, 1975.

———. *Object Relations Theory and Clinical Psychoanalysis.* New York: Jason Aronson, 1976.

———. *Internal World and External Reality: Object Relations Theory Applied.* New York: Jason Aronson, 1980.

———. *Severe Personality Disorders: Psychotherapeutic Strategies.* New Haven, Conn.: Yale University Press, 1984.

————. "Identification and Its Vicissitudes as Observed in Psychosis." *The International Journal of Psycho-Analysis* 67 (1986): 147–159.

KHAN, M. MASUD R. Review of *On Not Being Able to Paint,* by Joanna Field. *The International Journal of Psycho-Analysis* 35 (1954): 333–336.

————"Donald W. Winnicott: Obituary." *The International Journal of Psycho-Analysis* 52 (1971): 225–226.

————. "Mrs Alix Strachey." *The International Journal of Psycho-Analysis* 54 (1973): 370.

————. *Privacy of the Self: Papers on Psychoanalytic Theory and Technique.* London: Hogarth; New York: International Universities Press, 1974.

————. Introduction to *Through Paediatrics to Psycho-Analysis,* by D. W. Winnicott. London: Hogarth, 1975.

————. *Hidden Selves: Between Theory and Practice in Psychoanalysis.* London: Chatto and Windus, 1983.

KHAN, M. MASUD R.; JOHN A. DAVIS; and MADELEINE E. V. DAVIS. "The Beginnings and Fruitions of the Self—An Essay on D. W. Winnicott." *Scientific Foundations of Paediatrics,* February 20, 1974, pp. 626–640.

KING, PEARL H. M. "The Contributions of Ernest Jones to the British Psycho-Analytical Society." *The International Journal of Psycho-Analysis* 60 (1979): 280–284.

————. "The Education of a Psycho-Analyst." Scientific Bulletin, The British Psycho-Analytical Society, February 1981, pp. 1–20. Mimeo.

————. "Identity Crises: Splits or Compromises—Adaptive or Maladaptive." In *The Identity of the Psychoanalyst,* edited by Edward D. Joseph and Daniel Widlöcher. International Psycho-Analytical Association Monographs, no. 2. New York: International Universities Press, 1983.

————. "The Life and Work of Melanie Klein in the British Psycho-Analytical Society." *The International Journal of Psycho-Analysis* 64 (1983): 251–260.

————. "Paula Heimann and the British Psychoanalytical Society." Scientific Bulletin, The British Psycho-Analytical Society, June 1983. Mimeo.

KLEIN, GEORGE S. *Psychoanalytic Theory: An Exploration of Essentials.* New York: International Universities Press, 1976.

KLEIN, MELANIE. Most of the works listed below are, an indicated, in one of these two volumes: *The Writings of Melanie Klein,* under the general editorship of Roger Money-Kyrle, in collaboration with Betty Joseph, Edna O'Shaughnessy, and Hanna Segal. 4 vols. Vol. 1, *Love, Guilt and Reparation and Other Works 1921–1945.* Vol. 3, *Envy and Gratitude and Other Works 1946–1963.* London: Hogarth, 1975.

————. "The Development of a Child" (1921). In *Love, Guilt and Reparation.*

————. "Inhibitions and Difficulties at Puberty" (1922). In *Love, Guilt and Reparation.*

————. "Early Analysis" (1923). In *Love, Guilt and Reparation.*

————. "The Role of School in the Libidinal Development of the Child" (1923). In *Love, Guilt and Reparation.*

————. "A Contribution to the Psychogenesis of Tics" (1925). In *Love, Guilt and Reparation.*

————. "The Psychological Principle of Early Analysis" (1926). In *Love, Guilt and Reparation.*

———. "Criminal Tendencies in Normal Children" (1927). In *Love, Guilt and Reparation.*

———. Contribution to "Symposium on Child Analysis" (1927). In *Love, Guilt and Reparation.* (For the complete "Symposium," *see* Klein et al.)

———. "Early Stages of the Oedipus Conflict" (1928). In *Love, Guilt and Reparation.*

———. "Infantile Anxiety-Situations Reflected in a Work of Art and in the Creative Impulse" (1929). In *Love, Guilt and Reparation.*

———. "Personification in the Play of Children" (1929). In *Love, Guilt and Reparation.*

———. "The Importance of Symbol-Formation in the Development of the Ego" (1930). In *Love, Guilt and Reparation.*

———. "The Pychotherapy of the Psychoses" (1930). In *Love, Guilt and Reparation.*

———. "A Contribution to the Theory of Intellectual Inhibition" (1931). In *Love, Guilt and Reparation.*

———. "The Early Development of Conscience in the Child" (1933). In *Love, Guilt and Reparation.*

———. "On Criminality" (1934). In *Love, Guilt and Reparation.*

———. "A Contribution to the Psychogenesis of Manic-Depressive States" (1935). In *Love, Guilt and Reparation.*

———. "Weaning" (1936). In *Love, Guilt and Reparation.*

———. "Love, Guilt and Reparation" (1937). In *Love, Guilt and Reparation.*

———. "Mourning and Its Relation to Manic-Depressive States" (1940). In *Love, Guilt and Reparation.*

———. "The Oedipus Complex in the Light of Early Anxieties" (1945). In *Love, Guilt and Reparation.*

———. "Notes on Some Schizoid Mechanisms" (1946). In *Envy and Gratitude.*

———. "On the Theory of Anxiety and Guilt" (1948). In *Envy and Gratitude.*

———. "On the Criteria for the Termination of a Psycho-Analysis" (1950). In *Envy and Gratitude.*

———. "The Mutual Influences in the Development of Ego and Id" (1952). In *Envy and Gratitude.*

———. "On Observing the Behaviour of Young Infants" (1952). In *Envy and Gratitude.*

———. "The Origins of Transference" (1952). In *Envy and Gratitude.*

———. "Some Theoretical Conclusions Regarding the Emotional Life of the Infant" (1952). In *Envy and Gratitude.*

———. "On Identification" (1955). In *Envy and Gratitude.*

———. "The Psycho-Analytic Play Technique: Its History and Significance" (1955). In *Envy and Gratitude.*

———. "Envy and Gratitude" (1957). In *Envy and Gratitude.*

———. "On the Development of Mental Functioning" (1958). In *Envy and Gratitude.*

———. "Our Adult World and Its Roots in Infancy" (1959). In *Envy and Gratitude.*

———. "A Note on Depression in the Schizophrenic" (1960). In *Envy and Gratitude.*

―――. "On Mental Health" (1960). In *Envy and Gratitude*.

―――. "On the Sense of Loneliness" (1963). In *Envy and Gratitude*.

―――. "Some Reflections on *The Oresteia*" (1963). In *Envy and Gratitude*.

―――. *The Writings of Melanie Klein*. Vol. 2, *The Psycho-Analysis of Children*. Translated by Alix Strachey. London: Hogarth, 1975.

―――. *The Writings of Melanie Klein*. Vol. 4, *Narrative of a Child Analysis*. London: Hogarth, 1975.

KLEIN, MELANIE; JOAN RIVIERE; M. N. SEARL; ELLA F. SHARPE; EDWARD GLOVER; and ERNEST JONES. "Symposium on Child-Analysis." *The International Journal of Psycho-Analysis* 8 (1927): 331–391. (Klein's contribution is also published in *Love, Guilt and Reparation. See* Klein.)

KNIGHT, ISABEL F. "Freud's 'Project': A Theory for *Studies on Hysteria*." Journal of the History of the Behavioral Sciences 20 (1984): 340–358.

KOHON, GREGORIO, ed. *The British School of Psychoanalysis: The Independent Tradition*. London: Free Association Books, 1986.

KOHUT, HEINZ. *The Analysis of the Self: A Systematic Approach to the Psychoanalytic Treatment of Narcissistic Personality Disorders*. Psychoanalytic Study of the Child Monographs, no. 4. New York: International Universities Press, 1971.

―――. *The Restoration of the Self*. New York: International Universities Press, 1977.

―――. "The Two Analyses of Mr Z." *The International Journal of Psycho-Analysis* 60 (1979): 3–27.

―――. *How Analysis Cures*. Edited by Arnold Goldberg, with the collaboration of Paul Stepansky. Chicago: University of Chicago Press, 1984.

KOHUT, HEINZ, and ERNEST S. WOLF. "The Disorders of the Self and Their Treatment: An Outline." *The International Journal of Psycho-Analysis* 59 (1978): 413–425.

KONNER, MELVIN. *The Tangled Wing: Biological Constraints and the Human Spirit*. New York: Holt, Rinehart and Winston, 1982.

KRAFFT-EBING, RICHARD VON. *Psychopathia sexualis, mit besonderer Berücksichtigung der conträren Sexualempfindung. Eine medizinisch-gerichtliche Studie für Ärtze und Juristen*. 12th ed. Stuttgart: F. Enke, 1903. (Translated by Franklin S. Klaf as *Psychopathia Sexualis, With Especial Reference to the Antipathic Sexual Instinct: A Medico-Forensic Study*. New York: Bell, 1965.)

KRIS, ERNST. Introduction to *The Origins of Psychoanalysis, Letters to Wilhelm Fliess, Drafts and Notes: 1887–1902,* by Sigmund Freud. Edited by Marie Bonaparte, Anna Freud, and Ernst Kris; translated by Eric Mosbacher and James Strachey. New York: Basic Books, 1954.

KUHN, THOMAS S. *The Structure of Scientific Revolutions*. 2d ed. Chicago: University of Chicago Press, 1970.

―――. *The Essential Tension: Selected Studies in Scientific Tradition and Change*. Chicago: University of Chicago Press, 1977.

LAING, R. D. *The Divided Self: An Existential Study of Sanity and Madness*. London: Tavistock, 1960.

LAKATOS, IMRE, and ALAN MUSGRAVE, eds. *Criticism and the Growth of Knowledge*. Cambridge: Cambridge University Press, 1970.

LANGS, ROBERT. "The Kleinian Concept of Transference." In *The Therapeutic*

Interaction, vol. 2, *A Critical Overview and Synthesis,* by Robert Langs. New York: Jason Aronson, 1976.

LAPLANCHE, J., and J.-B. PANTALIS. *The Language of Psycho-Analysis.* Translated by Donald Nicholson-Smith. London: Hogarth, 1980.

LEHRMAN, D. S. "Semantic and Conceptual Issues in the Nature-Nurture Problem." In *Development and Evolution of Behavior: Essays in Memory of T. C. Schnierla,* edited by Lester R. Aronson and Ethel Tobak. San Francisco: Freeman, 1970.

LEIGH, DENIS. *The Historical Development of British Psychiatry.* London: Pergamon, 1961.

LEVIN, KENNETH. *Freud's Early Psychology of the Neuroses: A Historical Perspective.* Pittsburgh, Pa.: University of Pittsburgh Press, 1978.

LEVY, ELYSE. *Susan Issacs: An Intellectual Biography.* Ann Arbor, Mich.: University Microfilms, 1977.

LINDON, JOHN A. "Melanie Klein's Theory and Technique: Her Life and Work." In *Tactics and Techniques. See* James 1972.

LITTLE, MARGARET I. *Transference Neurosis and Transference Psychosis: Toward Basic Unity.* New York: Jason Aronson, 1981.

————. "Winnicott Working in Areas Where Psychotic Anxieties Predominate: A Personal Record." *Free Associations: Psychoanalysis, Groups, Politics, Culture* 3 (1985): 9–42.

LLOYD, ELISABETH A. "The Nature of Darwin's Support for the Theory of Natural Selection." *Philosophy of Science* 50 (1983): 112–129.

LOEWALD, HANS. "On the Therapeutic Action of Psychoanalysis." *The International Journal of Psycho-Analysis* 41 (1960): 463–472.

MACINTYRE, A. C. *The Unconscious: A Conceptual Analysis.* London: Routledge and Kegan Paul; New York: Humanities Press, 1958.

MACKAY, NIGEL. "Melanie Klein's Metapsychology: Phenomenological and Mechanistic Perspective." *The International Journal of Psycho-Analysis* 62 (1981): 187–198.

MADISON, PETER. *Freud's Concept of Repression and Defense. Its Theoretical and Observational Language.* Minneapolis: University of Minnesota Press, 1961.

MAHLER, MARGARET; FRED PINE; and ANNI BERGMAN. *The Psychological Birth of the Human Infant: Symbiosis and Individuation.* New York: Basic Books, 1975.

MANDLER, GEORGE. *Mind and Emotion.* New York: John Wiley, 1975.

MARKILLIE, R. E. D. "Observations on Early Ego Development." *The British Journal of Medical Psychology* 36 (1963): 131–140.

MASSON, JEFFREY MOUSSAIEFF. *The Assault on Truth: Freud's Suppression of the Seduction Theory.* New York: Farrar, Straus and Giroux, 1984.

MAYR, ERNST. *The Growth of Biological Thought: Diversity Evolution, and Inheritance.* Cambridge, Mass.: Harvard University Press, 1982.

MCDOUGALL, JOYCE, and SERGE LEBOVICI. *Dialogue with Sammy: A Psychoanalytical Contribution to the Understanding of Child Psychoses.* Edited by Martin James. London: Hogarth, 1969.

MCINTOSH, DONALD. "The Ego and the Self in the Thought of Sigmund Freud." *The International Journal of Psycho-Analysis* 67 (1986): 429–449.

MEISEL, PERRY, and WALTER KENDRICK, eds. *Bloomsbury/Freud: The Letters of James and Alix Strachey 1924–1925.* New York: Basic Books, 1985.

MEISSNER, W. W. "A Note on Internalization as Process." *The Psychoanalytic Quarterly* 45 (1976): 374–393.

———. "A Note on Projective Identification." *Journal of the American Psychoanalytic Association* 28 (1980): 43–67.

MELTZER, DONALD. *The Kleinian Development: Part I, Freud's Clinical Development (Method-Data-Therapy)*. Perthshire, Scotland: Clunie, 1978.

———. *The Kleinian Development: Part II, Richard Week-by-Week*. Perthshire, Scotland: Clunie, 1978.

———. "The Kleinian Expansion of Freud's Metapsychology." *The International Journal of Psycho-Analysis* 62 (1981): 177–185.

MENDEZ, ANITA M., and HAROLD J. FINE. "A Short History of the British School of Object Relations and Ego Psychology." With comments by Harry Guntrip. *Bulletin of the Menninger Clinic* 40 (1976): 357–382.

MIDDLEMORE, M. *The Nursing Couple*. London: Hamish Hamilton, 1941.

MILLER, G. A.; E. H. GALANTER; and K. PRIBRAM. *Plans and the Structure of Behavior*. New York: Holt, 1960.

MILNER, MARION [JOANNA FIELD, PSEUD.]. *A Life of One's Own*. London: Chatto and Windus, 1934. (Reprint. London: Virago, 1986.)

———. [Joanna Field, pseud.]. *An Experiment in Leisure*. London: Chatto and Windus, 1937. (Reprint. London: Virago, 1986.)

———. "A Suicidal Symptom in a Child of Three." *The International Journal of Psycho-Analysis* 25 (1944): 53–61.

———. "Some Aspects of Phantasy in Relation to General Psychology." *The International Journal of Psycho-Analysis* 26 (1945): 143–152.

———. [Joanna Field, pseud.]. *On Not Being Able to Paint*. London: Heinemann, 1950.

———. "The Role of Illusion in Symbol Formation." In *New Directions in Psycho-Analysis*. See Heimann 1955.

———. "The Communication of Primary Sensual Experience (The Yell of Joy)." *The International Journal of Psycho-Analysis* 37 (1956): 278–281.

———. "Psycho-Analysis and Art." In *Psychoanalysis and Contemporary Thought. See* Bowlby 1958, "Psycho-Analysis."

———. *The Hands of the Living God: An Account of a Psycho-Analytic Treatment*. London: Hogarth, 1969.

———. "D. W. Winnicott and the Two-Way Journey." In *Between Reality and Fantasy. See* Flew.

MITCHELL, JULIET. *Women: The Longest Revolution*. New York: Pantheon, 1984.

MITCHELL, STEPHEN A. "The Origin and Nature of the 'Object' in the Theories of Klein and Fairbairn." *Contemporary Psychoanalysis* 17 (1981): 374–398.

MODELL, ARNOLD H. *Object Love and Reality: An Introduction to A Psychoanalytic Theory of Object Relations*. New York: International Universities Press, 1968.

———. "The Transitional Object and the Creative Act." *The Psychoanalytic Quarterley* 39 (1970): 240–250.

———. "The Ego and the Id: Fifty Years Later." *The International Journal of Psycho-Analysis* 56 (1975): 57–68.

———. "Does Metapsychology Still Exist?" *The International Journal of Psycho-Analysis* 62 (1981): 391–401.

MOLL, ALBERT. *Perversions of the Sex Instinct: A Study of Sexual Inversion Based on*

Clinical Data and Official Documents. Translated by Maurice Popkin. Newark, N.J.: Julian, 1931.

————. *Untersuchungen über die Libido sexualis.* Berlin. Fischer's Medizinsche Buchhandlung, 1897. (Translated and abridged by David Berger as *Libido Sexualis: Studies in the Psychosexual Laws of Love Verified by Clinical Sexual Case Histories.* New York: American Ethnological Press, 1933.)

MONEY-KYRLE, ROGER E. "Melanie Klein and Kleinian Psychoanalytic Theory." In *American Handbook of Psychiatry,* edited by Silvano Arieti, vol. 3. New York: Basic Books, 1966.

MORA, GEORGE. "The Historiography of Psychiatry and Its Development: A Re-evaluation." *Journal of the History of the Behavioral Sciences* 1 (1965): 43–52.

————. "History of Psychiatry and Psychiatric Treatment." In *Treating Mental Illness: Aspects of Modern Therapy,* edited by Alfred M. Freedman and Harold I. Kaplan. New York: Atheneum, 1972.

MORSE, STEPHEN J. "Structure and Reconstruction: A Critical Comparison of Michael Balint and D. W. Winnicott." *The International Journal of Psycho-Analysis* 53 (1972): 487–500.

MUNRO, LOIS. "Joan Riviere: Obituary." *The International Journal of Psycho-Analysis* 44 (1963): 233–235.

NEISSER, ULRIC. *Cognitive Psychology.* New York: Appleton-Century-Crofts, 1967.

NETZER, CAROL. "Annals of Psychoanalysis: Ella Freeman Sharpe." *Psychoanalytic Review* 69 (1982): 207–219.

OGDEN, THOMAS H. *The Matrix of the Mind: Object Relations and the Psychoanalytic Dialogue.* Northvale, N.J.: Jason Aronson, 1986.

ORNSTON, DARIUS GRAY. "Strachey's Influence: A Preliminary Report." *The International Journal of Psycho-Analysis* 63 (1982): 409–426.

————. "Freud's Conception Is Different from Strachey's." *Journal of the American Psychoanalytic Association* 33 (1985): 379–412.

————. "The Invention of 'Cathexis' and Strachey's Strategy." *The International Review of Psycho-Analysis* 12 (1985): 391–399.

O'SHAUGHNESSY, EDNA. "Words and Working Through." *The International Journal of Psycho-Analysis* 64 (1983): 281–289.

OWEN, A. R. *Hysteria, Hypnosis and Healing: The Work of J.-M. Charcot.* London: Dennis Dobson, 1971.

PADEL, JOHN. "The Contributions of W. R. D. Fairbairn (1889–1964) to Psychoanalytic Theory and Practice." *Bulletin of the European Psycho-Analytic Federation* 2 (1973).

————. "No Man's Formula." *Bulletin of the European Psycho-Analytic Federation* 8 (1976): 10–13.

————. "Positions, Stages, Attitudes, or Modes of Being?" *Bulletin of the European Psycho-Analytic Federation* 12 (1978): 26–31.

————. "Ego in Current Thinking." *The International Review of Psycho-Analysis* 12 (1985): 273–282.

PARKES, COLIN MURRAY, and JOAN STEVENSON-HINDE, eds. *The Place of Attachment in Human Behaviour.* London: Tavistock, 1982.

PAYNE, SYLVIA M. "Ella Freeman Sharpe: Obituary." *The International Journal of Psycho-Analysis* 28 (1947): 54–56.

————. "Dr. John Rickman: Obituary." *The International Journal of Psycho-Analysis* 33 (1952): 54–60.

PETERFREUND, EMANUEL. *Information, Systems, and Psychoanalysis.* Psychological Issues Monographs, nos. 25/26. New York: International Universities Press, 1971.

PETERS, UWE HENRIK. *Anna Freud: A Life Dedicated to Children.* New York: Schocken Books, 1985.

PETOT, JEAN-MICHEL. *Melanie Klein, premières découvertes, premier système, 1919–1932.* Paris: Dunod, 1979.

————. "L'archaïque et le profond dans la pensée de Melanie Klein." *Nouvelle Revue de Psychanalyse* 26 (1982): 253–271.

————. *Melanie Klein, le moi et le bon objet, 1932–1960.* Paris: Dunod, 1982.

POPPER, KARL R. "Philosophy of Science: A Personal Report." In *British Philosophy in the Mid-Century,* edited by C. Mace. London: Allen and Unwin, 1957.

————. *Conjectures and Refutations: The Growth of Scientific Knowledge.* 2d ed. London: Routledge and Kegan Paul, 1965.

PRIBRAM, KARL H. "The Neuropsychology of Sigmund Freud." In *Experimental Foundations of Clinical Psychology,* edited by Arthur J. Bachrach. New York: Basic Books, 1962.

————. "Freud's Project: An Open Biologically Based Model for Psychoanalysis." In *Psychoanalysis and Current Biological Thought. See* Holt 1965.

————. "The Foundation of Psychoanalytic Theory: Freud's Neuropsychological Model." In *Brain and Behavior,* vol. 4, *Adaption,* edited by Karl H. Pribram. Harmondsworth, England: Penguin Books, 1969.

————. *Languages of the Brain.* Englewood Cliffs, N.J.: Prentice-Hall, 1971.

PRIBRAM, KARL H., and MERTON M. GILL. *Freud's 'Project' Reassessed: Preface to Contemporary Cognitive Theory and Neuropsychology.* New York: Basic Books, 1976.

PUTNAM, HILARY. "The 'Corroboration' of Theories." In *Mathematics, Matter and Method: Philosophical Papers,* by Hilary Putnam, vol. 1. Cambridge: Cambridge University Press, 1975.

RACKER, H. *Transference and Countertransference.* London: Hogarth; New York: International Universities Press, 1968.

RADÓ, SÁNDOR. "The Problem of Melancholia." *The International Journal of Psycho-Analysis* 9 (1928): 420–438.

RAPAPORT, DAVID. *The Structure of Psychoanalytic Theory.* Psychological Issues Monographs, no. 6. New York: International Universities Press, 1960.

REICH, WILHELM. "Character Formation and the Phobias of Childhood." *The International Journal of Psycho-Analysis* 12 (1931): 219–230.

REYNOLDS, PETER C. *On the Evolution of Human Behavior: The Argument from Animals to Man.* Berkeley, Los Angeles, London: University of California Press, 1981.

RICKMAN, JOHN. "Susan Sutherland Isaacs: Obituary." *The International Journal of Psycho-Analysis* 31 (1950): 279–285.

————. "Reflections on the Function and Organization of a Psychoanalytic Society." *The International Journal of Psycho-Analysis* 32 (1951): 218–237. (Also published in *Selected Contributions. See* Rickman 1957.)

———. *Selected Contributions to Psycho-Analysis.* Compiled by W. Clifford M. Scott. London: Hogarth, 1957.

RICOEUR, PAUL. *Freud and Philosophy: An Essay on Interpretation.* Translated by Denis Savage. New Haven, Conn.: Yale University Press, 1970.

RIEFF, PHILIP. *Freud: The Mind of the Moralist.* New York: Viking, 1959.

RIESE, WALTER. "The Neuropsychologic Phase in the History of Psychiatric Thought." In *Historic Derivations of Modern Psychiatry,* edited by Iago Gladston. New York: McGraw-Hill, 1967.

RINSLEY, DONALD B. "Object Relations Theory and Psychotherapy with Particular Reference to the Self-Disordered Patient." In *Technical Factors in the Treatment of the Severely Disturbed Patient,* edited by Peter L. Giovacchini and L. Bryce Boyer. New York: Jason Aronson, 1982.

RITVO, LUCILLE B. "Carl Claus as Freud's Professor of the New Darwinian Biology." *The International Journal of Psycho-Analysis* 53 (1972): 277–283.

———. "The Impact of Darwin on Freud." *The Psychoanalytic Quarterly* 43 (1974): 177–192.

RIVIERE, JOAN. "Womanliness as a Masquerade." *The International Journal of Psycho-Analysis* 10 (1929): 303–313.

———. "Jealousy as a Mechanism of Defence." *The International Journal of Psycho-Analysis* 13 (1932): 414–424.

———. "A Contribution to the Analysis of the Negative Therapeutic Reaction." *The International Journal of Psycho-Analysis* 17 (1936): 304–320.

———. "On the Genesis of Psychical Conflict in Earliest Infancy." *The International Journal of Psycho-Analysis* 17 (1936): 398–422. (Also published in *Developments in Psycho-Analysis. See* Heimann 1952, "Certain Functions.")

———. "Hate, Greed and Aggression." In *Love, Hate, and Reparation,* edited by Melanie Klein and Joan Riviere. London: Hogarth, 1937.

———. General Introduction to *Developments in Psycho-Analysis. See* Heimann 1952, "Certain Functions."

———. "The Inner World of Ibsen's *Master Builder.*" *The International Journal of Psycho-Analysis* 33 (1952): 173–180. (Also published in *New Directions in Psycho-Analysis. See* Heimann 1955.)

———. "The Unconscious Fantasy of an Inner World Reflected in Examples from English Literature." *The International Journal of Psycho-Analysis* 33 (1952): 160–172. (Also published in *New Directions in Psycho-Analysis. See* Heimann 1955.)

———. "A Character Trait of Freud's." In *Psycho-Analysis and Contemporary Thought. See* Bowlby 1958, "Psycho-Analysis."

ROAZEN, PAUL. *Freud and His Followers.* New York: Knopf, 1975.

ROBBINS, MICHAEL. "Current Controversy in Object Relations Theory as Outgrowth of a Schism Between Klein and Fairbairn." *The International Journal of Psycho-Analysis* 61 (1980): 477–492.

ROSENBLATT, ALLAN D., and JAMES T. THICKSTUN. "A Study of the Concept of Psychic Energy." *The International Journal of Psycho-Analysis* 51 (1970): 265–278.

———. *Modern Psychoanalytic Concepts in a General Psychology.* Psychological Issues Monographs, nos. 42/43. New York: International Universities Press, 1977.

ROSENFELD, HERBERT. "An Investigation into the Psychoanalytic Theory of Depression." *The International Journal of Psycho-Analysis* 40 (1959): 105–129.

———. *Psychotic States: A Psycho-Analytic Approach.* London: Hogarth; New York: International Universities Press, 1965. (Reprint. London: Karnac, Maresfield Reprints, 1982.)

———. "On the Treatment of Psychotic States by Psychoanalysis: An Historical Approach." *The International Journal of Psycho-Analysis* 50 (1969): 615–632.

———. "A Discussion of the Paper by Ralph R. Greenson on 'Transference: Freud or Klein.' " *The International Journal of Psycho-Analysis* 55 (1974): 49–51.

———. "Negative Therapeutic Reaction." In *Tactics and Techniques,* vol. 2, *Countertransference. See* Joseph 1975.

ROTHSTEIN, ARNOLD. *The Structural Hypothesis: An Evolutionary Perspective.* New York: International Universities Press, 1983.

RUBENS, RICHARD L. "The Meaning of Structure in Fairbairn." *The International Review of Psycho-Analysis* 11 (1984): 429–440.

RUBINSTEIN, BENJAMIN B. "Psychoanalytic Theory and the Mind-Body Problem." In *Psychoanalysis and Current Biological Thought. See* Holt 1965.

———. "Freud's Early Theories of Hysteria." In *Physics, Philosophy and Psychoanalysis. See* Glymour.

RUDWICK, MARTIN J. S. *The Great Devonian Controversy: The Shaping of Scientific Knowledge among Gentlemanly Specialists.* Chicago: University of Chicago Press, 1985.

RUSE, MICHAEL. *The Philosophy of Biology.* London: Hutchinson, 1973.

RUSTIN, MICHAEL. "The Social Organization of Secrets: Towards a Sociology of Psychoanalysis." *The International Review of Psycho-Analysis* 12 (1985): 143–159.

RYCROFT, CHARLES. Review of *Personality Structure and Human Interaction,* by Harry Guntrip. *The International Journal of Psycho-Analysis* 43 (1962): 352–355.

———. *Anxiety and Neurosis.* London: Allen Lane, 1968.

———. *A Critical Dictionary of Psychoanalysis.* New York: Basic Books, 1968.

———. *Imagination and Reality.* London: Hogarth; New York: International Universities Press, 1968.

———. *The Innocence of Dreams.* London: Hogarth, 1979.

———. *Psychoanalysis and Beyond.* London: Chatto and Windus and Hogarth, 1985.

SANDLER, JOSEPH. "Unconscious Wishes and Human Relationships." *Contemporary Psychoanalysis* 17 (1981): 180–196.

———. "Reflections on Some Relations Between Psychoanalytic Concepts and Psychoanalytic Practice." *The International Journal of Psycho-Analysis* 64 (1983): 35–45.

———. *The Analysis of Defense: The Ego and the Mechanisms of Defense Revisited.* New York: International Universities Press, 1985.

SANDLER, JOSEPH; CHRISTOPHER DARE; and ALEX HOLDER. "Frames of Reference in Psychoanalytic Psychology. I. Introduction." *The British Journal of Medical Psychology* 45 (1972): 127–131.

———. "Frames of Reference in Psychoanalytic Psychology. II. The Historical Context and Phases in the Development of Psychoanalysis." *The British Journal of Medical Psychology* 45 (1972): 133–142.

———. "Frames of Reference in Psychoanalytic Psychology. III. A Note on the Basic Assumptions." *The British Journal of Medical Psychology* 45 (1972): 143–147.

———. "Frames of Reference in Psychoanalytic Psychology. IV. The Affect-Trauma Frame of Reference." *The British Journal of Medical Psychology* 45 (1972): 265–272.

———. "Frames of Reference in Psychoanalytic Psychology. V. The Topographical Frame of Reference: The Organization of the Mental Apparatus." *The British Journal of Medical Psychology* 46 (1973): 29–36.

———. "Frames of Reference in Psychoanalytic Psychology. VI. The Topographical Frame of Reference: The Unconscious." *The British Journal of Medical Psychology* 46 (1973): 27–43.

———. "Frames of Reference in Psychoanalytic Psychology. VII. The Topographical Frame of Reference: The Preconscious and The Conscious." *The British Journal of Medical Psychology* 46 (1973): 143–153.

SANDLER, JOSEPH; ALEX HOLDER; and DALE MEERS. "The Ego Ideal and the Ideal Self." *The Psychoanalytic Study of the Child* 18 (1963): 139–158.

SANDLER, JOSEPH; HANSI KENNEDY; and ROBERT L. TYSON, eds. *The Technique of Child Psychoanalysis: Discussions with Anna Freud.* London: Hogarth, 1980.

SANDLER, JOSEPH, and HUMBERTO NAGERA. "Aspects of the Metapsychology of Fantasy." *The Psychoanalytic Study of the Child* 18 (1963): 159–194.

SANDLER, JOSEPH, and BERNARD ROSENBLATT. "The Concept of the Representational World." *The Psychoanalytic Study of the Child* 17 (1962): 128–145.

SANDLER, JOSEPH, and ANNE-MARIE SANDLER. "On the Development of Object Relationships and Affects." *The International Journal of Psycho-Analysis* 59 (1978): 285–296.

SCHAFER, ROY. *Aspects of Internalization.* New York: International Universities Press, 1968.

———. "Internalization: Process or Fantasy?" *The Psychoanalytic Study of the Child* 27 (1972): 411–436.

———. *A New Language for Psychoanalysis.* New Haven, Conn.: Yale University Press, 1976.

———. *The Analytic Attitude.* New York: Basic Books, 1983.

SCHILLER, FRANCIS. *A Möbius Strip: Fin-de-Siècle Neuropsychiatry and Paul Möbius.* Berkeley, Los Angeles, London: University of California Press, 1982.

SCHMIDEBERG, MELITTA. "The Role of Psychotic Mechanisms in Cultural Development." *The International Journal of Psycho-Analysis* 11 (1930): 387–418.

———. "A Contribution to the Psychology of Persecutory Ideas and Delusions." *The International Journal of Psycho-Analysis* 12 (1931): 331–367.

———. "Some Unconscious Mechanisms in Pathological Sexuality and Their Relations to Normal Sexual Activity." *The International Journal of Psycho-Analysis* 14 (1933): 225–260.

———. "The Play-Analysis of a Three-Year-Old Girl." *The International Journal of Psycho-Analysis* 15 (1934): 245–264.

―――. "The Psycho-Analysis of Asocial Children and Adolescents." *The International Journal of Psycho-Analysis* 16 (1935): 22–48.

―――. "A Contribution to the History of the Psycho-Analytic Movement in Britain." *British Journal of Psychiatry* 118 (1971): 61–68.

SCHUR, MAX. *Freud: Living and Dying.* London: Hogarth; New York: International Universities Press, 1972.

SCHUR, MAX, and LUCILLE B. RITVO. "The Concept of Development and Evolution in Psychoanalysis." In *Development and Evolution of Behavior. See* Lehrman.

SEARL, M. N. "The Flight to Reality." *The International Journal of Psycho-Analysis* 10 (1929): 280–291.

―――. "The Psychology of Screaming." *The International Journal of Psycho-Analysis* 14 (1933): 193–205.

SEARLES, HAROLD F. "An Epic Struggle with Schizophrenia: A Review of Marion Milner's *The Hands of the Living God.*" In *Countertransference and Related Subjects: Selected Papers,* by Harold F. Searles. New York: International Universities Press, 1979.

SEGAL, HANNA. *Introduction to the Work of Melanie Klein.* Enl. ed. London: Hogarth, 1978.

―――. *Melanie Klein.* New York: Viking, 1980.

―――. *The Work of Hanna Segal: A Kleinian Approach to Clinical Practice.* New York: Jason Aronson, 1981.

―――. "Early Infantile Development as Reflected in the Psychoanalytical Process: Steps in Integration." *The International Journal of Psycho-Analysis* 63 (1982): 15–22.

―――. "Some Clinical Implications of Melanie Klein's Work: Emergence from Narcissism." *The International Journal of Psycho-Analysis* 64 (1983): 269–276.

SEGAL, HANNA, and DONALD MELTZER. Evaluation of *Narrative of A Child Analysis,* by Melanie Klein. *The International Journal of Psycho-Analysis* 44 (1963): 507–513.

SHARPE, ELLA FREEMAN. *Dream Analysis: A Practical Handbook for Psycho-Analysts.* London: Hogarth, 1937.

―――. *Collected Papers on Psycho-Analysis.* Edited by Marjorie Brierley. London: Hogarth, 1950.

SHERWOOD, MICHAEL. *The Logic of Explanation in Psychoanalysis.* New York: Academic, 1969.

SMIRNOFF, VICTOR. *The Scope of Child Analysis.* Translated by Stephen Corrin. London: Routledge and Kegan Paul, 1971.

SMITH, DAVID L. "Freud's Developmental Approach to Narcissism: A Concise Review." *The International Journal of Psycho-Analysis* 66 (1985): 489–497.

SOLMS, MARK, and MICHAEL SALING. "On Psychoanalysis and Neuroscience: Freud's Attitude to the Localizationist Tradition." *The International Journal of Psycho-Analysis* 67 (1986): 397–416.

SPENCE, DONALD P. *Narrative Truth and Historical Truth: Meaning and Interpretation in Psychoanalysis.* New York: Norton, 1982.

SPILLIUS, ELIZABETH BOTT. "Some Developments from the Work of Melanie Klein." *The International Journal of Psycho-Analysis* 64 (1983): 321–332.

STEINER, RICCARDO. "Some Thoughts about Tradition and Change Arising from an Examination of the British Psychanalytical Society's Controversial Discussions (1943–1944)." *The International Review of Psycho-Analysis* 12 (1985). 27–71.

STENGEL, ERWIN. Introduction to *On Aphasia: A Critical Study*, by Sigmund Freud. Translated by Erwin Stengel. New York: International Universities Press, 1953.

———. "A Re-evaluation of Freud's Book 'On Aphasia': Its Significance for Psycho-Analysis." *The International Journal of Psycho-Analysis* 35 (1954): 85–89.

STEPHEN, ADRIAN. "A Note on Ambivalence." *The International Journal of Psycho-Analysis* 26 (1945): 55–58.

STERN, DANIEL N. *The First Relationship: Mother and Infant.* Cambridge, Mass.: Harvard University Press, 1977.

———. *The Interpersonal World of the Infant: A View from Psychoanalysis and Developmental Psychology.* New York: Basic Books, 1985.

STEWART, WALTER A. *Psychoanalysis: The First Ten Years 1888–1898.* New York: Macmillan, 1967.

STRACHEY, ALIX. "A Note on the Use of the Word 'Internal.' " *The International Journal of Psycho-Analysis* 22 (1941): 37–43.

STRACHEY, JAMES. "The Nature of the Therapeutic Action of Psycho-Analysis." *The International Journal of Psycho-Analysis* 15 (1934): 127–159.

———. "Joan Riviere: Obituary." *The International Journal of Psycho-Analysis* 44 (1963): 228–230.

———. "Notes on Some Technical Terms Whose Translation Calls for Comment." In *Standard Edition*, vol. 1. *See* Freud.

SUGARMAN, ALAN. "Object-Relations Theory: A Reconciliation of Phenomenology and Ego Psychology." *Bulletin of the Menninger Clinic* 41 (1977): 113–130.

SULLOWAY, FRANK J. *Freud, Biologist of the Mind: Beyond the Psychoanalytic Legend.* New York: Basic Books, 1979.

SUPPE, FREDERICK, ed. *The Structure of Scientific Theories.* 2d ed. Urbana: University of Illinois Press, 1977.

SUTHERLAND, JOHN D. "Object-Relations Theory and the Conceptual Model of Psychoanalysis." *The British Journal of Medical Psychology* 36 (1963): 109–124.

———. "W. R. D. Fairbairn: Obituary." *The International Journal of Psycho-Analysis* 46 (1965): 245–247.

———. "The British Object Relations Theorists: Balint, Winnicott, Fairbairn, Guntrip." *Journal of the American Psychoanalytic Association* 28 (1980): 829–860.

SUTTIE, IAN. *The Origins of Love and Hate.* London: K. Paul, Trench, Trubner, 1935.

SYMINGTON, NEVILLE. *The Analytic Experience: Lectures from the Tavistock.* London: Free Association Books, 1986.

SZASZ, T. S. *The Myth of Mental Illness: Foundations of a Theory of Personal Conduct.* New York: Harper and Row, 1961.

TIZARD, J. P. M. "Donald W. Winnicott: Obituary." *The International Journal of Psycho-Analysis* 52 (1971): 226–227.

TOULMIN, STEPHEN. *Human Understanding.* Vol. 1. *General Introduction and Part I.* Princeton, N.J.: Princeton University Press, 1972.

VEITH, ILZA. *Hysteria: The History of a Disease.* Chicago: University of Chicago Press, 1965.

VOLKAN, VAMIK D. *Primitive Internalized Object Relations; A Clinical Study of Schizoid, Borderline, and Narcissistic Patients.* New York: International Universities Press, 1976.

——. *What Do You Get When You Cross a Dandelion with a Rose? The True Story of a Psychoanalysis.* New York: Jason Aronson, 1984.

WAELDER, ROBERT. "The Principle of Multiple Function: Observations on Over-Determination." *The Psychoanalytic Quarterly* 5 (1936): 45–62.

——. "The Problem of Freedom in Psycho-Analysis and the Problem of Reality Testing." *The International Journal of Psycho-Analysis* 17 (1936): 89–108.

——. "The Problem of the Genesis of Psychical Conflict in Earliest Infancy: Remarks on a Paper by Joan Riviere." *The International Journal of Psycho-Analysis* 18 (1937): 406–473.

WAHL, CHARLES WILLIAM. "Edward Glover: Theory of Technique." In *Psychoanalytic Pioneers. See* Glover 1966.

——. "Ella Freeman Sharpe: The Search for Empathy." In *Psychoanalytic Pioneers. See* Glover 1966.

WALLERSTEIN, ROBERT S. "How Does Self Psychology Differ in Practice?" *The International Journal of Psycho-Analysis* 66 (1985): 391–404.

WEININGER, O. *The Clinical Psychology of Melanie Klein.* Springfield, Ill.: Charles C. Thomas, 1984.

WINNICOTT, CLARE. "D. W. W.: A Reflection." In *Between Reality and Fantasy. See* Flew.

——. "Fear of Breakdown: A Clinical Example." *The International Journal of Psycho-Analysis* 61 (1980): 351–357.

WINNICOTT, D. W. Most of the works listed below are, as indicated, in one of these two volumes: *Collected Papers: Through Paediatrics to Psycho-Analysis,* by D. W. Winnicott. London: Tavistock, 1958. *The Maturational Processes and the Facilitating Environment: Studies in the Theory of Emotional Development,* by D. W. Winnicott. London: Hogarth, 1965.

——. *Clinical Notes on Disorders of Childhood.* London: William Heinemann, 1931.

——. "Fidgetiness" (1931). In *Collected Papers.*

——. "A Note on Normality and Anxiety" (1931). In *Collected Papers.*

——. "The Manic Defence" (1935). In *Collected Papers.*

——. "Appetite and Emotional Disorder" (1936). In *Collected Papers.*

——. "The Observation of Infants in a Set Situation" (1941). In *Collected Papers.*

——. "Child Department Consultations" (1942). In *Collected Papers.*

——. "Ocular Psychoneuroses of Childhood" (1944). In *Collected Papers.*

——. "Primitive Emotional Development" (1945). In *Collected Papers.*

——. "Hate in the Countertransference" (1947). In *Collected Papers.*

——. "Paediatrics and Psychiatry" (1948). In *Collected Papers.*

——. "Reparation in Respect of Mother's Organized Defence against Depression" (1948). In *Collected Papers.*

——. "Birth Memories, Birth Trauma, and Anxiety" (1949). In *Collected Papers.*

———. "Mind and Its Relation to the Psyche-Soma" (1949). In *Collected Papers*.

———. Review of *On Not Being Able to Paint*, by Joanna Field. *The British Journal of Medical Psychology* 24 (1951): 75–76.

———. "Transitional Objects and Transitional Phenomena" (1951). In *Collected Papers*. (Also published in *Playing and Reality*. *See* Winnicott 1971.)

———. "Anxiety Associated with Insecurity" (1952). In *Collected Papers*.

———. "Psychoses and Child Care" (1952). In *Collected Papers*.

———. "Symptom Tolerance in Paediatrics: A Case History" (1953). In *Collected Papers*.

———. "The Depressive Position in Normal Emotional Development" (1954). In *Collected Papers*.

———. "Metapsychological and Clinical Aspects of Regression within the Psycho-Analytical Set-Up" (1954). In *Collected Papers*.

———. "Withdrawal and Regression" (1954). In *Collected Papers*.

———. "A Case Managed at Home" (1955). In *Collected Papers*.

———. "Clinical Varieties of Transference" (1955–1956). In *Collected Papers*.

———. "The Anti-Social Tendency" (1956). In *Collected Papers*.

———. "Paediatrics and Childhood Neurosis" (1956). In *Collected Papers*.

———. "Primary Maternal Preoccupation" (1956). In *Collected Papers*.

———. *The Child and the Family: First Relationships*. London: Tavistock, 1957.

———. *The Child and the Outside World: Studies in Developing Relationships*. London: Tavistock, 1957.

———. "On the Contribution of Direct Child Observation to Psycho-Analysis" (1957). In *Maturational Processes*.

———. "The Capacity to Be Alone" (1958). In *Maturational Processes*.

———. "Child Analysis in the Latency Period" (1958). In *Maturational Processes*.

———. "Psycho-Analysis and the Sense of Guilt" (1958). In *Maturational Processes*.

———. "Classification: Is There a Psycho-Analytic Contribution to Psychiatric Classification?" (1959–1964). In *Maturational Processes*.

———. "Counter-Transference" (1960). In *Maturational Processes*.

———. "Ego Distortion in Terms of True and False Self" (1960). In *Maturational Processes*.

———. "String: A Technique of Communication" (1960). In *Maturational Processes*.

———. "The Theory of the Parent-Infant Relationship" (1960). In *Maturational Processes*.

———. "The Aims of Psycho-Analytical Treatment" (1962). In *Maturational Processes*.

———. "Ego Integration in Child Development" (1962). In *Maturational Processes*.

———. "A Personal View of the Kleinian Contribution" (1962). In *Maturational Processes*.

———. "Providing for the Child in Health and Crisis" (1962). In *Maturational Processes*.

———. "Communicating and Not Communicating Leading to a Study of Certain Opposites" (1963). In *Maturational Processes*.

———. "Dependence in Infant-Care, in Child-Care, and in the Psycho-Analytic Setting" (1963). In *Maturational Processes.*

———. "The Development of the Capacity for Concern" (1963). In *Maturational Processes.*

———. "From Dependence Towards Independence in the Development of the Individual" (1963). In *Maturational Processes.*

———. "Hospital Care Supplementing Intensive Psychotherapy in Adolescence" (1963). In *Maturational Processes.*

———. "The Mentally Ill in Your Caseload" (1963). In *Maturational Processes.*

———. "Morals and Education" (1963). In *Maturational Processes.*

———. "Psychiatric Disorder in Terms of Infantile Maturational Processes" (1963). In *Maturational Processes.*

———. "Psychotherapy of Character Disorder" (1963). In *Maturational Processes.*

———. "Training in Child Psychiatry" (1963). In *Maturational Processes.*

———. *The Child, the Family, and the Outside World.* Harmondsworth, England: Penguin Books, 1964.

———. *The Family and Individual Development.* London: Tavistock, 1965.

———. "Psycho-Somatic Illness in Its Positive and Negative Aspects." *The International Journal of Psycho-Analysis* 47 (1966): 510–516.

———. "Envy and Jealousy." Scientific Bulletin, The British Psycho-Analytical Society 29 (1969): 1–3. Mimeo.

———. "James Strachey: Obituary." *The International Journal of Psycho-Analysis* 50 (1969): 129–131.

———. "The Mother-Infant Experience of Mutuality." In *Parenthood: Its Psychology and Psychopathology,* edited by E. James Anthony and Therese Benedek. Boston: Little, Brown, 1970.

———. *Playing and Reality.* London: Tavistock, 1971.

———. *Therapeutic Consultations in Child Psychiatry.* London: Hogarth, 1971.

———. "Mother's Madness Appearing in the Clinical Material as an Ego-alien Factor." In *Tactics and Techniques. See* James 1972.

———. "Delinquency as a Sign of Hope." In *Adolescent Psychiatry,* vol. 2, *Developmental and Clinical Studies,* edited by Sherman C. Feinstein and Peter L. Giovacchini. New York: Basic Books, 1973.

———. "Fear of Breakdown." *The International Review of Psycho-Analysis* 1 (1974): 103–107.

———. *The Piggle: An Account of the Psychoanalytic Treatment of a Little Girl.* New York: International Universities Press, 1977.

———. *Deprivation and Delinquency.* London: Tavistock, 1984.

———. *Holding and Interpretation: Fragment of an Analysis.* London: Hogarth, 1986.

———. *Home Is Where We Start From: Essays by a Psychoanalyst.* New York: Norton, 1986.

———. *The Spontaneous Gesture: Selected Letters of D. W. Winnicott.* Edited by F. Robert Rodman. Cambridge, Mass: Harvard University Press, 1987.

———. Clinical Papers. Archives of Psychiatry, The New York Hospital–Cornell Medical Center, New York.

———. Correspondence, boxes 1–4. Archives of Psychiatry, The New York Hospital–Cornell Medical Center, New York.

WINNICOTT, D. W., and M. MASUD R. KHAN. Review of *Psychoanalytic Studies of the Personality,* by W. R. D. Fairbairn. *The International Journal of Psycho-Analysis* 34 (1953): 329–333.

WISDOM, J. O. "Fairbairn's Contribution on Object Relationship, Splitting, and Ego Structure." *The British Journal of Medical Psychology* 36 (1963): 145–159.

———. "Freud and Melanie Klein: Psychology, Ontology, and Weltanschauung." In *Psychoanalysis and Philosophy,* edited by Charles Hanley and Morris Lazerowitz. New York: International Universities Press, 1970.

———. "What Is Left of Psychoanalytic Theory?" *The International Review of Psycho-Analysis* 11 (1984): 313–326.

WOLLHEIM, RICHARD. *Freud.* London: Fontana Books, 1971.

———. "The Mind and the Mind's Image of Itself." In *On Art and the Mind: Essays and Lectures,* by Richard Wollheim. London: Allen Lane, 1973.

———, ed. *Freud: A Collection of Critical Essays.* Garden City, N.Y.: Doubleday, 1974.

WOLLHEIM, RICHARD, and JAMES HOPKINS, eds. *Philosophical Essays on Freud.* Cambridge: Cambridge University Press, 1982.

WORTIS, JOSEPH. *Fragments of an Analysis with Freud.* New York: Simon and Schuster, 1954.

YANKELOVICH, DANIEL, and WILLIAM BARRETT. *Ego and Instinct: The Psychoanalytic View of Human Nature—Revised.* New York: Random House, 1970.

YORKE, CLIFFORD. "Some Suggestions for a Critique of Kleinian Psychology." *The Psychoanalytic Study of the Child* 26 (1971): 129–155.

YOUNG, J. Z. *A Model of the Brain.* Oxford: Clarendon, 1964.

YOUNG, ROBERT M. *Mind, Brain and Adaptation in the Nineteenth Century: Cerebral Localization and Its Biological Context from Gall to Ferrier.* Oxford: Clarendon, 1970.

———. *Darwin's Metaphor: Nature's Place in Victorian Culture.* Cambridge: Cambridge University Press, 1985.

ZETZEL, ELIZABETH R. "Ernest Jones: His Contribution to Psycho-Analytic Theory." *The International Journal of Psycho-Analysis* 39 (1958): 311–318.

———. *The Capacity for Emotional Growth.* London: Hogarth; New York: International Universities Press, 1972.

ZILBOORG, GREGORY, in collaboration with GEORGE W. HENRY. *A History of Medical Psychology.* New York: Norton, 1941.

Index

Hughes, Judith M.
    Reshaping the psychoanalytic domain.

    Bibliography: p.
    Includes index.
    1. Psychoanalysis—Great Britain—History.
2. Klein, Melanie. 3. Fairbairn, W. Ronald D.
(William Ronald Dodds) 4. Winnicott, D. W.
(Donald Woods), 1896–1971. 5. Freud, Sigmund,
1856–1939. I. Title. [DNLM: 1. Klein, Melanie.
2. Fairbairn, W. Ronald D. (William Ronald Dodds).
4. Psychoanalysis. 5. Psychoanalytic Theory.
WM 460 H893r]
BF173.H785   1989   150.19'5'0922   88-29537

ISBN 0-520-06480-1 (alk. paper)

Designer: Linda M. Robertson
Compositor: Huron Valley Graphics, Inc.
Text: 10/12 Baskerville
Display: Helvetica
Printer: Braun-Brumfield, Inc.
Binder: Braun-Brumfield, Inc.